Relationship Marketing

The Marketing Series is one of the most comprehensive collections of books in marketing and sales available from the UK today.

Published by Butterworth-Heinemann on behalf of the Chartered Institute of Marketing, the series is divided into three distinct groups: *Student* (fulfilling the needs of those taking the Institute's certificate and diploma qualifications); *Professional Development* (for those on formal or self-study vocational training programmes); and *Practitioner* (presented in a more informal, motivating and highly practical manner for the busy marketer).

Formed in 1911, the Chartered Institute of Marketing is now the largest professional marketing management body in Europe with over 24,000 members and 28,000 students located worldwide. Its primary objectives are focused on the development of awareness and understanding of marketing throughout UK industry and commerce and in the raising of standards of professionalism in the education, training and practice of this key business discipline.

Books in the series

Relationship Marketing

Bringing quality, customer service and
marketing together

Martin Christopher, Adrian Payne and
David Ballantyne

*Published in association with
the Chartered Institute of Marketing*

BUTTERWORTH
HEINEMANN

Butterworth-Heinemann
Linacre House, Jordan Hill, Oxford OX2 8DP
A division of Reed Educational and Professional Publishing Ltd

ℝ A member of the Reed Elsevier plc group

OXFORD   BOSTON   JOHANNESBURG
MELBOURNE   NEW DELHI   SINGAPORE

First published 1991
First published as a paperback edition 1993
Reprinted 1994 (twice), 1996

© Martin Christopher, Adrian Payne and David Ballantyne 1991

British Library Cataloguing in Publication Data
Christopher Martin
Relationship Marketing: Bringing quality,
customer service and marketing together.
– (The marketing series)
I. Title II. Payne, Adrian
III. Ballantyne, David IV. Series
658.8

ISBN 0 7506 0978 8

Photoset by Deltatype Ltd, Ellesmere Port, Cheshire
Printed in Great Britain by Clays Ltd, St Ives plc

CONTENTS

PREFACE

Over the past decade many organizations have recognized the importance of developing a marketing orientation. Similarly, many companies claim to be marketing oriented, customer focused, customer oriented or marketing led. In discussions with literally thousands of middle and senior managers it has become clear to us that only a relatively small percentage, perhaps 30 per cent, practise what they preach. Hence our concern that companies come to terms with the requirements of market leadership.

Customer service became one of the key business and management issues of the 1980s and within sectors such as retail financial services virtually all companies adopted some form of 'customer care' programme. Despite this the results have been far from an obvious success. One recent North American study showed that while 77 per cent of service industry companies had some form of customer service programme in place, less than 20 per cent believed it had any significant impact on profit performance or shareholder value. At the same time many quality assurance and quality systems initiatives have focused on the internal dimensions of quality rather than external customer perceived measures of quality. Additionally many companies adopting quality programmes have not embraced the idea of total quality across all functions, nor addressed the motivational and organizational issues.

While quality improvement programmes and customer service initiatives are to be welcomed wherever they are found it is our view that they should be firmly embedded in the overall marketing strategy of the firm. This is the major challenge for the emerging redefinition of marketing as being primarily concerned with the establishment of enduring and mutually profitable relationships between the firm and its customers.

In a sense the separation of quality, customer service and marketing is rather like three spotlights shining on a stage and beaming light – often of different intensity – at different points on that stage. The task facing the organization is to bring about an alignment of the three beams so that the impact on the customer is more effective.

Relationship marketing has emerged as a concept to help this realignment to be achieved. Traditionally marketing has been about getting customers. Relationship marketing addresses the twin concerns – getting and keeping customers. With this in mind we seek in this book to emphasize three issues:

- Relationship marketing strategies are concerned with a broader scope of external 'market' relationships which include suppliers, business referral and 'influence' souces.
- Relationship marketing also focuses on the internal (staff) relationships critical to the success of (external) marketing plans. 'Internal marketing' aims to achieve continuous improvement in marketing performance.
- Improving marketing performance ultimately requires a resolution (or realignment) of the competing interests of customers, staff and shareholders, by changing the way managers 'manage' the activities of the business.

Our claim is that relationship-based marketing and the resulting long-term retention of customers' attention leads to significantly improved financial and market performance. Relationship marketing represents a new opportunity for organizations to gain a competitive edge in the turbulent business environment of the 1990s. Our hope is that this book will encourage others to add to the growing body of knowledge and experience that is now emerging in this exciting area.

David Ballantyne
Martin Christopher
Adrian Payne

PART ONE

1. *RELATIONSHIP MARKETING*

The decade of the 1980s saw considerable attention directed towards customer service. The customer revolution can be traced, at least in part, to the Peters and Waterman's study of excellent companies published as *In Search of Excellence* – a book which featured as a best-selling non-fiction work and drew attention to the efforts top performing companies were placing on 'getting closer to the customer'. The results of this increased attention on the customer has diffused rapidly through western organizations. In the UK, among the examples most publicized are British Airways and Rank Xerox, but no business sector has been unaffected. In the financial services sector virtually every major player in retail financial services has adopted some form of 'customer care' programme, albeit many without noticeable success. Much attention has been directed at customer service in a wide range of industries from the hospitality sector to public utilities. With so much attention, why have the results

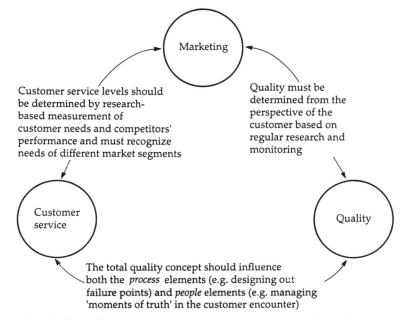

Figure 1.1 *Linkages between marketing, customer service and quality*

often been slow to materialize? We believe, in spite of good intentions, there has often been a noticeable lack of company-wide alignment of purpose towards meeting the customer's requirements. We consider the traditional perspective of marketing must bear some responsibility for this.

Marketing is concerned with exchange relationships between the organization and its customers and quality and customer service are key linkages in this relationship. Figure 1.1 shows the linkages between marketing, customer service and quality that must be exploited to achieve total customer satisfaction and long-term relationships. The challenge to the organization is to bring these three critical areas into closer alignment. So often in the past they have been treated as separate and unrelated. As a result of this lack of alignment the relationship marketing concept is emerging (see Figure 1.2) as the new focal point integrating customer service and quality with a market orientation. Relationship marketing has as its concern the dual focus of getting and keeping customers. Traditionally, much of the emphasis of marketing has been directed towards the 'getting' of customers rather than the 'keeping' of them. Relationship marketing aims to close the loop.

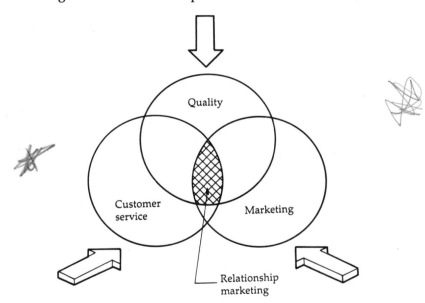

Figure 1.2 *The relationship marketing orientation: bringing together customer service, quality and marketing*

Customer service and total (company-wide) quality decisions take place in the context of competitive marketing strategy. Historically, customer service has been seen from a somewhat narrow perspective. This narrow perspective suggests that the primary role of customer service is concerned with getting the right product to the right place at the right time and the focus was primarily from a distribution and logistics viewpoint. However, a new vision of customer service has started to emerge. This view of customer service places it in a much broader context as a multi-dimensional issue with an impact on **relationships** with specific target groups across a broad range of a company's activities.

The source of quality, as well as customer service, is also undergoing review. The traditional production concept of 'conformance to specifications' is giving way to a customer orientation of quality, i.e. perceived quality. Also the idea of total quality **across all functions** focuses the scope of quality on the total relationship between the firm and its customers, suppliers and other key markets, on an ongoing basis.

In this chapter, to set the context of relationship marketing, we explore the traditional concept of marketing and describe how it must be broadened to apply to all key markets with which the firm interacts and how it should include the wider perspectives of customer service and quality.

The role of customer service

Many companies have different views of customer service. La Londe and Zinszer[1] found a range of views existed as to the definition of customer service. These included:

- All the activities required to accept, process, deliver and build customer orders and to follow up on any activity that erred.
- Timeliness and reliability of getting materials to customers in accordance with a customer's expectation.
- A complex of activities involving all areas of the business which combine to deliver and invoice the company's products in a fashion that is perceived as satisfactory by the customer and which advances our company's objectives.
- Total order entry, all communications with customers, all shipping, all freight, all invoicing and total control of repair of products.
- Timely and accurate delivery of products ordered by customers with accurate follow up and enquiry response including timely delivery of invoice.

These views illustrate the extent to which the meaning of customer service varies considerably from one company to another.

Our view of customer service is that it is broader than any of these definitions and that it is concerned with the building of **bonds** with customers and other markets or groups to ensure long-term **relationships** of mutual advantage. Customer service can be seen as a process which provides time and place utilities for the customer and which involves pre-transaction, transaction and post-transaction considerations relating to the exchange process with the customer.[2] The provision of quality customer service involves understanding what the customer buys and determining how additional value can be added to the product or service being offered.

Customer service decisions are made in the context of a larger marketing strategy. Marketing deals with the development of exchange relationships with customers and customer service should form a key interface with this activity.

The role of quality

The typical approach to quality is moving from one of final inspection to one of assessing whether critical processes are in control and giving guidance to others in the techniques involved. This change of focus from inspecting production **outputs** to monitoring the variation in process **during the process**, has special significance in distribution and service industries, where traditional quality inspection techniques always were inappropriate or ineffective.

As quality management techniques expand from the factory floor to the purchasing department on the one hand, and distribution on the other, this highlights the need for clear communication and planning in new ways. There is a role here for marketing, in liaison with operations and personnel managers, to get the quality planning cycle and the communications right.

This change in the role of quality has been a long time coming. Dr Walter Shewhart of the Bell Laboratories (USA) first made the distinction between 'controlled' and 'uncontrolled' variation in work processes in the 1920s. He used statistical control charts to monitor the performance quality of a process. According to the type of process, this measurement might be temperature, units, dimensions, or error rate, etc. W. Edwards Deming and J. M. Juran are widely regarded as the men who taught the Japanese to achieve high quality at low cost. Deming had worked with Shewhart in the USA before the Second World War and his methods were used extensively during that War. Afterwards, markets for US goods sought volume, and quality was put to one side. Meanwhile, the Japanese faced a 'do or die' economic situation, and they listened to Deming, Juran and others.

Over the next forty years, both Deming and Juran developed from their immediate post-war experience in Japan distinctive management philosophies now known as total quality management (TQM). In Deming's case in particular, the message to management has become more blunt and urgent: the basic cause of sickness in industry and resulting unemployment is the failure of management to manage.

The need for quality goods and services is so well understood by consumers that it is perhaps puzzling that quality is a 'problem', indeed so great a problem in marketing today that 'fixing' the problem is now seen as a source of competitive advantage. Because quality is part of our everyday vocabulary the word easily takes on personal meaning and in so doing loses focus in terms of its measurement and management. This does not mean that quality can be ignored on the grounds that its meaning is subjective, but that is why its achievement takes a variety of forms, according to the perceptions of individual customers. We shall emphasize throughout the book that quality, from a relationship marketing perspective, must be perceived from the viewpoint of the customer.

The role of marketing

Traditionally, marketing has been seen as a process of perceiving, understanding, stimulating and satisfying the needs of specially selected target markets by channelling an organization's resources to meet those needs. Marketing is concerned with the dynamic interrelationships between a company's products and services, the customer's wants and needs and the activities of the competition. The marketing framework can be considered as consisting of:

- The marketing mix – the important elements or ingredients that make up a marketing programme.
- Market forces – the opportunities and threats which bear on the marketing operation of an organization.
- A matching process – the strategic and managerial process of ensuring that the marketing mix and internal policies are appropriate to the market forces.

The term marketing mix has been used to describe the important elements or ingredients that make up a marketing programme. The origins of the concept of the marketing mix lie in work done by Borden at the Harvard Business School in the 1960s. He suggested the following twelve elements should be considered in formulating a marketing programme:

- Product planning
- Pricing
- Branding
- Channels of distribution
- Personal selling
- Advertising
- Promotions
- Packaging
- Display
- Servicing
- Physical handling
- Fact finding and analysis

Over time the concept of the marketing mix has gained wide acceptance. In discussing this acceptance Borden remarked:

> I've always found it interesting to observe how an apt or colourful term may catch on, gain wide usage, and help to further understanding of a concept that has already been expressed in less appealing and communicative terms. Such has been true of the phrase 'marketing mix', which I began to use in my teaching and writing some 20 years ago. In a relatively short time this has come to have wild usage.[3]

The wide acceptance of the marketing mix concept in the business sector is due in part to the simplification of Borden's rather long list into a much shorter one. Over time the list of marketing mix decisions has been simplified under four headings which became known as the 'Four Ps'. This fixed list of four categories has now become 'enshrined' in marketing theory but perhaps less so in marketing practice.

The 'Four Ps' include:

- 'Product' – the product or service being produced.
- 'Price' – the price charged and terms associated with its sale.
- 'Promotion' – promotion and communications activities associated with marketing the product.
- 'Place' – the distribution and logistics function that needs to be considered in making the product or service available.

It has been suggested that this offers a seductive sense of simplicity to students, teachers and practitioners of marketing, which has resulted in a lack of empirical study into the key marketing variables, how they are perceived and used by marketing managers and a neglect of process in favour of structure.[4]

Each of the 'Four Ps' is, of course, a collection of subactivities (for example, promotion includes both advertising and personal selling). However, it is important to recognize that this simplified list can be misleading if it focuses attention on the generic categories of product, price, promotion and place rather than undertaking a full analysis of their subactivities and related elements. As such the basic 'Four Ps' model does not really capture the full extent and complexity of marketing in practice, neither does it explicitly recognize the essential inter-relationships between the elements of the mix.

The evolution of relationship marketing

The formal study of marketing has focused on an evolving range of marketing sectors over the past few decades as shown in Figure 1.3.

In the 1950s, marketing interest was primarily focused on consumer goods. In the 1960s, increased attention also started to be directed towards industrial markets. In the 1970s, considerable academic effort was placed on the area of non-profit or societal marketing. In the 1980s, attention started to be directed at the services sector, an area of marketing that had received remarkably little attention in view of its importance in the overall economy. In the 1990s, we believe that relationship marketing is the area that will receive increasing attention. This involves two major considerations. First, at a macro level, the recognition that marketing impacts on a wide range of areas including customer markets, employee markets, supply markets, internal markets, referral markets and 'influencer' markets such as the governmental and financial markets; and second, at the micro level, the recognition that the nature of interrelations with customers is changing. The emphasis is moving from a **transaction** focus to a **relationship** focus. These changes are characterized below.

Figure 1.3 *The changing focus of marketing*

Transaction marketing
- Focus on single sale
- Orientation on product features
- Short time-scale
- Little emphasis on customer service
- Limited customer commitment
- Moderate customer contact
- Quality is primarily a concern of production

Relationship marketing
- Focus on customer retention
- Orientation on product benefits
- Long time-scale
- High customer service emphasis
- High customer commitment
- High customer contact
- Quality is the concern of all

While this relationship focus has been present in some firms' marketing activities for many years, it is by no means a common philosophy throughout industrial and service firms today. The 1990s will see a much increased acceptance of the relationship concept.

Historically, much of marketing theory has evolved from a study of consumer markets. However, the study of industrial and service markets has suggested a new perspective is called for. For example, Gummesson[5] points out how industrial firms' international operations are not so much primarily concerned with the manipulation of the Four Ps, as used in consumer goods marketing, rather they are concerned with reaching a critical mass in terms of the relations with customers, distributors, suppliers, public institutions, individuals, etc. In the new theory of industrial marketing, 'network-interaction marketing' has been defined as 'all activities by the firm to build, maintain and develop customer relations'[6] and builds on many years by the IMP group in Europe. The notion of interactive marketing and building interactive relationships is closely related to the concept of relationship marketing.

One of the key issues which has emerged from the study of industrial markets is the notion of the buying centre. This model suggests that the 'customer' comprises of a number of individuals who have different roles in the purchase decision process. These include users, influencers, deciders, buyers and gatekeepers. The roles of these buying unit members, based on Webster and Wind,[7] are shown in Figure 1.4.

- *Users* Users are the members of the organization who will use the product or service. In many cases, the users initiate the buying proposal and help define the product specifications.
- *Influencers* Influencers are persons who influence the buying decision. They often help define specifications and also provide information for evaluating alternatives. Technical personnel are particularly important as influencers.
- *Deciders* Deciders are persons who have the power to decide on product requirements and/or on suppliers.
- *Approvers* Approvers are persons who must authorize the proposed actions of deciders or buyers.
- *Buyers* Buyers are persons with formal authority for selecting the supplier and arranging the terms of purchase. Buyers may help shape product specifications, but they play their major role in selecting vendors and negotiating. In more complex purchases, the buyers might include high-level officers participating in the negotiations.
- *Gatekeepers* Gatekeepers are persons who have the power to prevent sellers or information from reaching members of the buying centre. For example, purchasing agents, receptionists, and telephone operators may prevent salespersons from talking to users or deciders.

Figure 1.4 *The buying centre concept*

While this model was proposed in the context of the purchase of industrial products the same concept, sometimes referred to as the decision making unit (DMU), has applicability to the purchase of many services and consumer goods.

The contributions from services marketing also emphasize the importance of long-term relationships. The relationship issues which surface in a consideration of industrial and service markets are exposed in a more explicit context than with their consumer goods counterparts. Many of them, however, have relevance in the context of consumer markets.

A consideration of the above issues, which derive from examination of industrial and services markets as well as consumer markets, suggests that the Four Ps model can be too restrictive in that it focuses attention narrowly on four elements of the marketing mix and thus fails to capture the broader complexity inherent in relationship marketing. Gronroos[8] has pointed out that Borden indicated his original list of twelve marketing mix elements probably had to be reconsidered in every given situation. However, our experience suggests this is not often done.

A number of authors have suggested modifying the Four Ps framework. Brookes[9] has argued that customer service should be added as a 'Fifth P'. Booms and Bitner[10] suggest seven elements of the marketing mix need to be considered. Their marketing framework, developed for services marketing, includes the identification of three additional areas for attention – people, physical evidence and processes. Wind[11] considers that eleven elements should be considered in the marketing mix.

The consideration of the appropriate marketing mix elements and the amount of emphasis that needs to be placed on them will always vary according to the context being considered. When considering relationship marketing across different sectors, we need to identify marketing mix elements which are generic and have applicability to all areas of marketing, not just, say, consumer goods or services. Although the Four Ps framework is the most universally known it has been argued that there is no widely accepted list that can be used by marketers.[12] While the Four Ps are important in most marketing situations, the environment in which the business is operating dictates that the marketing mix ingredients need to be adapted to the needs of that particular marketing place. Thus marketing managers should place appropriate emphasis on those marketing mix elements which are important in the context of their company's operation. The key issue in consideration of whether or not a particular element should be included in the firm's marketing mix should be based on whether it offers the customer some form of **value satisfaction**.

Managers need to make their own judgement as to whether a specific ingredient deserves a separate existence in the marketing mix. Majaro[13] has identified three factors which help determine if any ingredient deserves a separate existence:

- **The level of expenditure spent on a given ingredient of the marketing mix.** Basically it is question of resources allocated to each ingredient which matters. Thus a firm that spends an insignificant amount of money on publicity would be fully justified to add that small budget to the total promotional budget or to the advertising budget. Similarly, a firm that spends very little on packaging would not bother to give this ingredient a separate existence. It would attach it to the 'product' or to the 'promotional' mix, which ever appears more appropriate in the circumstances. In other words, every ingredient involving a significant expenditure would normally earn its separate identity.
- **The perceived level of elasticity in customer responsiveness.** Where the marketer knows that a change in the level of expenditure, either up or down, of an ingredient would affect results it must be treated as a separate element of the mix. Price is invariably important as an

element of the marketing mix, especially where the marketer is able to alter the supply–demand relationship through price changes if he knows that elasticity exists and reduces prices, he would probably have to reduce the allocation of other resources to the ingredients of the marketing mix and in fact develop a new marketing mix. Conversely a firm enjoying a monopoly, or where the price is fixed by government edict may justify it exclusion from the marketing mix. It can cease to be a controllable element.

- **Allocation of responsibilities.** Invariably a well-defined and well-structured marketing mix reflects a clear-cut allocation of responsibilities. Thus, where the firm requires the services of a specialist to help to develop or design new packaging, as in the case of cosmetics firms, it is perfectly proper to say that 'packaging' is an important and integral part of the mix and deserves separate existence therein.

Thus the decision as to which of the ingredients of the marketing mix to include depends on a combined analysis of the most effective and results oriented way of allocating funds and responsibilities coupled with a thorough understanding of what would provide the maximum responsiveness from the final arbiter, the customer.

The expanded marketing mix

We have suggested that the Four Ps model is unnecessarly restrictive. The framework for an expanded marketing mix shown in Figure 1.5 enables the complexity associated with relationship marketing to be addressed. The marketing mix in Figure 1.5 suggests seven elements –the traditional Four Ps of product, price, promotion and place, plus three additional elements of people, processes and the provision of customer service need to be considered.

In the broader context of relationship marketing we consider that the provision of customer service, which creates a clearly differentiated and superior value proposition, to specific customer segments, becomes a central focus on which to consider the other marketing mix elements.

Customer service

There is some disagreement among writers as to whether customer service should be included separately as an element of the marketing mix or whether it forms part of one or more elements of the marketing mix. For example, Kotler[14] says that customer service is another element of product strategy and suggests its importance will be dependent on which of the following four categories the product falls under:

- **A pure tangible good.** Here the offer consists primarily of a tangible good such as soap, toothpaste or salt. No services accompany the product.
- **A tangible goods with accompanying services.** Here the offer

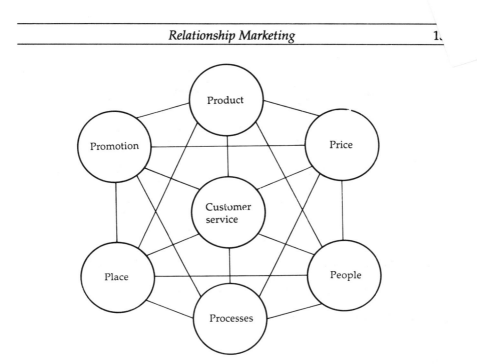

Figure 1.5 *The expanded marketing mix*

consists of a tangible good accompanied by one or more services to enhance its consumer appeal.

- **A major service with accompanying minor goods and services.** Here the offer consists of a major service along with some additional services and/or supporting goods.
- **A pure service.** Here the offer consists primarily of a service.

However, customer service is now often seen as falling in the province of the distribution and logistics function. The view of customer service as the outcome of the distribution and logistics functions seeks to explain its significance in terms of the way in which products or services are delivered and the extent to which customers are satisfied especially in the context of reliability and speed of delivery. Earlier definitions of customer service such as 'a system organized to provide a continuing link between the time that the order is placed and the goods are received with the objective of satisfying customers' needs on a long-term basis' have expanded somewhat in recent years. For example, La Londe, Cooper and Noordewier's[15] study sees the logistics function as being subsumed within the customer service function. The results of their study show the relative importance of customer service in a range of industries including food, chemicals, petrochemicals, autos, paper, electronics, clothing and textiles contrasted with other elements of the marketing mix including advertising, promotion, and sales effort. (See Figure 1.6.)

VARIABLES	Food 1987	Food 1990	Chemical 1987	Chemical 1990	Pharmaceutical 1987	Pharmaceutical 1990	Auto 1987	Auto 1990	Paper 1987	Paper 1990	Total response 1987	Total response 1990
a. Product (quality, breadth of line, etc.)	34.8	34.7	33.0	30.4	36.9	34.8	26.8	26.1	23.2	30.0	33.3	32.7
b. Price (base price, competitiveness, etc.)	25.8	23.4	34.8	36.5	29.4	28.2	29.8	29.3	35.8	34.5	29.9	28.8
c. Customer service	20.0	23.0	19.1	22.3	17.3	19.5	33.5	35.9	28.9	28.3	22.4	24.9
d. Advertising promotion, sales effort	19.4	18.9	13.1	10.8	16.4	17.5	9.9	8.7	12.1	7.2	14.4	13.6
Total	100.0	100.0	100.0	100.0	100.0	100.0	100.0	100.0	100.0	100.0	100.0	100.0

VARIABLES	Electronic 1987	Electronic 1990	Cloth/tex. 1987	Cloth/tex. 1990	Other mfg. 1987	Other mfg. 1990	Total mfg. 1987	Total mfg. 1990	Merchandise 1987	Merchandise 1990
a. Product (quality, breadth of line, etc.)	41.3	41.9	34.7	35.2	32.6	31.8	33.2	32.8	32.9	31.8
b. Price (base price, competitiveness, etc.)	26.5	23.8	22.0	20.5	33.7	33.8	30.0	29.1	27.9	22.6
c. Customer service	21.8	24.5	22.8	27.8	23.6	24.9	22.6	24.7	21.3	28.1
d. Advertising promotion, sales effort	10.4	9.8	20.5	16.5	10.1	9.5	14.2	13.4	17.9	17.5
Total	100.0	100.0	100.0	100.0	100.0	100.0	100.0	100.0	100.0	100.0

Figure 1.6 *Relative importance of customer service*

Source: La Londe B. J., Cooper M. C. and Noordewier T. G. (1988). *Customer Service: A Management Perspective*. Council of Logistics Management. Oak Brook, Illinois

Respondents were asked to distribute 100 points among a set of marketing mix variables, including customer service, and to indicate the importance of each in generating sales. As noted earlier the importance of customer service varies from company to company and industry to industry, however, it was generally considered important by most respondents. Overall, it is rated ahead of advertising, promotion and sales effort in terms of importance and ranked third behind product and price. There are, however, significant differences in relative importance at the individual industry level. In the automotive industry, for example, customer service is considered to be the most important marketing variable ahead of product and price variables. In the pharmaceutical industry, by contrast, customer service is considered relatively less important. For every industry examined, with the exception of the paper industry, customer service was predicted to be more important in 1990 than in 1987 when the survey was undertaken.

In relationship marketing customer service needs to be seen in the context of the supply/marketing channel, shown in Figure 1.7. This view of the supply/marketing channel suggests that customer service should be seen not just in the context of the company and its relationship with its customers but also in its **downstream** relationship with its ultimate consumers as well as its **upstream** relationships with suppliers and perhaps even the supplier's suppliers.

Figure 1.7 *The supply/marketing channel*

For a manufacturer supplying branded goods to distribution companies, the physical distribution component may represent much of the customer service element. Similarly, Cunningham and Roberts[16] showed that the ability of suppliers to be able to meet quoted delivery schedules was the most frequently mentioned service attribute quoted by buyers in the pump and valve industries.

While to a distributor, delivery schedules may be of paramount importance, other service elements may be relevant to the final consumer. It is for this reason that warranties, unconditional service guarantees, intelligible instruction books and free 'phone-in advice centres such as General Electric's 'phone-in centre, become critical to customer service.

Not all writers are narrow in their perspective of customer service. O'Shaughnessy states 'service is . . . essentially any back-up the firm gives to customers to maintain their custom or secure a sale'.[17]

We consider several arguments support the choice of customer service as a separate element of the marketing mix. These include:

- **Changing customer expectations.** In almost every market the customer is now more demanding and more sophisticated than he or she was, say, thirty years ago. This is equally if not more true in industrial markets. Industrial purchasers are becoming more professional and increasing use is being made of vendor appraisal systems and suppliers are now confronted with a need to provide 'Just-In-Time' delivery performance.

- **The increased importance of customer service.** With changing customer expectations, competitors are seeing customer service as a competitive weapon with which to differentiate their sales. The issue and importance of customer service has been commented on by many writers. Quantitative evidence for this is provided in the La Londe study.
- **The need for a relationship strategy.** To ensure a customer service strategy that will create a value proposition for customers is formulated, implemented and controlled it is necessary to establish it as having a central role and not one that is subsumed in various elements of the marketing mix.

Based on Majaro's criteria for including ingredients as elements in the core marketing mix of a firm these arguments give strong support to a consideration of customer service as being included as a key element of the marketing mix. Further evidence for incorporating customer service as an element in the marketing mix is supplied by Blenel and Bender who state that 'More people in the United States today are engaged in technical and customer service than in industrial sales, with service organisations ranging in size from the independent repair person to corporate divisions with tens of thousands of employees.'[18]

Our proposition is that effective relationship marketing is predicated on the choice of marketing mix elements that are mutually supportive and integrated together so that a synergistic effect is achieved. We believe this implies that **customer service strategy** should be seen as a crucial and separate element of the marketing mix.

We have dicussed the reason for inclusion of customer service as a marketing mix element in some detail. The two other areas – people and processes are central to the achievement of quality performance and as such are discussed in greater detail in Chapter 3. However, as elements in our expanded marketing mix we outline their contribution at this point.

People

It has been pointed out by Judd[19] that substantive attempts to conceptualize the employees of an organization as an element of the organization's marketing strategy are notably absent from academic marketing literature. While the expression 'our employees are our greatest asset' is increasingly being heard among companies, it is clear that this statement is often a platitude. We believe that by recognizing the contribution of people to getting and keeping customers, within the overall marketing mix, the company's competitive performance will be substantially enhanced.

An essential aspect of seeing people as part of the marketing mix is to recognize the different roles which the employees of an organization have in impacting on both the marketing task and also customer contact. Judd has developed a categorization scheme based on the degree of frequency of customer contact and the extent to which staff are involved with conventional marketing activities. This categorization results in four groups: contractors, modifiers, influencers and isolateds shown in Figure 1.8.

	Involved with conventional marketing mix	Not directly involved with marketing mix
Frequency or periodic customer contact	Contactors	Modifiers
Infrequent or no customer contact	Influencers	Isolateds

Figure 1.8 *Employee influence on customers*

Contactors have frequent or periodic customer contact and are heavily involved with conventional marketing activities. They hold a range of positions including selling and customer service roles. Whether they are involved in planning or execution of marketing strategy they need to be well versed in the marketing strategies of the firm. They must be well trained, prepared and motivated to serve the customers on a day-to-day basis in a responsive manner. They should be recruited based on their potential to be responsive to customer needs and be evaluated and rewarded on this basis.

Modifiers are people such as receptionists, credit department and switchboard personnel, and while not directly involved with conventional marketing activities to a great degree, nevertheless have frequent customer contact. As such they need to have a clear view of the organization's marketing strategy and the role that they can play in being responsive to customers' needs. They have a vital role to play especially, but not exclusively, in service businesses. Modifiers need to develop high levels of customer relationship skills. Training and monitoring of performance are especially important here.

Influencers while involved with elements of the conventional marketing mix have infrequent or no customer contact. However, they are very much part of the implementation of the organization's relationship marketing strategy. They include roles such as research and development, market research, the shipping department, etc. In recruitment of influencers people with the potential to develop a sense of customer responsiveness should be pursued. Influencers should be evaluated and rewarded according to customer oriented performance standards and opportunities to enhance the level of customer contact should be programmed into their job activities.

Isolateds are the various support functions which neither have frequent customer contact nor a great deal to do with the conventional marketing activities. However, as support people their activities critically affect performance of the organization's activities. Staff falling within this category include purchasing department, personnel and data processing. Such staff should be sensitive to the fact that internal customers as well as external customers have needs which must be satisfied. They need to understand the company's overall marketing strategy and how their functions contribute to the quality of delivered value to the customer. How people may be involved in the quality improvement process is dealt with in Chapter 5.

This suggests that people form an important part of the differentiation which can create added value for the customer. By conceptualizing people as a separate element of the marketing mix the appropriate level of attention can be directed on maximizing the impact of their activities and motivating and rewarding them to make the desired contribution. Ultimately, it is people who develop and achieve competitive advantage.

Processes

Process should also assume a separate role within the marketing mix. All work activity is process. Process management involves the procedures, task schedules, mechanisms, activities and routines by which a product or service is delivered to the customer. It involves policy decisions about customer involvement and employee discretion. Identification of process management as a separate activity is a prerequisite to quality improvement. The importance of this element is especially highlighted in service businesses where inventories cannot be stored. Banks provide a good example of this. By reconfiguring the way they deliver service through the introduction of automatic teller machines (ATMs) banks have been able to free up staff to handle more complex customer needs by diverting cash-only customers to the ATMs.

While the people element is important in customer service, no amount of attention and effort from staff will overcome continued unsatisfactory process performance. This is an area where the 'smile training' approach to customer service adopted by many companies is fundamentally flawed. If the process supporting product or service delivery cannot, for example, achieve quickly repaired equipment following breakdown, a supply of goods with agreed quality standards, or a meal within a defined period, an unhappy customer will be the result. This suggests a close cooperation is needed between marketing and operations staff who are involved in process management. By identifying process as a separate marketing mix element, we recognize its importance in product and service quality.

Each of these marketing mix elements interact with each other and a key issue is the integration of the various elements of the mix so that they are mutually supportive in gaining the best possible match between the internal environment of the organization and the external customer environment.

Market forces and the matching process

In developing a marketing mix strategy those responsible have to consider various market forces. The important forces acting on the marketing mix include:

- **The customer** – buying behaviour in terms of their motivation to purchase, buying habits, environment, size of market and buying power.
- **The industry's behaviour** – the behaviour of retailer and wholesaler and other members of the logistics chain in terms of their motivations, structure, practice and attitudes.
- **Competitors** – their position and behaviour as influenced by industry structure and the nature of competition.
- **Government and regulatory** – controls over marketing which relate to both marketing activities and competitive practices.

The job of the manager in developing a marketing programme is to assemble elements of the marketing mix to ensure the best match between the internal capabilities of the company and the external market environment. A key issue with respect to the marketing programme is the recognition that the elements of the marketing mix are largely controllable by managers within the organization, and the market forces in the external environment are largely uncontrollable. The success of a marketing programme will largely depend on the degree of match between the external and internal environment as shown in Figure 1.9.

The external forces are not stable. The forces can alter quickly and dramatically. While changes in these forces can have adverse effects on the organization's existing marketing efforts, it can also create marketing opportunities. Thus marketing executives should constantly monitor the external environment and be prepared to alter the marketing mix to capitalize on opportunities provided by this change. The marketing programme can be characterized as a **matching** process. Customer service provides a key linkage in this marketing process. If any mismatch occurs between the expectations of what the customer wants and what the customer receives there is a perceived 'quality gap'. The issue of quality and customers' expectations and the notion of quality gaps is addressed later in the book.

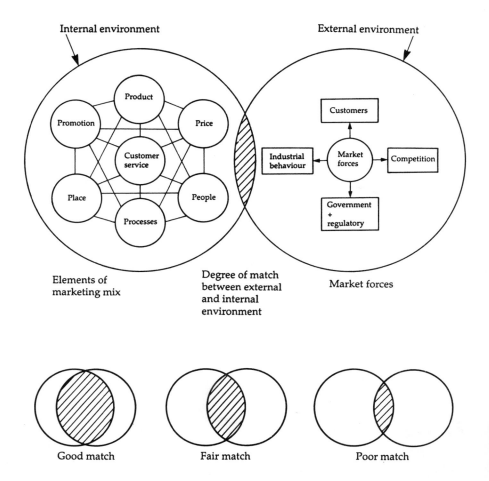

Figure 1.9 *The marketing programme as a matching process*

Relationship marketing: a broader view

Traditionally marketing has been seen from the perspective of managing relationships with **customer** groups. However, a much broader view-point is appropriate in relationship marketing. In order to provide the best value proposition in terms of both the product and customer service it is necessary to consider a wider range of markets. The 'six markets' model in Figure 1.10 illustrates this broadened view of marketing. This figure suggests that companies have a number of markets to whom they need to direct marketing activity and formulate marketing plans. In addition to formulating marketing activity directed at existing and potential customers, a company should also consider supplier markets,

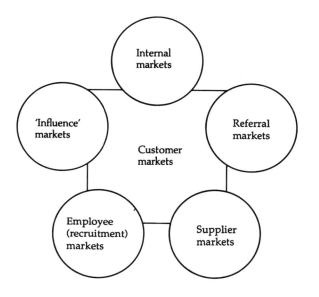

Figure 1.10 *The six markets model: a broadened view of marketing*

employee markets, referral markets, 'influencer' and internal markets. Each of these markets will now be discussed.

Customer markets

There is no doubt that the primary focus of marketing was and remains on the customer. More recently there has been a changing emphasis in the focus of marketing from transactional marketing that emphasizes the individual sale to relationship marketing which emphasizes long-term lasting relationships.

Our experience, and those of other practitioners and researchers, suggests that the greater part of most companies' marketing activity is directed at seeking new customers. While a focus on gaining new customers is necessary to the development of all businesses it is also essential to ensure that ongoing marketing activity is directed at existing customers. By placing too much focus on marketing activities directed at new customers, companies often experience the 'leaking bucket' effect,

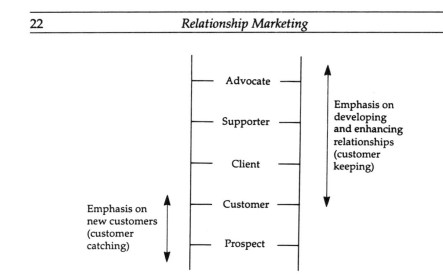

Figure 1.11 *The relationship marketing ladder of customer loyalty*

where customers are being lost because insufficient marketing activity generally, and customer service specifically, is being directed to them. Davidow has pointed out this problem:

> It has always been incredible to me how insensitive companies can be to their customers. Most of them don't seem to understand that their future business depends on having the same customer come back again and again.[20]

Too many companies, having secured a customer's order, then turn their attention to seeking new customers without understanding the importance of maintaining and enhancing the relationships with their existing customers.

Figure 1.11 shows the relationship marketing ladder of customer loyalty. This suggests that too many firms over-emphasize the identification of prospects and focus on trying to convert them into customers. By contrast, underemphasis is placed on generating repeat business. The objective of relationship marketing is to turn new customers into regularly purchasing clients, and then to progressively move them through being strong supporters of the company and its product, and finally to being active and vocal advocates for the company thus playing an important role as a referral source. Customer service has a pivotal role to play in achieving this progression up the ladder of customer loyalty. It should be obvious that the traditional marketing mix elements of product, price, promotion and place are the principal elements used to turn prospects into customers, while the other additional elements we have suggested of customer service, people and process are those which are used to move customers into clients, supporters, and ultimately advocates for our company's products and services. In moving clients up the ladder it is essential to understand in an in-depth and explicit manner exactly what the customer is buying and how we can offer augmentation to differentially improve our offering to the customer. We shall address this topic in more detail in Chapter 2. To achieve the transition from customer to advocate this augmentation should aim at taking them beyond mere 'customer satisfaction' to 'customer delight' by delivering products or services that exceed expectations.

Referral markets

It has been said that the best form of marketing is to get your customers to do the marketing for you. This suggests the importance of developing the referral sources or advocates referred to above. Existing customers need, of course, to be managed to provide greater opportunities for customer referrals. However, there are many other possible referral sources as well as a company's customers.

An example will serve to illustrate this point. One of the authors recently worked with an overseas bank. Historically, little attention had been directed at trying to manage relationships with referral sources in this bank. Marketing efforts were mainly directed at entertainment, with the referral sources being invited to an annual party and being taken out to the occasional lunch. In an environment of increasing competition it was decided to explore the potential of improved marketing via these referral sources. It was concluded that referral markets should form the subject of major marketing effort by the bank.

A study team examined five major areas of the bank's non-retail activities to identify the percentage of business that had been acquired through referral sources and how this pattern had changed over the past five years. In some cases research had to be done to clarify this. Estimates were made as to how this mix would change over the forthcoming five years. The findings were considered at a retreat held for the board of directors and top twenty officers in the bank. There was considerable surprise among the officers as to the extent of the importance of their referral sources. At the same retreat several key referral sources had been invited to describe their process in making judgements as to which bank to refer business to and the levels of customer service that had been provided by the bank and its key competitors to themselves and also to the ultimate customer.

The executives of the bank, a highly profitable one, arrived at the retreat confident that they were providing their referral sources and customers with high levels of service, responsiveness and customer satisfaction. The referral sources then spoke at length of problems experienced in dealings with the bank and the executives left the retreat with a different perspective after learning the referral sources views of their customer service. As a result, a task force was established to consider how formal relationships could be better developed with referral sources, and a marketing plan to deal with their referral market was established. The plan to overcome the problems was shared throughout the bank and a high priority was accorded to building better relationships with these referral sources. Over a period of six months noticeable and continued improvement in business generated by the referral sources resulted from the implementation of the plan.

These referral markets are referred to under various names within different industry sectors, including: intermediaries, connectors, multipliers, third-party markets, agencies, networks and referral sources. In most industries they have two things in common, they are becoming more important and there are more of them. We should start by identifying the key referral sources.

In the case of the bank, these included insurance companies, property brokers, accountants, solicitors, surveyors and valuers, other banks, as well as existing customers and internal referrals. The present and likely future importance of these referral sources should be identified and a specific plan developed to determine the appropriate levels of marketing resources that should be devoted to each of them. Additionally, efforts should be made to evaluate results and the cost benefit of marketing effort and resources directed at them. While a highly focused pilot scheme can sometimes suggest where the greatest benefit can be obtained it should be emphasized that the development of these relationships takes time and all the benefits of such marketing activity may not be realized for some time.

Supplier markets

There is mounting evidence of a movement from the traditional adversarial relationship between suppliers and their customers towards a new form of relationship based on cooperation. This emphasizes a long-term very close relationship and a win–win philosophy rather than the win–lose philosophy inherent in adversarial relationships.

In the past, firms have typically focused on trying to extract the best price from suppliers, but the unknown costs of this has often been variability in supply or quality, or both. Many firms see this as a process of playing one supplier off against another. This approach is slowly being revised and is being replaced with a more enlightened approach whereby suppliers are viewed as collaborators and recognition is being made that there is a need to establish greater partnership in the marketing channel between companies and their suppliers.

Relatively few organizations in either the private or public sector spend less than about 20 or 30 per cent of their total budget on goods or services from outside suppliers. For manufacturers in the USA the average is over 60 per cent of total revenue.[21] The supply function is often looked on largely as a clerical function and such things as new product introductions are planned and specifications drawn up without supplier input. However, this can often result in high costs or poor quality and a more strategic attitude is appropriate.

This new attitude to supplier markets is described by a number of labels such as 'co-makership' (Philips), the 'vendorship partnership' (AT&T), 'co-marketing' and 'relationship marketing' (used in a narrower sense than we have described in this chapter).

The principle of co-makership is based on the concept of both parties agreeing and as a result creating a better future for each of them. Companies who are adopting a co-makership approach to suppliers such as Philips and AT&T are doing so because of serious threats from global competition, initiatives such as quality improvement programmes and a general effort to operate more effectively.

There is increasing evidence of the value of such approaches. A study by Masson of two electronics companies examined one firm that had adopted a co-makership relationship with suppliers and another which had a traditional adversarial relationship. The suppliers to both manufacturers were the same. The firm who had developed a co-maker relationship was outperforming the other firm and its suppliers were performing to a much higher standard with them than they were for its competitor who did not have the benefit of a co-makership relationship.[22]

Co-makership is concerned with the establishment and enhancement of longer term relationships with a limited number of suppliers on the basis of developed mutual confidence. The objectives of co-makership include.[23]

- **Reliability in agreements.** This corresponds to the delivery of high quality products at exactly indicated points of time.
- **Obligations to deliver in time:**
  –in smaller lot sizes – meeting the requirements as much as possible
  –rapid change of versions, and
  –shorter set up times.
- **Flexibility in deliveries.**
- **An optimal product** – involving an exchange of ideas between purchaser and maker.
- **At the lowest costs.**

Co-makership is based on the concept that traditional company contact with suppliers is characterized by friction about quality, price and delivery. Companies and their suppliers are now realizing their business can be much more profitable if they abandon the traditional relationship and replace it with a new spirit of cooperation. The idea of co-makership suggests very close cooperation with comprehensive communication embracing the areas of development, quality, engineering and logistics. Mutual trust, continuity of the relationship and a willingness of each party to create a profitable business for the other are the foundations on which the relationship is built.

This involves considerable cooperation from the supplier and includes design, development and production stages of the customer. The co-makership approach can have an impact on a number of specific areas:

- **Product specification.** By working together customer and supplier can ensure that a product is designed that fits a supplier's manufacturing capabilities and the customers needs. It can avoid over-specification, and can lead to greater standardization, lower reject levels, less rework by both customer and supplier, high delivery performance, lower costs, and greater satisfaction on the part of both the supplier and the customer.
- **Quality.** In co-makership quality is built in at the design stage and improved continuously with effective process control. Both supplier

and customer work together to contribute to the raising of the quality of the product and reducing inspection to a minimum. In some cases the partners analyse each other's quality control procedures and agree on measuring standards, both in the development phase and in actual production.

- **Mix and volume flexibility.** This aspect of co-makership is concerned with achieving mix and volume flexibility with the shortest possible lead time. The supplier and customer need to work together so that manufacturing and supply processes of both parties are harmonized.[24]

The move towards improved supplier relationships involves a company marketing these principles both externally to their suppliers and internally within the company itself.

Employee markets

Increasingly, companies are finding strong competition in their efforts to attract a sufficient number of suitably motivated and trained employees into their ranks. Many firms are today learning that the limiting factor to their success is far more predicated on the availability of satisfactorily skilled people to work in their organizations than the availability of other resources such as capital or raw materials.

This problem will worsen considerably in the decade of the 1990s. There is a worldwide structural shift underway. In the USA one writer[25] shows the percentage of people in the 16–24 age group falling from around 20 per cent in 1985 to 16 per cent in 2000 and in the 25–34 age group from 23 per cent to 19 per cent over the same period.

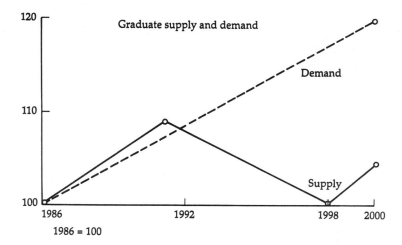

Figure 1.12 *Graduate supply and demand in the UK*
Source: Institute of Manpower Studies

This is a worldwide trend in western developed countries. Figure 1.12 shows the supply and demand of graduates in the UK from an Institute of Manpower Studies survey illustrating a significant gap between supply and demand over the next decade.

The reducing pool of available labour will create special problems for customer service delivery in the years ahead. Despite recognizing this problem many firms have not responded to this problem by development of a plan aimed at improving their competitive edge in employee markets. A brief case study illustrates this point.

A large and well-known firm of accountants had considerable problems in attracting new graduate recruits to work for their firm. A review of their recruitment practices suggested why. For years they had produced extremely poor quality recruitment brochures both in terms of content and visual impact. On recruitment visits to university campuses they sent an old and uninspiring partner to give talks to those expressing possible interest in joining the firm. He was accompanied by two disinterested administrative staff from the personnel department. As a result this firm's recruiting success was disappointing and it lamented the 'average' quality of people accepting places with the firm and the inadequate number of interested prospects.

Some years passed before this was recognized as a marketing problem and appropriate attention and resources placed behind the marketing task. A marketing plan was developed to increase the quality and number of staff accepting places with the firm. This involved production of a much more professional brochure, and a direct mailing of it to prospective students completing their accountancy studies; sponsorship of awards and prizes at key universities from which they sought to recruit and the establishment of a trained team to give presentations at university campuses.

Recent graduates working in the firm were involved in the design and copy of the recruitment brochure and also in the interviewing process. Mail shots followed up those attending the talks and then follow up by telephone was made to see if any further information could be provided to prospective employees. Presentations at the campuses were seen as of the highest importance and the brightest partners, who wherever possible were graduates of that university, visited the campus in question. They are accompanied by managers also who have attended that university. The managers chosen were ones who had been promoted rapidly to management and/or who had some especially interesting experiences, e.g.: secondment overseas, working on a particularly interesting and high profile client, etc. As a result of a formal marketing plan directed at potential employees the firm's offers to acceptances ratio increased by nearly 200 per cent within two years.

While in times of high unemployment some companies will have adequate personnel resources at the clerical and blue collar levels the demographics of young people and graduates argue this will be a critical area for relationship marketing over the next decade.

'Influence' markets

The above examples do not, of course, include all the groups to whom marketing activity may need to be directed. Other examples of where marketing activity may need to be directed include finance markets, regulatory markets and the government. These can be described as 'influence' markets – additional markets which, depending on their circumstances, may need to be addressed. With respect to finance markets one leading British manufacturing company developed an integrated marketing activity at improving its market perception and share price. The chairman and deputy chairman spent a high proportion of their time with key figures including stockbrokers, bankers, investment associations and financial journalists. They **marketed** their strategy for the future of the company which included plans for a series of ambitious acquisitions. The company's acquisition plans were extremely well thought through and details of them in broad scope were made available to these groups as part of the presentation. After the period of a year or two of such activity the financial community directed considerable interest at this particular company and the acquisitions it made. There was much favourable commentary in stockbrokers circulars and in the financial press. As a result, share prices improved by some 20 per cent and it is believed that much of this was a direct result of this marketing activity aimed at financial markets. The company consequently purchased a number of companies. Although some criticism was made of certain of the acquisitions, in terms of paying too high a premium, the firms were purchased mainly through share placement and because of the increased share price the total cost to the company was relatively less.

Similarly, marketing activity may need to be directed at government or regulatory bodies. Gummesson[26] has pointed out how such things are of particular importance for companies who sell equipment of an infrastructural character, such as nuclear reactors, telephone systems and defence products. These are products which may impact on the country's economic performance, employment levels or financial status or may be important from a political point of view. Companies involved in such sensitive fields as defence or the North Sea may well recognize the importance of these target markets but may well not have formulated detailed and coherent marketing strategies to gain maximum advantage from these relationships. Such plans are essential to sustained success in such markets. These plans, whether described internally as public relations or marketing, will benefit from the application of a strategic marketing approach.

Internal markets

In the past decade the term **internal marketing** has emerged in many companies to describe the application of marketing internally within the firm. This seems to be an area where practice appears ahead of theory. Despite the existence of many internal marketing programmes no books, at least in English, have been published on internal marketing and only a handful of articles have addressed this important and emerging area. There are two key aspects to this. One involves the notion of the internal customer. That is, every person working within an organization has both a supplier and a customer. Here we are concerned with getting staff to recognize that both individuals and departments have customers and then determining what can be done to improve levels of customer service and quality levels within the organization.

The second aspect is concerned with making certain that all staff work together in a manner that is attuned to the company's mission, strategy and goals. The importance of this has become particularly transparent in service firms where there is a close interface with the customer. The idea behind internal marketing, in this context, is to ensure that all members of the staff provide the best representation of the company and successfully handle all telephone, mail, electronic, and personal interactions with the customer. Thus this forms part of quality management and customer service and is highly dependent on the coordination of people and process improvement strategies.

A pilot study on internal marketing at the Cranfield School of Management[27] suggests that **formalized** internal marketing rarely exists. In practice, a diverse range of activities constitute 'internal marketing', however, such activities tend not to be labelled as 'internal marketing' by organizations. Respondents were asked in semi-structured interviews to describe the internal marketing programmes established in their organizations. Specific questions were asked in relation to the length of time an internal marketing programme had been running, whether the programme was formal, if it had a name, the job title of the person in charge of internal marketing, whether this was a full-time or part-time appointment and the number of staff involved in internal marketing, and who it reported to. Additionally respondents were asked to describe the critical success factors of the internal marketing programme and to describe modifications to the programme, employee perceptions and potential future developments.

Some initial findings from the pilot study suggest:

- Internal marketing is generally not a discrete activity, but is implicit in quality initiatives, customer service programmes and broader business strategies.
- Internal marketing comprises formal structured activities accompanied by a range of less formal ad hoc initiatives.
- Communication is critical to successful internal marketing.
- Internal marketing performs a critical role in competitive differentiation.
- Internal marketing has an important role to play in reducing conflict between the functional areas of the organization.
- Internal marketing is an experiential process, leading employees to arrive at conclusions themselves.
- Internal marketing is evolutionary, it involves the slow erosion of barriers.

- Internal marketing is used to facilitate an innovative spirit.
- Internal marketing is more successful when there is commitment at the highest level, the cooperation of all employees and an open management style.
- Overt packaging of the internal marketing concept may be less successful than a subtle approach that permeates the organization and becomes part of the business philosophy.

Internal marketing in all its forms was recognized as an important activity in developing a customer-focused organization. In practice, internal marketing is concerned with communications, with developing responsiveness, responsibility and unity of purpose. Fundamental aims of internal marketing are to develop internal and external customer awareness and remove functional barriers to organizational effectiveness.

Internal marketing is at an embryonic stage of development and one where practitioners lead academic research. While little has been codified regarding internal marketing practice it is clear a consideration of internal markets is essential. Where internal marketing is concerned with the development of a customer orientation, the alignment of internal and external marketing ensures coherent relationship marketing. Further, it plays an important role in employee motivation and retention. This area is one which should receive considerable attention over the next five years and research is needed to identify success factors and barriers, particularly in areas of structures, systems and people.

Integrating relationship marketing in the firm

We have argued that relationship marketing implies a consideration of not just better relationships with customer markets but also the development and enhancement of relationships with supplier, employee, referral, 'influencer' and internal markets. Not all these markets necessarily need a formal marketing plan drawn up around them although some firms will benefit from a written plan. For example, the accounting firm mentioned earlier benefited significantly from having a formal marketing plan directed at the task of recruiting graduates. Nevertheless, companies will need to have some form of strategy developed to address each of these markets. In some cases this may be implicit. However, there is a risk associated with such implicit strategy unless it is deeply ingrained and understood by all staff within the organization.

At the same time, efforts should be made to ensure the relationship strategy within each of the markets is realized. Equal if not greater attention needs to be placed on the implementation of the desired strategy than with the creation of a written plan. In some cases this may be counter-productive. For example, a written marketing plan for internal markets may not capture the behavioural and motivational processes which need to be initiated to ensure that, for example, customer contact staff are motivated and empowered to deliver the requisite level of service quality.

Marketing, customer service and quality

To avoid the danger that customer service will be confined to the province of the distribution or the complaints department and not seen as a company-wide opportunity, this chapter has argued that customer service should be considered as a full element of the marketing mix. Traditionally there has been little written about customer service as a separate element of the marketing mix and in part this has been because it has been subsumed in the other elements of the mix. However, the increasing importance of customer service is obvious from both an observation of what is happening in the business environment and a study of the focus of current academic research. Customer service has emerged as having an important role within relationship marketing and thus deserving explicit examination as a marketing mix element in its own right.

The increasing sophistication of customers, both industrial and consumers, suggests increasing attention needs to be placed on customer service. Customer service has an important part to play in both the pre-sale, sale and post-sale stages of the relationship with the customer. While virtually all the literature on customer service is concerned with the relationship between a company and its customers, it should now be apparent that customer service has a role to play in the other markets outlined. Members of supply markets, referral markets, employee markets, internal markets and 'influence markets' need to be served in the same way that customer markets are. The concepts of customer service have application in establishing and maintaining relationships with all these key markets.

Thus the concept of relationship marketing involves both a consideration of the six market areas and the creation of a bond with each market through the delivery of value satisfactions as represented by the quality of the ongoing relationship as well as the quality of products and services being produced. It is this notion of total quality, in the sense of providing customer perceived value, that creates an opportunity to turn transaction-based marketing into relationship-based marketing.

References

1 La Londe B. J. and Zinszer, P. H. (1976). *Customer Service: Meaning and Measurement*, Chicago: NCPDM.

2 Christopher M. G., Schary, P. P. and Skjott-Larsen, T. (1979). *Customer Service and Distribution Strategy*, Associated Business Press.

3 Borden N. H. (1965). The concept of the marketing mix. In *Science in Marketing*, (Schwartz G. ed.) John Wiley, pp. 386–397.

4 Kent R. A. (1986). Faith in the four Ps: an alternative. *Journal of Marketing Management*, Vol 2, No 2, pp. 145–154.

5 Gummesson E. (1987). The new marketing – developing long term interactive relationships. *Long Range Planning*, **20**, 4, 10–20.

6 *op. cit.* For a discussion of the work of Hakansson and his *IMP*

colleagues see: Hakansson H. (ed.) (1982) *International Marketing and Purchasing of Industrial Goods*, Wiley.

7   Webster F. E., Jr and Wind Y. (1972). *Organisational Buying Behaviour*, Prentice Hall, pp. 78–80.

8   Gronroos C. (1989). Fundamental research issues in services marketing. In *Designing a Winning Service Strategy* (Bitner M. J. and Crosby L. A. eds) American Marketing Association, pp. 9–10.

9   Brookes R. (1988). *The New Marketing*, Gower Press.

10 Booms B. H. and Bitner M. J. (1981). Marketing strategies and organisation structures for service firms. In *Marketing of Services* (Donnelly J. and George W. R. eds) Chicago: American Marketing Association, pp. 47–51.

11 Wind Y. (1986). Models for marketing planning and decision making. In *Handbook of Modern Marketing* 2nd edn (Buell V. P. ed.): McGraw Hill, pp. 49.1–49.12.

12 Baker M. (1985). *Marketing Strategy and Management*, Macmillan, p. 179.

13 Majaro S. (1982). *Marketing in Perspective*. George Allen & Unwin.

14 Kotler P. (1984). *Marketing Management: Analysis, Planning and Control*, 5th edn. Prentice Hall, pp. 492–3.

15 La Londe B. J., Cooper, M. C. and Noordewier, T. G. (1988). *Customer Service: A Management Perspective*. Council of Logistics Management.

16 Cunningham M. T. and Roberts D. A. (1974). The role of customer service in industrial marketing. *European Journal of Marketing*. **8**, 1, pp. 15–28.

17 O'Shaughnessy J. *Competitive Marketing: A Strategic Approach*. George Allen & Unwin, p. 184.

18 Blenel W. H. and Bender H. E. (1980). *Product Service Planning*. AMA Conference, p. 12.

19 Judd V. C. (1987). Differentiate with the 5th P: People. *Industrial Marketing Management*. **16**, pp. 241–247.

20 Davidow W. H. (1986). *Marketing High Technology*. The Free Press, p. 172.

21 Leenders M. R. and Blenkhorn, D. L. (1988). *Reverse Marketing: The New Buyer–Supplier Relationship*. The Free Press, p. 8.

22 Masson R. J. (1985). User–vendor relationships in the Scottish electronics industry. *International Journal of Quality and Reliability Management*, **3**, 2, pp. 31–37.

23 Philips Industries (1986). *Co-Makership: Reader on Co-Makership, and its Consequences in Forwarding, Purchasing Benelux*. The following material on co-makership is based on this report.

24 *op. cit.*, pp. 7–8.

25 Maister D. H. (1989). *Professional Service Firm Management*, 4th edn: Maister Associates Inc., p. 78.

26 Gummesson E., *op. cit.*

27 Payne A. F. T. and Walters D. (1990). Internal marketing: myth or magic, Draft Paper. Cranfield School of Management.

28 Buzzell R. D. and Gale B. T. (1987). *The PIMS Principles.*: **The Free Press.**
29 Peters T. and Austin N., *op. cit.*, p. 53.

2. DEVELOPING A RELATIONSHIP STRATEGY

The strategic process

In this chapter we examine some of the key considerations in the formulation of strategy and discuss how the relationship marketing concept interrelates with them; we explore the process of strategy, examine the concept of 'what the customer buys', and review the central importance of quality to a relationship strategy. Underpinning the whole concept of strategy is the notion of a strategic focus relating to the **delivery of value** to the customer. This focus on value delivery to the customer should pervade both the formulation and implementation of strategy. While most companies recognize the importance of strategy, relatively few actively develop a formal strategy with the notion of relationships constantly in mind. We use the term 'relationship strategy' to emphasize the need to be constantly focused on the relationships outlined in the previous chapter when developing a business strategy.

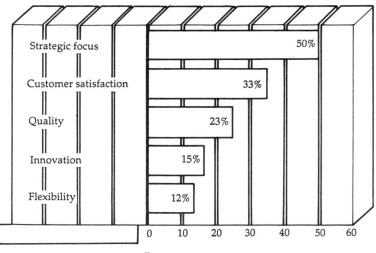

Percentage response

Figure 2.1 *Chief executives' view of critical success factors*

Source: KPMG Peat Marwick/Business International/Crosby Associates Surveys reported in Arrington, L. (1990) 'The Customer is God', *Managing Service Quality*, **1**, 1, 24

How important is this strategic focus in developing a relationship strategy? A study was recently conducted among nearly 500 chief executives in Europe, North America and Asia on competing effectively during the 1990s and into the 21st century by KPMG Peat Marwick, Business International and Crosby Associates. The study identified the chief executives' views of critical factors for success and these are shown in Figure 2.1. It shows, across the wide range of industries and countries studied, that strategic focus was considered the most important critical success factor for competing in the future. The importance of customer satisfaction (which results from effective marketing and customer service) and quality followed closely in second and third place in the survey. The findings of this study are consistent with our view of relationship marketing. This suggests that a tactical focus on customer service and quality is necessary but not sufficient. A relationship strategy, based on strategic marketing considerations, is also necessary to bring about the desired delivery of value to the customer.

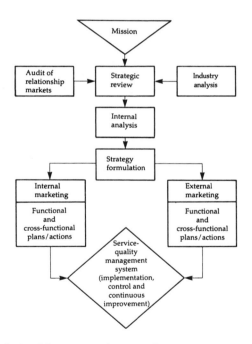

Figure 2.2 *Relationship strategy framework*

Many approaches to understanding the process of strategy have been suggested.[1] However, most of them are based on a similar series of steps. Figure 2.2 incorporates these steps within a relationship strategy framework. These steps consist of: formulation of a mission or purpose statement; a strategic review which involves an audit of relationship markets and an industry analysis of both the customer markets and competition; an internal analysis of the firm; the formulation of a strategy based on decisions about how and where to compete in the marketplace involving the development of plans aimed at both external and internal markets; and the implementation of the relationship strategy supported by a service-quality management system.

This chapter reviews each of the formulation steps in the strategic process. This relationship strategy is applicable at the broad level of formulation and implementation of a corporate level strategy or at a more specific level such as formulation and implementation of a business unit strategy. While this model implies sequential development of strategy it should be emphasized that, in reality, strategy is developed iteratively. The 'people' and 'process' issues leading to service-quality implementation are discussed in Chapters 5 and 6.

Mission statements

If a strategic focus is viewed as the most important critical success factor in business today it is appropriate to address this first. The process which provides this strategic focus commences with the identification and articulation of a company mission statement. Such a statement should explicitly reflect the underlying beliefs, values and aspirations and strategies of the organization. It has been pointed out, however, that many companies' mission statements display bland similarity and consist of generalizations rather than reflect a unique commitment to the values and corporate direction that is intended.[2]

Statements of company mission need not be long and platitudinous. Tom Watson, the founder of IBM, articulated his company's philosophy in the phrase 'IBM means service'. The corporate philosophy described by Watson was simple: not just to be a *good* service company, but to be the *best* service company – in *any* industry, in the *world*. Tom Watson argued the basic philosophy of the organization had a great deal more to do with its performance than did technological or economic resources, organizational structure, innovation or timing.

Some organizations spell out their mission in more detail. For example, British Airways outlines its mission and goals (see Figure 2.3) at some length under a number of themes which include corporate charisma, creativity, business capability, competitive stance and training philosophy. Ultimately the company's mission needs to reflect the shared value systems which are held within the organization as part of its strategic focus. Within the industry sectors it competes, British Airways aims to be 'the worldwide symbol of creativity, value, service and quality'.

A company mission can be defined as a statement of purpose that distinguishes the organization from other firms and which outlines the scope of that company's values and beliefs as well as its strategic field of operations in product and market terms. The mission statement is an important device for focusing activity in an organization. It provides a framework to enable the diverse staff of an organization to work in a coordinated manner towards the achievement of the overall objectives and philosophy of the enterprise and thus is consistent with the concept of relationship marketing that we have described.

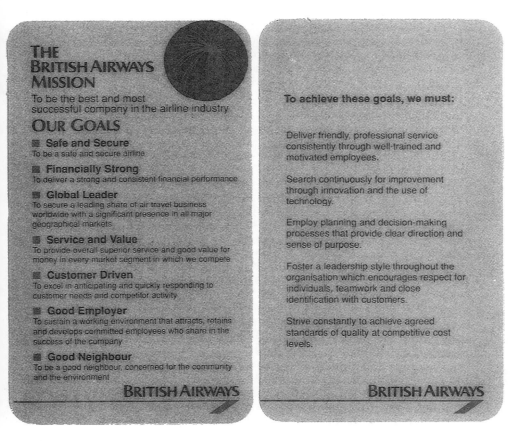

THE BRITISH AIRWAYS MISSION

To be the best and most successful company in the airline industry

OUR GOALS

■ **Safe and Secure**
To be a safe and secure airline

■ **Financially Strong**
To deliver a strong and consistent financial performance

■ **Global Leader**
To secure a leading share of air travel business worldwide with a significant presence in all major geographical markets

■ **Service and Value**
To provide overall superior service and good value for money in every market segment in which we compete

■ **Customer Driven**
To excel in anticipating and quickly responding to customer needs and competitor activity

■ **Good Employer**
To sustain a working environment that attracts, retains and develops committed employees who share in the success of the company

■ **Good Neighbour**
To be a good neighbour, concerned for the community and the environment

BRITISH AIRWAYS

To achieve these goals, we must:

Deliver friendly, professional service consistently through well-trained and motivated employees.

Search continuously for improvement through innovation and the use of technology.

Employ planning and decision-making processes that provide clear direction and sense of purpose.

Foster a leadership style throughout the organisation which encourages respect for individuals, teamwork and close identification with customers.

Strive constantly to achieve agreed standards of quality at competitive cost levels.

BRITISH AIRWAYS

Figure 2.3 *British Airways' mission and goals*

Unfortunately, many companies' mission statements don't conform to these requirements. Common problems with mission statements are that they consist of 'motherhood' statements, fail to support a relationship focus, or are unnecessarily broad, or restrictingly narrow, and may prevent management taking advantage of new opportunities.

A mission statement should articulate the desired long-term direction of the organization by indicating the basic products to be provided, major markets to be served, and means of serving those markets. In developing a mission statement, Christopher et al[3] point out a number of factors that should be considered in formulating a mission statement. They argue a mission statement should:

- Be specific enough to have an impact on the behaviour of individuals throughout the business.
- Be focused more on customer-need satisfaction than upon products or services.
- Reflect the distinctive competences of the business and be based upon an objective recognition of the company's strengths and weaknesses.
- Recognize the opportunities and threats in the competitive environment, trends in resource and consumption markets and the company's vulnerabilities.
- Be realistic and attainable.
- Be flexible.

It is particularly important to avoid mission statements that are product-oriented. That is, the business's mission should be defined in a way that reflects customer needs rather than product features and attributes. The dangers of product-oriented mission statements become obvious when manufacturers of products such as candlesticks and slide rules, which have seen their markets largely disappear, are considered. In the long run, companies which appreciate that they are in the business of satisfaction of underlying market needs such as illumination or computational aids, rather than in manufacture of specific products, are likely to be much more successful than companies that are product-oriented.

It is a focus around shared corporate values and customer needs that signals the likely commitment by staff to a relationship strategy. Figure 2.4 shows the mission statement for the Royal Trust Bank, a leading Canadian bank based in London. The strategic process of development of a mission statement should, and in this case did, involve detailed consideration and input from the board and senior management team. In the Royal Trust Bank this led to a reappraisal of the key business areas and a refocusing of the bank's activities. In particular the bank recognized the importance of customer service **at the strategic level** and its role 'as a leading relationship bank'.

Mission statements can be an empty statement on a piece of paper or can reflect and underpin fundamental values of an organization in pursuit of its strategy. In Royal Trust Bank's case the importance of a **relationship strategy** has been emphasized as the primary means by which their basic business objectives will be achieved.

Of particular importance is the explanation and communication of the rationale and purpose of the mission statement. In the bank's case each employee received a copy of the mission statement together with a letter from the chief executive explaining it. This was followed up by small group workshops for **all** staff, from receptionists and secretaries up to board level, in which the mission statement was discussed, the bank's strategy as a leading relationship bank was explained and key customer service strategies were identified. This formed part of an ongoing relationship strategy programme aimed at both external and internal customer markets.

A focus on the customer is pivotal to a relationship strategy and this

ROYAL TRUST BANK

MISSION STATEMENT

We aim to strengthen and focus our role in the United
Kingdom as a leading relationship bank offering our
clients selected lending and investment products
together with fiduciary and advisory services designed
for developing companies, wealth-producing
entrepreneurs and professional individuals.

We will create wealth for our clients, employees
and shareholder.

Our aim will be achieved by:
Earning the loyalty of our clients and their
recommendation of our people through:
- quality products and good advice
- dependable delivery
- efficient administration

Giving our employees purpose and pride through:
- training
- authority commensurate with responsibility
- recognition for performance

Maintaining the confidence and support of our
shareholder through:
- prudence
- forsight
- progress

Figure 2.4 *Corporate mission statement for Royal Trust Bank*
Source: Royal Trust Bank

customer orientation should be apparent in the mission statement. Peter Drucker has summed up the importance of this focus on the customer.

> It is a customer who determines what a business is. It is the customer alone whose willingness to pay for a good or service converts economic resources into wealth and things into goods. What a business thinks it produces is not of first importance, especially not to the future of the business and to its success. What the customer thinks he/she is buying, what he/she considers value, is decisive – it determines what a business is, what it produces, and whether it will prosper. And what the customer buys and considers value is never a product. It is always utility, meaning what a product or service does for him. The customer is the foundation of a business and keeps it in existence.[4]

This customer orientation is highlighted in a section of the ICL (International Computers Limited) mission statement entitled 'Commitment to Customers':

- The overriding importance of the needs and expectations of our customers should condition all our thinking and govern all our planning. We are now a company driven by the business needs of our market. We all have to become steeped in the concept that 'there is nothing too good for our customers.'
- We owe them 100 per cent quality. 100 per cent reliability and 100 per cent service. Our 'zero defects' standards illustrate this commitment to our customers. We cannot be satisfied with less.
- All work units within the company also have to adopt the same attitude towards their in-house customers. Staff people towards their field customers: development divisions towards the sales force that will sell their systems and provide them with market intelligence: these too should adopt an attitude of 100 per cent service.
- The customer matters most and comes first in everything we do. We must never allow our own problems to distract us from understanding and solving his.

It is noticeable in ICL that the internal customers within the company as well as external customers are identified as groups for 'zero defects' standards.

A common mistake with mission statements is for them to be framed in the Boardroom and not to be related to functional, cross-functional and operational activities in the organization. Mission statements should be promulgated with a view to creating unity of purpose throughout the organization. Two approaches can be used to do this. Firstly, an amplification of the mission statement can be made at lower levels. This involves the amplification of how the mission statement applies to the activities of, say, a particular division or department. This enables all levels to relate the corporate mission statement to their specific activities and responsibilities.

Secondly, mission statements can be specifically developed for divisional or departmental levels. In this way they could be developed, for example, at a business unit level or a functional level or could cover key cross-functional activities such as customer service.

Mission

The Dynamics Division of British Aerospace is a world-wide leader in both the design and manufacture of guided weapons and high technology equipments.

Our mission is one of continuous improvement of our products, our product range and services to satisfy our customers' needs, allowing us to prosper as a business, thus securing long term employment, and provide the Company's shareholders, many of whom are also employees, with a reasonable return on their investment.

Values

How we accomplish our mission is as important as the mission itself. Fundamental to success for the Company are these basic values:

People – People are our most important resource. They provide our corporate intelligence and determine our reputation and vitality. Involvement and teamwork are our core human values.

Products – Our products are the end result of our efforts, and they should be the best in serving customers world-wide.

Profits – are required for survival and growth, they are the source of finance for enhancing our product range and capital investment programmes.

Guiding Principles

Quality Comes First – To achieve customer satisfaction, the quality of our products and services must be our number one priority.

Customers are the reason for our existence – They must be convinced that our products and services provide value for money and are superior to those offered by our competitors.

Continuous improvement is essential to our success – We must strive for excellence in everything we do; in our products, in their safety and value in our services, our human relations, our competitiveness and our profitability.

Employee involvement is our way of life – We are a team. We must treat each other with trust and respect. Our managers and supervisors have, as a major responsibility, the creation of a quality environment in which continued improvement can flourish.

Dealers and suppliers are our partners – The Company must maintain mutually beneficial relationships with dealers, suppliers, and our other business associates. They play a vital role in assisting us to achieve our mission. They, therefore, need to have a full understanding of what our mission is.

Integrity is never compromised – The conduct of our Company world-wide must be pursued in a manner that is socially responsible and commands respect for this integrity and for its positive contributions to society.

Figure 2.5 *British Aerospace (Dynamics) Limited's Mission, Value and Guiding Principles*

Source: British Aerospace. Reproduced with permission

Some mission statements are long and cumbersome. Further they may make perfect sense to a business graduate or senior manager in head office but not to a front-line teller in a bank or a leading hand on the shop floor of a factory. Consequently it may be worthwhile considering an alternative version of a mission statement which captures the essential elements of the corporate mission in terms that can be meaningfully communicated at lower levels within the organization.

An example of this is the version of a mission statement for the branch banking unit of ANZ Bank in Australia:

- To not only be known for quality customer service, but to be renowned for it.
- To know our customers.
- Give them the service and products they want.
- And do it better than anyone.

Such a version of the corporate mission may not include the strategic focus element for the firm in terms of its business scope but does get across the **relationship** message to front-line staff.

A customer service mission statement, for example, expresses the company's philosophy and commitment to customer service and is derived from the increasing recognition that service quality is an important means of gaining competitive advantage. In some cases customer service and quality missions are stated separately but often they are combined as part of the statement of a firm's overall mission. Figure 2.5 provides an example of a statement of mission and values for a manufacturing organization – in this case the Dynamics Division of British Aerospace, prior to its creation as a wholly-owned subsidiary of BAe. It highlights the role of both quality and customers service as well as relationships with suppliers, dealers and employees as well as customers.

Relationships are based on both personal inter-reactions and supporting systems. By acknowledgement of the key role of quality and customer service in the corporation's mission statement, recognition is placed on the role all levels of the business have in making a relationship strategy happen, including:

- Senior management who set company-wide priorities and are ultimately responsible for their achievement.
- Middle management who manage front-line and support staff to ensure relationship policies and goals are met.
- Front-line service and support staff who are responsible for service quality on a day-to-day basis.

Strategic review and internal analysis

The strategic review and internal analysis follows from the development of a mission statement and are key steps in the process of developing a relationship strategy. A broad audit covers a number of key areas including competitor analysis and benchmarking, market and customer analysis, a consideration of the six market areas outlined in Chapter 1, environmental analysis and internal analysis. However, from a relationship strategy perspective we are especially concerned with analysis from the competitive and market perspectives. To undertake a thorough strategic review and internal analysis a number of useful approaches and frameworks can be utilized. These include industry and relationship analysis, value chains and market analyses and segmentation.[5] Each of these approaches will now be discussed.

Industry and relationship analysis

An industry and relationship analysis including an examination of competitors is an essential step prior to making a decision about your own strategy. In undertaking an analysis of any industry, its characteristics and long-term prospects can be analysed in terms of five dimensions: the nature and degree of competition, the barriers to entry to that business, the competitive power of substitute products, the degree of buyer power, and the degree of supplier power. The industry analysis framework, developed by Porter,[6] is shown in Figure 2.6. Through analysis of these five dimensions insights can be gained into relationship with a number of key market areas for both opportunities and threats as well as the specific key factors for success in the industry under consideration.

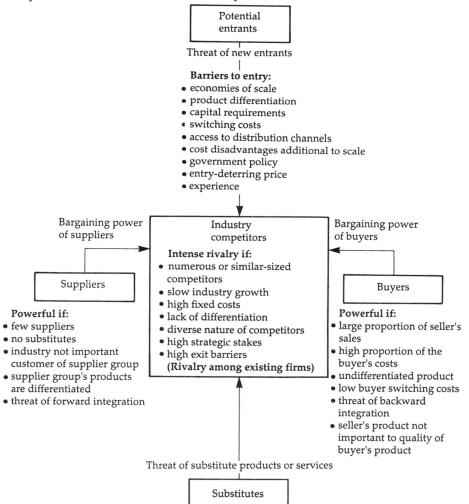

Figure 2.6 *The Porter industry analysis model*

Source: Based on Porter Michael E. (1980), Techniques for Analysing Industries and Competitors, *Competitive Strategy*. New York: Free Press

The five forces which contribute to industry profitability, include:

- **Potential entrants.** Two factors determine how strong this force will be: the existing barriers to entry and the likelihood of a strong competitive reaction from established competitors. If the threat of entry tends to be low, if barriers to entry are high and/or aspiring new entrants can expect extremely hostile retaliation from the established firms within the industry. If the threat of entry is low, profitability of the industry tends to be high.
- **Buyers.** The bargaining power of customers (or buyers) is high when a number of critical factors are present. These include: the products that a company purchase form a large proportion, in terms of cost, of its own product; if the buyer group is operating in an industry of low profitability; if the products supplied are undifferentiated and it is easy for the buyer to switch between suppliers at little cost; if the products are purchased in large volumes; or if the buyers have the potential to integrate backwards. Such conditions of high buyer power will result in lower industry profitability.
- **Suppliers.** Similarly, the bargaining power of suppliers can be high if there are relatively few suppliers; if the industry is not an important customer of the supplier group; if the supplier has the potential to integrate forward into the customer's business; if there are few or no direct substitutes for the product; if the industry is dominated by only a few suppliers; or if the supplier group's products are sufficiently differentiated so that the firm being supplied the goods cannot easily switch to another supplier. Conditions of high supplier power lead to reduced industry profitability.
- **Substitute products.** In many markets it is possible to identify products which can serve as substitutes. In industries ranging from telecommunications to car making, the threat of substitution is present. The higher the threat of substitution, the lower the profitability is likely to be within the industry. This is because threat of substitution generally sets a limit on the prices that can be charged. The factors which influence the threat of substitution include the substitute product price – performance trade-off; and the extent of switching costs associated with changing from one supplier to the supplier of the substitute. If the threat of substitution is low, industry profitability will tend to be high.
- **Industry competition.** The degree of industry competition is characterized by the amount of rivalry between existing firms. This can vary considerably and is not related necessarily to whether or not the industry is highly profitable. Intense rivalry can exist if there is slow growth within the industry; if competitors are evenly balanced in size and capability; where switching costs are low; where there is a high fixed cost structure and companies need to keep volumes high; where exit barriers are high such that unprofitable companies may still remain within the industry; and where competitors have different strategies – the result of which is that some firms may be willing to

pursue a strategy that results in considerable conflict within the industry. A common outcome of this is price wars. A high degree of rivalry depresses industry profitability.

Porter argues that the goal of the corporate strategist is to find a position in his industry where his company can best defend itself against these five forces, or alternatively influence them in his favour.

A complete and balanced analysis of the competitive environment in which a firm is operating would include an examination of barriers to entry, the relative power of buyers and suppliers, the power of substitute, and the degree of rivalry within the industry. This would lead to a good understanding of the key factors for success within that industry. Such an analysis makes a major impact on managers' understanding of the strengths and weaknesses, opportunities and threats within their industry.

The importance of relationships become apparent when these five forces impacting on probability are examined. We have already described relationships with customers and relationships with suppliers in the previous chapter. It is also of importance to consider relationships with competitors. The type of relationships with competitors are often the result of the degree of rivalry and the competitive structure of the industry. Rivalry is usually strong where there are numerous or equally balanced competitors but may also be intense under other conditions. Day[7] illustrates the poor relationships between the two major competitors in the market for industrial lasers in the USA. The poor relationships between Specra-Physics and Coherent Radiation manifests itself in deep-seated antagonism between the firms in the way they use their resources to attack one another. As a result neither firm is profitable.

Adoption of a better relationship between these two seemingly implacable rivals is needed to restore industry profitability in this sector. Porter points to the need to adopt strategies relating to competitors that could be called 'cooperative' and that makes the industry as a whole better off.

Porter's model explicitly examines two market areas, suppliers and customers in the context of the competitive environment. The audit of relationship markets and internal analysis, see Figure 2.2, acts as a reminder of the necessity to also audit the potential employee, 'influencer', referral and internal market relationships.

The value chain

Competitive advantage can be gained from focusing on the individual activities and work processes within a business. To consider the strengths and weaknesses of a business, its activities should be divided into the various steps by which value is added. Porter's value chain[8] is a useful means of doing this. Identification of the value chain for a business helps understand the relative importance of the constituent activities by disaggregating the business into activities which are of significance from a strategic perspective.

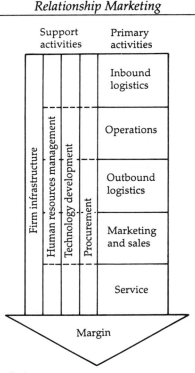

Figure 2.7 *The value chain*

Value chain activities, shown in Figure 2.7, can be categorized into two types – primary activities (inbound logistics, operations, outbound logistics, marketing and sales, and service) and support activities (infrastructure, human-resource management, technology development, and procurement). These support activities are integrating functions that 'cut across' the various primary activities within the firm.

It may also be useful to further subdivide specific primary activities within the value chain. For example, the marketing and sales activity in Figure 2.7 can be expanded further into constituent activities of marketing management, which include advertising, sales-force administration, sales-force operations, and promotion.

Competitive advantage grows out of the way in which firms organize and perform the discrete activities within the value chain. To gain competitive advantage over its rivals a firm must promote value to its customers through performing activities more efficiently than its competitors (lower cost advantage) or by performing activities in a unique way that creates greater buyer value (differentiation advantage).

The process activities within a value chain should not be considered in isolation. It is essential to consider the linkages where the performance of one activity impacts the cost or effectiveness of other activities. In a manufacturing company improved product design may reduce the need for inspection and result in significantly reduced after-sales service costs. Cross-functional coordination of linked activities may reduce time to perform them and result in less inventories, etc. Reconfiguration of the value chain by relocating, reordering, regrouping or even carefully eliminating activities may represent an opportunity for major improvement in competitive position.

The objective of strategy is to create increased shareholder wealth through the development of a sustainable competitive advantage. A firm can possess or develop two types of competitive advantage – **cost advantage or differentiation**. Thus, each element of the value chain should be investigated thoroughly to identify existing or potential means through which the firm can achieve their relative cost position (cost advantage) or affect their level of uniqueness (differentiation), or both.

The value chain is a graphic model of the firm's activities that enable managers to review the many complex factors that effect their business. Relationship marketing is an integrating concept which ensures an external focus, as well as in internal focus, is placed on all the value-adding activities in the business. At the same time it recognizes the importance of the linkages between discrete activities in the value chain and the role that internal marketing has to play.

Within each of the primary and support activities of the value chain, the area concerned has two forms of internal customer/supplier relationship. First there is the customer/supplier relationship between that activity and other primary and support activities. Second there is the customer/supplier relationship **within** the primary or support activity. A relationship marketing orientation can diminish traditional rivalries between different primary activities (e.g. the production department and the marketing department) and between support and primary activities (e.g. finance and production).

Market analyses and segmentation

When a critical review of any market is undertaken it soon becomes clear that the notion of a single market for a given product or service is of limited use. All markets are made up of market segments and even if the product supplied is identical from a physical point of view, a consideration should be made of how the total offer can be differentiated from competitive offers. Many companies following a market aggregation strategy, (i.e. not recognizing market segments) are increasingly considering means of appealing to different segments. Thus companies, such as McDonalds, offer different product ranges in different countries, banks recognize the value of different delivery systems for standard products, and manufacturers of 'commodity' products are seeking differentiation through customer service.

The process of market segmentation is one of dividing a total market up into a series of submarkets (or market segments). The marketing segmentation approach is concerned with first considering the alternative bases for segmentation; second, choosing specific segments (or a single segment) within that base and finally determining appropriate service levels for these segments. Three criteria are commonly used in selecting target segments. Market segments should be:

i) Accessible – it should be possible to communicate with segment markets with a minimum of overlap with other segments and distribution channels should be available to reach them.

ii) Measurable – it should be possible to measure or estimate the size of the segment and to quantify the impact of varying marketing mix strategies on that segment.

iii) Size – the segment should be sufficiently large, to make it financially worthwhile to service.

Seven broad bases have traditionally been used in market segmentation.

Geographic segmentation

An approach whereby customers are differentiated on the basis of where they are located. Thus a customer may be segmented into urban, suburban or rural groups. A common geographic segmentation may divide customers into areas on the basis of postcodes which might also represent different groups in terms of relative wealth, socio-economic and other factors.

Demographic and socioeconomic segmentation

Demographic and socio-economic segmentation is based on a wide range of factors including age, sex, family size income, education, social class and ethnic origins. It is thus helpful in indicating the profile of people who purchase a company's product or services.

Psychographic segmentation

Psychographic segmentation involves an analysis of lifestyle characteristics, attitudes and personality. Recent research in several coun-tries suggests that the population can be divided into between ten and fifteen groups, each having an identifible set of lifestyle, attitude and personality characteristics.

Benefit segmentation

Benefit segmentation involves grouping customers together on the basis of the benefits they are seeking from a product. For example, purchasers of motor cars seek widely varying benefits. For example, they may seek fuel economy, size, bootspace, performance, reliability or prestige.

Usage segmentation

Usage segmentation, a very important variable for many products, usually divides consumers into heavy users, medium users, occasional users or non-users of the product being considered. Marketers are often concerned with the heavy-user segment who consume many times the amount of the product compared with occasional users.

Loyalty segmentation

Loyalty segmentation is concerned with identifying the relative loyalty a customer has to a particular product or brand. Customers can be divided into groups who are very loyal, moderately loyal and unloyal. These groups are then examined in an attempt to identify any common characteristics they have so the product can be targeted at prospectively loyal customers.

Occasion segmentation

Occasion segmentation recognizes that customers may vary in their usage of a product or brand depending on the situation. For example, a beer drinker may drink light beer with his workmates before driving home, a conventional beer in his home and a premium or imported beer at a special dinner in a licensed restaurant.

These are the more common forms of segmentation. However, there are obviously many other ways in which markets may be segmented. For example, in listing thirty variables for segmentation, Twedt[9] points out that his list is intended as being illustrative rather than complete.

Segmentation by service

One area of potential which has received relatively little attention is the consideration of how customers respond to varying service offerings. In a sense this may be considered as a subset of benefit segmentation, but we consider it of sufficient importance to be addressed separately. The various elements of customer service that can be offered, and possible differentiation in terms of service levels within these elements, represent considerable opportunity to design service packages appropriate to different market segments.

Segmenting markets by service involves addressing these issues:

- Can groupings of customers be identified with similar service requirements?
- Can we differentiate our service offering?
- Do all our products require the same level of service?

In a study of the scientific instrument and supplies industry, Gilmour[10] examined the response of five customer segments to a range of nine customer service elements. The results of his study are partly summarized in Figure 2.8 which shows the response of both the suppliers and the five customer segments, as well as the composite results for all customers. The results show some disparity between the customers and their suppliers' perception of the importance of certain customer service elements, particularly in the areas of sales service and back-up and efficient telephone handling of orders and queries. The table also shows several important differences between market segments. For example, two government markets – government instrumentalities and secondary schools, showed very marked differences in the importance attached to a wide range of service elements including availability, after-sales service

Customer service element	Suppliers	All customers	Private companies	Government instrumentalities	Secondary schools	Universities and CAEs	Hospitals
Availability of item	1	1	1	5	1	1	1
After-sales service and back-up	5	2	5	1	7	2	2
Efficient telephone handling of orders and queries	2	6	4	6	4	7	7
Ordering convenience	7	7	8	9	2	6	8
Competent technical representatives	3	5	5	2	8	5	3
Delivery time	5	4	2	6	5	3	5
Reliability of delivery	4	3	3	4	3	4	4
Demonstrations of equipment	8	7	7	3	9	7	5
Availability of published material	9	9	9	8	6	9	8

Figure 2.8 *Average importance ratings for customer service elements for different market segments*

Source: Gilmour P. (1977). Customer segmentation: differentiating by market segment. *International Journal of Physical Distribution*, 7, 3, 146

and back-up, ordering convenience, competent technical representatives, and demonstrations of equipment.

By explicitly measuring the perceived importance of different customer service elements across market segments, the supplier is much better placed to respond to that segment's identified needs and allocate the service offering appropriate to it. This particular study suggested that highly qualified technical representation was appropriate to servicing the government and hospitals segments, but not the others where a less-technically qualified salesman would suffice. Also a highly efficient and responsive handling of orders was appropriate for private companies and secondary schools, but was less necessary for other customer segments.

Studies such as the one outlined above suggest that policy decisions to increase or reduce customer service levels should not be made equally across the entire customer base or across service factors. Considerable potential exists in many companies by adopting an approach to reduce customer service costs and/or improve levels of service to the customer by recognizing differentiated service requirements by customer segment.[11]

At the heart of the relationship strategy is the careful segmenting of the market and the development of an approach that minimizes competitors' strengths while maximizing those of your own firm.

This section has focused on the role of segmentation as part of the strategic review and internal analysis. Segmentation is perhaps the most important aspect of market analysis from a relationship strategy perspective as it provides the opportunity to **tailor** the relationship to the needs of specific segments. It is also equally reluctant to segmentation of internal markets. While market segmentation is typically viewed as part of the marketing plan[12] its impact on a firm's fortunes is so profound that top management would not be performing its strategic function if it were to dissociate itself from the detailed process of evaluating segmentation policies.[13] It is thus essential that segmentation should be considered within the framework of corporate strategy as well as marketing management.

The external market analysis and segmentation, and industry analysis, are then examined in the context of an internal analysis of the firm. This involves an in-depth review of the internal markets including strengths and weaknesses of the firm and how they relate to the external opportunities and threats identified as a result of the industry analysis and audit of the other relationship markets.

Strategy formulation

When the strategic review and internal analysis steps are complete the next step is strategy formulation. Strategy formulation is concerned with an examination of the alternative strategies available to an organization and involves two basic questions which must be addressed. These are: in what product-market areas should the company compete, and what strategy should be adopted within these product-market areas? A decision on the firm's key markets should have been made in determining the mission statement or will evolve from a consideration of it. To identify the product-market area in which to compete the firm can consider the following options:

- Market penetration
- Market development
- Product development
- Diversification

Each of these options are shown in the product–market matrix in Figure 2.9. Each cell in the matrix represents a core marketing strategy based on targeting combinations of existing or new markets and existing or new products. The company should review its strengths in considering moving beyond its present markets and products. Firms which have extremely close relationships with their existing markets may wish to develop new products for them and adopt a product development strategy. This strategy is also relevant for firms with a single product or service being offered to a particular customer group. We term this product development cell the 'relationship building box' where we can meet additional customer needs through the development of new products or services for existing clients. Firms with unique and proprietary products and technologies may consider offering them to new markets through a market development strategy. A diversification

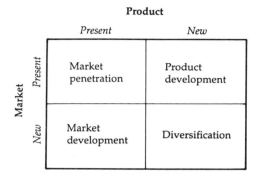

Figure 2.9 *The product–market matrix*

strategy, where a firm moves beyond its present markets and products, represents an area of high risk.

At the start of strategy formulation the firm's objectives should be developed and the planning assumptions identified. The planning assumptions will cover general aspects such as economic, social and technology issues as well as more specific ones dealing specifically with the industry and competition within it. Objectives need to be developed in terms of growth, profitability and degree of acceptable risk in the chosen product-market areas.

Generic strategies

There are several basic strategies which can be adopted once a decision has been made regarding which products and which markets to be involved in. Different writers have proposed various alternative natural or generic strategies which can be adopted by a firm. An approach developed by Porter[14] suggests that a choice of one of three generic strategies is appropriate for a given business. These include a cost-leadership strategy, a differentiation strategy, or a focus strategy.

- **Cost-leadership strategy.** A cost-leadership strategy requires a company to set out with the objective of being the lowest cost producer in the industry. Companies must seek economies of scale, proprietary technology not available to other firms, preferential access to raw materials and cost minimization over a wide range of areas.
- **Differentiation.** A second generic strategy that can be adopted by firms is one of differentiation. With a differentiation strategy a firm seeks to be different within the industry it is operating in by being unique on some dimension or set of dimensions of value to buyers. The company seeks one or more dimensions to differentiate itself on, and as a result hopes to earn premium price for its products or services.
- **Focus strategy.** A focus strategy involves concentrating on a particular buyer group, geographic area or product/market segment. Thus it

is a strategy of differentiation within a particular segment. By selecting a particular segment or group of segments the company attempts to tailor its strategy to serving the needs of its segment better than the competition. It is essentially a strategy of gaining competitive advantage in the target segment because their company is not likely to enjoy competitive advantage across the market as a whole.

Firms wishing to pursue a **cost-leadership strategy** should understand the concept of the experience curve.[15] The experience curve is an essential tool to help managers examine competitive cost structure in an industry. The experience curve is an empirically derived cost relationship which suggests that as accumulated volume of production doubles, cost **per unit** (in real terms) typically falls between 20 and 30 per cent. The experience curve suggests that a company whose products have a greater accumulated volume are likely to enjoy a better cost position than those of their competitors, provided their operations are managed efficiently. There have been hundreds of instances in many industries ranging from passenger car production, the beer market to the insurance industry, where this relationship has also been found to exist. Few strategic concepts have had greater acceptance than that of the experience curve which is used widely throughout manufacturing industry. Understanding of the experience curve concept is fundamental to determining if a company can adopt a cost-leadership strategy. For example, if it could be predicted that a firm would have a lower cost position than its competitors, and opportunity may exist to reduce prices and displace the higher cost competitor from the industry by aggressive pricing.

A **differentiation strategy** means that it is necessary to create differentiation that is perceived by the market as being different and unique. The appropriate means of differentiation varies considerably across different industries. Differentiation could be in terms of technology, features, customer service, dealer network used, styling, and product positioning. Mercedes Benz has, for example, differentiated itself from its competition by adopting a strategy on the basis of design, image, styling and engineering.

The approach adopted for a **focus strategy** varies considerably and can take many forms. The focus strategy is concerned with a specific market segment and is more concentrated than the differentiation approach which appeals to a wider market. While Japanese motor car manufacturers adopt a cost-leadership approach and manufacturers such as Mercedes a differentiation approach, other manufacturers such as Ferrari and Lamborgini focus on a very tightly defined market segment. The focus strategy is concerned with servicing a particular target market better than any of the other competitors within the industry who are adopting either focus strategies aimed at other segments or broader strategies of differentiation and cost leadership.

The challenge facing managers is to choose the strategy most appropriate to the relationship with the customer segments it has chosen to compete in. Should it be one of cost leadership, differentiation or focus? Figure 2.10 shows the commonly required skills and resources that are needed for each of these three strategies together with the common organizational requirements. It should be noted that attempting to follow more than one generic strategy at the same time is usually a considerable disadvantage. Firms which attempt to do this are 'stuck in the middle', a situation where you are likely to get run over. Porter uses the example of Laker Airways in the UK which began its operations with a clear cost-leadership strategy based on a 'no-frills' operation across the North Atlantic in a market segment which was extremely price sensitive.[16] He points out how Laker by adding additional frills, new services, new routes, ended up with a blurring of Laker's image and suboptimization in service and delivery systems. Faced with difficult business conditions the consequences led Laker to bankruptcy.

Generic strategy	Commonly required skills and resources	Common organizational requirements
Overall-cost leadership	Sustained capital investment and access to capital Process engineering skills Intense supervision of labour Products designed for ease in manufacture Low-cost distribution system	Tight cost control Frequent, detailed control reports Structured organization and responsibilities Incentives based on meeting strict quantitative targets
Differentiation	Strong marketing abilities Product engineering Creative flair Strong capability in basic research Corporate reputation for quality or technological leadership Long tradition in the industry or unique combination of skills drawn from other businesses Strong cooperation from channels	Strong coordination among functions in R & D, product development and marketing Subjective measurement and incentives instead of quantitative measures Amenities to attract highly skilled labour, scientists, or creative people
Focus	Combination of the above policies directed at the particular strategic target	Combination of the above policies directed at the particular strategic target

Figure 2.10 *Commonly required skills, resources and organizational requirements for generic strategies*
Source: Porter Michael E. (1980). Techniques for Analysing Industries and Competitors. *Competitive Strategy*. New York Free Press

The value delivery sequence

In order to assist the decision regarding the generic strategy chosen, we should constantly keep under review the relationship the company is

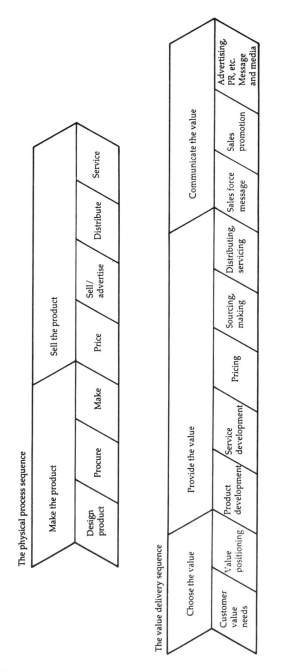

Figure 2.11 *The value delivery system*
Source: Bower M. and Garda R. A. (1985). 'The role of marketing in management', Chapter 1 in Buell, Victor. P. (ed.) *Handbook of Modern Marketing*, New York: McGraw-Hill (1986) pp. 1–10

seeking to establish and what **value** needs to be delivered to the customer to establish and maintain the relationship. McKinsey & Company have developed a framework called the **value delivery sequence** which recognizes companies who have shifted from their traditional view of business as a series of functional activities, to an externally oriented view as seeing the business as being concerned with value delivery.[17] Figure 2.11 shows the value delivery sequence. This builds on the idea that the customers buy promises of satisfaction and they only purchase products because they are of some value to them. We shall return to this concept of 'what the customer buys' in more detail later in this chapter.

They emphasize relationships through a marketing strategy that is directed 'first – factually, constantly, resolutely and imaginatively – to the customer and his or her needs rather than the product given to the marketer to sell'. The value delivery sequence argues that focusing on the traditional physical process sequence of 'make the product and sell the product' can be suboptimal. The value delivery sequence, by contrast, depicts the business as viewed from the customer's perspective rather than a series of internally oriented functions.

The value delivery sequence consists of three key steps – choose the value, provide the value and communicate the value.

- **Choose the value.** It can be argued that customers select products and services because they believe they offer superior value. The pre-requisite here is an understanding of changing customer needs in terms of the forces driving demand as well as customer economics and the buying process and also understanding how well the competition serves those needs particularly in terms of the products, the service and price charged.
- **Provide the value.** The second stage, providing the value, is concerned with developing a product/service package that creates clear and superior value. This involves a focus on things such as product quality and performance, service cost and responsiveness, manufacturing cost and flexibility, channel structure and performance, and price structure.
- **Communicate the value.** This involves the various aspects of promotional activity needed to persuade customers that the values are better than those offered by competitors. It involves not only the issues of organizing sales promotion, advertising and the sales force, but also of providing outstanding service in a way that is continually recognized by the target audience.

Superior value delivery can be defined as providing a product or service that the customer considers gives a net positive value greater than that offered by competitors. Thus the value proposition of IBM is that data processing managers buy their greater **reliability** (not their marketing and not state-of-the-art computer technology). Thus IBM provide a fundamental benefit that appeals to an attractive customer segment which is prepared to pay a price premium for greater perceived reliability. Similarly the value proportion delivered by Volvo of high levels of safety and reliability at a modest price premium has resulted in superior perceived value in the eyes of a significant customer segment.

Adoption of the value delivery sequence approach should result in a specific value proposition for a company. McKinsey suggest that companies wishing to implement a value proposition approach should adopt a three-step sequence.[18]

- Analysing and segmenting the markets by values customers desire
- Vigorously assessing opportunities in each segment to deliver a superior value
- Explicitly choosing the value proposition that optimizes these opportunities.

Lanning and Michaels[19] point out, that success is not just a matter of choice of value proposition but is largely concerned with the thoroughness and innovation with which it is both provided and communicated throughout the organization. Creating the culture so that the value is really provided and communicated is challenging but may well be something which is also very difficult for competitors to replicate. Hence, it can be a source of sustainable competitive advantage. They also argue that the value delivery system helps integrate the different functions within a company and gives added meaning to teamwork whereby every employee is concerned with a contribution to the delivery of the chosen value.

What the customer buys – external and internal marketing

In considering what the customers buy we need to consider external marketing as well as the supporting internal marketing activities discussed in Chapter 1. A consideration of the value delivery sequence suggests that we put aside distinctions between goods and services. Customers do not buy products or services – when they buy they expect benefits and value from the *total offering*. This is not just a semantic point, it is an important distinction which can be strategically vital for the long-term survival of the firm. There are many examples of companies who have taken a narrow view and defined their business purely in terms of the traditional products or services. As a result they were forced out of business when a competitor or competitors effectively reshaped the market by not only getting customers, but by keeping them!

The offer

For an effective relationship strategy an understanding of exactly what the customer is buying is critical. Customers essentially derive benefits from the purchase of either goods or services (hereafter called 'the offer' or the 'the offering'). An offer can be visualized as a molecule with the nucleus or core in the centre, surrounded by a series of both tangible and intangible attributes, features, and benefits. If you think of the core as offering the customer essential solutions, then the surrounding offer is about service support of various kinds. For example packaging, information, finance, delivery, warehousing, advice, warranty, reliability, styling, etc.

Levitt[20] has suggested the offer can be viewed at several levels. These include:

- **Core or generic.** For consumer or industrial products this consists of the basic physical product, i.e. 2 kg of sugar, a packet of self-tapping screws, or a camera. The core elements for a camera, for example, consist of the camera body, the viewer, the winding mechanism, the lens and the other core basic physical components which make up the camera. For a banking service, the core elements might be safety and transactional utility in the form of deposits and withdrawals.
- **Expected.** This consists of the generic product together with the minimal purchase conditions which need to be met. When a customer buys a video cassette recorder they expect an instruction book which explains how to programme it, a warranty for a reasonable period should it break down, and a service network so that it can be repaired.
- **Augmented.** This is the area which enables one offer to be diferentiated from another. For example, IBM have a reputation for excellent customer service although they may not have the most technologically advanced core product. They differentiate by 'adding value' to the core, in terms of service reliability and responsiveness.
- **Potential.** This consists of all potential added features and benefits that are or may be of utility to some buyers. The potential for redefinition of the product gives advantages in attracting new users or 'locking in' existing customers. This could make it difficult or expensive for customers to switch to another supplier.

Thus a firm's offer is a complex set of value-based promises. People buy to solve problems and they attach value to any offer in proportion to this perception of its ability to achieve particular ends. In other words, value is assigned by buyers in relationship to the perceived benefits they receive matched against their expectations.

Returning to the camera example above, the **expected offer** may include a series of lens choices, attractive packaging, easy-to-read operating instructions, a network of service agents, and so on. The **augmented offer** could include a wide range of differentiating factors such as longer warranties, etc. The **potential offer** involves creative options or innovations which will add value for the customer. This might involve new applications being worked on, new materials being used in the camera constitution, or new ideas for varying the camera's features for different user requirements.

Levitt's model allows us to reconcile the marketer's traditional view of the *product*, seen in the terms of various inputs and processes needed to produce it, and the consumer's view of the **offer**, as being a set of solutions and supporting benefits. This is referred to by Collins as the total product concept, but the idea is the same.[21] In Figure 2.12, Collins has used the example of the personal computer market for comparative analysis. The core product for a computer is a machine that permits input,

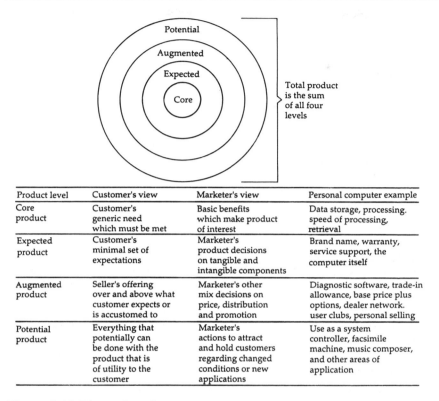

Product level	Customer's view	Marketer's view	Personal computer example
Core product	Customer's generic need which must be met	Basic benefits which make product of interest	Data storage, processing. speed of processing, retrieval
Expected product	Customer's minimal set of expectations	Marketer's product decisions on tangible and intangible components	Brand name, warranty, service support, the computer itself
Augmented product	Seller's offering over and above what customer expects or is accustomed to	Marketer's other mix decisions on price, distribution and promotion	Diagnostic software, trade-in allowance, base price plus options, dealer network. user clubs, personal selling
Potential product	Everything that potentially can be done with the product that is of utility to the customer	Marketer's actions to attract and hold customers regarding changed conditions or new applications	Use as a system controller, facsimile machine, music composer, and other areas of application

Figure 2.12 *The total product concept*

> Source: Collins B. (1989). Chapter 11 'Marketing for Engineers'. In *Management for Engineers* (Sampson D., ed.) Melbourne: Longman Cheshire, p. 372.

processing, storage and retrieval of data. This is the minimum requirement. The expected product consists of not just the above but also service support, warranty, a recognizable brand name and attractive packaging. The augmented product may include the supply of free diagnostic software, a generous trade-in allowance, user clubs and other augmentations which are valuable to personal computer buyers. The potential product may consist of future applications including a systems controller, facsimile machine or a music composer.

It is important to recognize that all customers' requirements are not the same. Customers want different configurations of benefits, features and attributes, and the **market segmentation**, discussed earlier, becomes an essential part of the relationship strategy formulation.

Differentiation and the value of brand names

The value of the brand image also becomes an important element of the augmented offer. Brands are a major determining element in the repeat purchase of consumer products, industrial products and services, and an important way of adding differentiation at the augmented level. The value of brand image can be illustrated by the taste test for Coke and Pepsi shown in Figure 2.13. The table shows the results of a survey of an open taste where the two products were placed in front of the respondents. Supposedly using their most discriminating taste sensibility, 65 per cent of those surveyed preferred Cokes, while 23 per cent preferred Pepsi, and 12 per cent of them ranked them equal/can't say.

	Open	Blind
Prefer Pepsi	23%	51%
Prefer Coke	65%	44%
Equal/can't say	12%	5%

Figure 2.13 *Importance of an image and brand name*

When a matched sample was subjected to a blind taste test (where the identity of the two colas was concealed) strikingly different results were obtained. The results of the blind taste test showed 44 per cent preferred Coke and 51 per cent preferred Pepsi, an increase in preference of Pepsi of over 220 per cent.

Significantly different results were obtained from the consumers in the two different controlled tests. How can this astonishing difference be explained? This suggests that customers 'taste' both the drink and its brand image. This brand image adds value to the offer in the mind of the consumer when they see the familiar Coke package and logo. The same phenomenon ws observed in the office supplies market. Manufacturers had traditionally packaged plain white cut paper in reams externally wrapped in brown paper. One manufacturer adopted a vivid colour coding for different paper grades on the wrapping paper and this resulted in dramatically increased sales!

Whilst these 'added values' may relate to an emotional level they are nevertheless real for the customer perceiving them. Value is added through the creation of brand image. The owners of strong brand names can command higher prices for their offerings.

Differentiation of a brand is achieved by adding value to the basic core offer. Figure 2.14 illustrates this concept. The idea is that the 'core', the essential elemental attributes, may represent 70 per cent of the costs of manufacturing but may only have 30 per cent of the total impact on the customer. By contrast the 'surround' may represent perhaps 30 per cent of the costs but may have 70 per cent of the total customer impact. This means that managers should give increased attention as to how they can differentiate the 'surround' and enlarge it. The larger the 'surround' the greater the likely differentiation of a product compared to its competitors. The cost/benefits must of course be worked out in particular cases.

A key issue which needs to be considered in the context of differentiation and brands is the **brand to commodity continuum**. This continuum

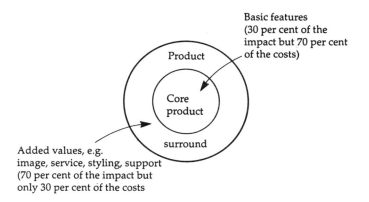

Basic features
(30 per cent of the
impact but 70 per cent
of the costs)

Product

Core
product

surround

Added values, e.g.
image, service, styling, support
(70 per cent of the impact but
only 30 per cent of the costs

Figure 2.14 *The product surround concept*

is shown in Figure 2.15. On one extreme is the speciality offer – often a highly differentiated brand – and on the other extreme is the commodity. When a totally new offering is introduced it is, by definition, a speciality. Over time, as new competitors emerge, there is a tendency for it to move towards commodity status. This 'speciality to commodity slide' through the life cycle results in reduced brand image and differentiation, lower prices and increased competition.

Competition in commodity markets is primarily based around prices and terms. By contrast, competition in speciality branded goods and services are based on the other elements of the marketing mix including customer service, advertising, brand name, guarantees, packaging, warranties, etc. A key issue then is how to impede (or reverse) this transition to ensure offerings remain differentiated, rather than slide into the commodity category.

This speciality to commodity slide is not inevitable. In a chapter entitled 'No such thing as a commodity', Peters and Austin[22] point out a wide range of examples of firms who have differentiated essentially identical generic core offers through the development and expansion of the 'surround'.

Yet we see many examples of once strong brands that have followed a path of erosion from branded proprietary speciality to commodity-like status. This has happened in the UK in the fruit drink market. Whereas fifteen or twenty years ago there were a number of very strong brands, including Suncrush, Kia-Ora and Jaffa Juice, these brands suffered as a consequence of a switch in marketing emphasis. Traditionally in this market, quality had been emphasized. However, in the 1960s price cutting became prevalent and emphasis was placed on below the line promotional activity and away from advertising which promoted the 'pure juice' **brand values**. Twenty years later, orange squash has been relegated to a commodity to such an extent that retailer's own label

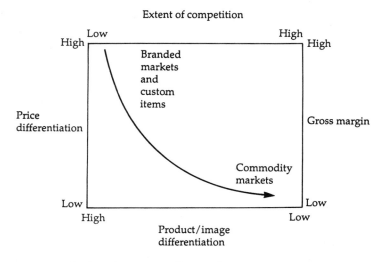

Figure 2.15 *The brand to commodity continuum*

products now account for a significant proportion of the total market. This opens up the question of 'what is quality?'

A good example of differentiation of a 'quality' product that is essentially a commodity is mineral water. Perrier have taken a commodity – naturally occurring spring water – and through packaging, promotion and the creation of internationally supported brand values have achieved brand loyalty and margins well in excess of those of its competitors. The controversy following impurity in the production of Perrier in 1989 and its subsequent withdrawal for a period from the market provided a good test of the strength of the brand and their commitment to 'quality'. The successful relaunch of Perrier was based in large part on the prompt attention to quality, in this case, the reliability of the purity of the spring water. It was this which underpinned customer **perceived quality** and mediated brand image.

People **expect** a brand to be consistent in image and performance. If your offer delivers what is expected, you have grounds to build (or sustain) a strong brand image. Your brand will, however, lose some of its power if expectations are not met, or met inconsistently.

Service quality management: the strategic dimensions of quality and retention

As noted earlier the discussion on implementation of a service quality management system is examined in Chapter 6. However, a discussion on developing a relationship strategy would not be complete without some comment on the strategic dimension of quality and retention.

There is considerable evidence that supports the focus on quality as a strategic issue. The profit impact of market strategy (PIMS) study correlated many variables with long-term financial performance. In describing PIMS, Buzzell and Gale conclude 'In the long run, the most single important factor affecting a business unit's performance is the quality of its products and services, relative to those of competitors.'[23]

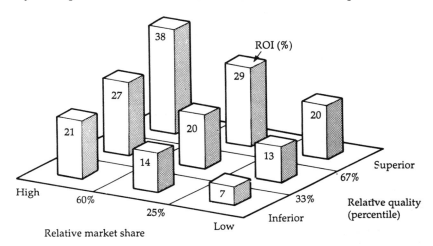

Figure 2.16 *The impact of quality and market share on profitability*
    Source: Buzzell, R. D. and Gale, B. T. (1987). *The PIMS Principles: Linking Strategy to Performance*. New York: Free Press

Figure 2.16 shows the relationship between quality, market share and profitability, measured as return on investment (ROI). The PIMS findings suggest that **relative perceived product quality** is more positively related to a company's financial performance than such things as relative market share. While a combination of high relative market share and superior relative quality yield the highest ROI (38 per cent) it is possible to obtain good profitability (21 per cent ROI) with a low relative market share through high relative quality.

Quality can be seen from two perspectives – an internal and an external one. Internal quality is based on conformance to specifications while external quality is based on relative customer perceived quality. The important point here is that quality must be seen from the customer's viewpoint, not the company's. It is essential that quality is measured by customers and is not measured by what managers within a company think their customers' views are.

A number of reasons have been identified as to why it is unsafe to rely on managerial opinions of customer perceptions. These include:

● Management may not know what specific purchase criteria users consider important. For example, customers frequently identify key purchase criteria not identified by management. Even when the criteria are correctly identified, management may misjudge the relative importance of individual criteria . . . sometimes by a factor of 3:1.

- Management may misjudge how users perceive the performance of competitive products on specific performance criteria. These differences in perception of performance may exist for the most basic of criteria.
- Management may fail to recognize that user needs have evolved in response to competitive product developments, technological advances, or other market or environmental influences.[24]

Thus external market research should be used to identify customer perceived quality.

A further finding of relevance is that high quality does **not** necessarily mean cost. PIMS research concludes that perceived quality variable has little effect on cost.[25]

In reviewing these findings Peters and Austin conclude that the winners emphasize customer expectations, research customer needs, use customer-based quality performance measures, and formulate quality control objectives for all functions. In contrast, losers downgrade the customer view, make high quality synonymous with technical tolerances, tie quality objectives to work flow, and formalize quality control objectives for production only.[26]

We have already described the importance of companies developing a relationship-rather than transaction-based aproach to their marketing. The consequence of this has recently been highlighted by research on customer retention reported by Reichheld of Bain & Co. and Sasser of Harvard Business School. They have described how reducing defections (or increasing the retention rate) by 5 per cent dramatically impacts on profitability.

By calculating the net present values of the profit streams for the average customer life at current defection rates and comparing this with the net present values of the profit streams for the average customer life at 5 per cent lower defection rates, the following profit impacts were identified.[27]

Industry	Profit income increase (%) for a 5% increase in retention
Mail order	20
Auto service chain	30
Software	35
Insurance brokerage	50
Credit card	125

It is noteable that Bain & Co., a leading strategy consulting firm, has identified customer retention as a practice area of major opportunity for themselves and their clients. Bain & Co. have developed a formal approach to customer retention that points out the tremendous profit improvement potential from a top management perspective.

To engage the attention of front-line staff as well as junior and middle management we need a device to dramatize its importance. Peters has captured the importance of retention management in his phrase 'treat the customer as an appreciating asset'. He suggests, his $1500 a month Federal Express account is worth $360 000 in terms of future custom.[28] He points out that $1500 per month is $18 000 per year or $180 000 over ten years – assuming a ten-year customer life time. Based on the concept of a satisfied customer becoming a supporter or an advocate (as described in Chapter 1) he or she will generate considerable repeat business through word-of-mouth recommendation. A conservative estimate of one acquaintance becoming a lifetime (ten-year) user of Federal Express increases the value of the current user from $180 000 to $360 000. Assuming the courier calls upon forty customers with a similar average sized sales this represents a customer portfolio of 40 × $360 000 or $14 million to Federal Express.

By viewing customers as an appreciating asset with the monetary values described above, this should suggest a different approach be taken by front-line staff dealing with customers. Further it supports the taking of a much more serious approach to hiring, training and compensation of a staff member who is managing, say, a $14 million portfolio of business. Whether an organization is selling motor cars, hospital beds, or pizza pies (to which we will return in Chapter 6) it should consider the role of a customer retention programme as part of its relationship strategy.

Thus the nature of customer retention changes from a position where it may be viewed as a tactical issue involving a marginal increase in sales for a salesman to an issue of strategic importance at board level. The way to deliver this, of course, is increased quality of products and service from each customer segment's viewpoint. This suggests quality should be seen as a competitive strategy – which we address in the next chapter.

References

1 For example, see Trotter W. D. (1981). *Strategic Planning Theory and Practice*, PhD Thesis. Lubin Graduate School of Business, Pace University, who discusses forty-three approaches to strategic planning.

2 For a further discussion of mission statements see Deane J. A., Robinson R. B., and Roth B. (1987). The company mission as a guide to strategic action. In *Strategic Planning and Management Handbook*, (King W. R. and Cleland D. I.). Van Nostrand Reinhold Company. See also David F. R. 1989, How companies define their mission. *Long Range Planning.* **22**, 1. pp. 90–97; and Campbell A. and Yeung S. (1990). *Do You Need a Mission Statement.* The Economist Publications.

3 Christopher M. G., Majaro S. and McDonald M. H. B. (1987). *Strategy Search: A Guide to Marketing for Chief Executives and Directors.* Gower Press, p. 8.

4 Drucker P. F. (1973). *Management: Tasks, Responsibilities, and Practices.* Harper & Row.

5 For additional and a more detailed review of approaches and frameworks see references 6, 7, and 8 below.

6 See Porter M. E. (1980). *Competitive Strategy*. Free Press, for a more detailed discussion.

7 Day G. S. (1990). *Market Driven Strategy: Processes for Creating Value*. The Free Press, p. 110.

8 See Porter M. E. (1985). *Competitive Advantage*. Free Press.

9 Twedt D. K. (1986). The concept of market segmentation. In *Handbook of Modern Marketing*, 2nd ed. (Buell V. P. ed.), pp. 8.3–8.12. For a more detailed discussion of segmentation see Bonoma T. V. and Shapiro, B. (1983). *Industrial Market Segmentation*. Lexington Books; and Weinstein A. (1987). *Market Segmentation*. Probus Publishing Co.

10 Gilmour P. (1977). Customer segmentation: differentiating by market segments. *International Journal of Physical Distribution*, 7, 3, pp. 141–8.

11 *Op. cit.*

12 Discussions of market analysis and marketing planning are widely available in the marketing literature. See for example McDonald M. (1989). *Marketing Plans – How to Prepare Them: How to Make Them*. Heinemann, 2nd ed.

13 Christopher M. G., Majaro S. and McDonald M., *op. cit.*, p. 57.

14 Porter M. E. (1985). *op. cit.*

15 For a detailed discussion of the experience curve see Day G. and Montgomery D. B. (1983). Diagnosing the experience curve. *Journal of Marketing*, 47, Spring, pp. 44–58.

16 Porter M. E. (1985). *op. cit.*

17 Bower M. and Garda, R. A. (1985). The role of marketing in management. *McKinsey Quarterly*, Autumn, pp. 34–46.

18 Lanning M. J. and Michaels E. G. (1988). A business is a value delivery system. *McKinsey Staff Paper*, July.

19 *Op. cit.*

20 Levitt T. (1983). *The Marketing Imagination*. The Free Press.

21 Collins B. (1989). Marketing for Engineers. In *Management for Engineers*, (Samson D. ed.) Longman Cheshire, pp. 347–409.

22 Peters T. and Austin N. (1985). *A Passion for Excellence*. Random House.

23 Buzzell R. D. and Gale B. T. (1987). *The PIMS Principles*. The Free Press.

24 Thompson P., De Souza G. and Gale B. T. (1985). The strategic management of service quality. *Pimsletter No. 33*. The Strategic Planning Institute.

25 Luchs R. (1986). Successful businesses compete on quality – not costs. *Long Range Planning*. 19, 1, pp. 12–17. Also see Buzzell and Gale *op. cit.* p. 108.

26 Peters T. and Austin N. A. *op. cit.*

27 Reichheld F. F. and Sasser W. E. Jr (1990). Zero defections: quality

comes to services. *Harvard Business Review*. September-October, pp. 105–111; and Buchanan R. W. J. (1990). Customer retention: the key link between customer satisfaction and profitability. Unpublished paper. Bain & Company.

28   Peters T. (1988). *Thriving on Chaos*. MacMillan.

3. QUALITY AS A COMPETITIVE STRATEGY

Competitive strategies in relationship marketing require an understanding of what customers value, or might value, and at what price. In other words, firms should aim to **position** themselves in their market to attract and keep customers, and may reshape the market in the process. In this way of course, they also position the firm to advantage, relative to its competitors.[1] The purpose of any relationship marketing strategy must be to change the market dynamics in favour of a particular firm (as a point of differentiation) by providing unique value in chosen markets, sustainable and profitable over time.

Relationship marketing and its association with **quality** as a competitive strategy seeks always to create enough value in the sale to bring customers back for more. If this sounds remarkably like any other form of marketing then we would say, yes, marketing in theory but not in practice. The quality we want to emphasize is quality at the right price, not quality in any absolute 'Rolls Royce' sense; quality in the sense of **customer perceived value**, with the kind of support and consideration that really does bring them back for more. In other words, the strategic emphasis in relationship marketing is as much on keeping customers as it is on getting them in the first place. This we believe is a radical shift in marketing practice.

One point we would emphasize here is that while relationship marketing requires a look sideways to the competition it also means looking straight ahead to the customer, and systematically building a relationship with them. This seems obvious enough but in practice we all know it is the exception, not the rule. Yes, if you don't have the right cost levels you can't achieve the right price levels. Yes, if you don't have a clear vision of where you want to go, you won't get to the right place. However, if you don't work on quality improvement and innovation, you may sell today but are less likely to sell to the same person or company again, or to any of their friends and associates.

In fractured deregulated markets, companies will not survive without quality. Quality is the means by which the firm **sustains** its position among competing offers over time. Quality is how the offer **gains** uniqueness and value in the eyes of the customer. **Quality is both the act of making the offer different and its evaluation by customers.**

What a firm offers can also be discussed in terms of 'outputs' and the customers' needs in terms of 'inputs'. Anything else the firm does, the way it organizes itself, the materials it uses, its processes and people, are all inputs to the design and delivery of outputs (see Figure 3.1). When we orientate our thinking this way, the quality of the offering can be understood in terms of the match or mismatch of output–input linkages, which represent the firm's offer on the one hand and each customer's need on the other.

Figure 3.1 *Basic process model*

The purpose of a relationship marketing strategy, as we have said, is to shape the market in your favour (to **create** the market if necessary) but there is no gain if the unique value of the offering has the effect of positioning the firm in a market that is likely to decline. Change is inevitable, growth is not. The fate of many high street 'niche' retailers in the UK comes to mind as they consider their positioning 'next to Next' and readjust to the conditions of the 1990s, amid shifting customer loyalties.

Every industry is potentially a 'service industry'

During the 1980s we saw a radical shift in management thinking. Interest in quality, which had some early and superficial expression as **customer care** in service industries, is being fuelled by new technology (information and delivery systems) and competitive action under open market conditions (deregulation). These rather 'revolutionary' events are interrelated and are now fused together as one rolling, cascading event, invading all markets.[2]

We need to make one thing clear about the nature of opportunities for relationship marketing. **Every industry is potentially a 'service' industry**. In relationship marketing, the aim is to lead and reshape the market to this end.[3] Every company has the opportunity to design and manage its own unique set of solutions to meet customer problems and this requires a mix of functional utility, service, support of various kinds, information and advice, and ongoing 'services'. To take the shift of marketing emphasis one step further, some companies already consider their products to be part of an emerging **experience industry**. Disneyland we can understand, but Toyota? Yes, Toyota! Making judgements about marketing opportunities needs this flexible view.

We admit to a dilemma we have with using terms like 'products' and 'services'. As a stand-alone term, 'product' reflects a backwards look to the production line and 'service' conjures up a long past history of masters and bonded slavery. Neither of these terms properly describe what is essentially a relationship between people and organizations.

The traditional image of 'service' is that it is 'performed' by individuals and yet this perspective is clearly untrue in particular cases. Is your bank's automatic telling machine delivering the product, or a service? In the world of fast foods, is the 'McDonald's experience' a product or a service? And why does it matter? Marketing literature is weighed down with classification schemes for services but every such classification is partially flawed because what is meant by 'service' is contingent on time, tangibility and tasks.

Production, a time-based work activity, builds up an accumulation of **values**, which of course, we traditionally call a 'product'. These values are amortized by the customer over the time-life of the product. What the customer gets from a product, or hopes to get, is 'service-ability'. Service in this sense, tends to occur after the point of sale. The differences drawn between 'products' and 'services' is therefore resolved in 'time', and indeed, over time.

We can pass by these fine time-biased distinctions when we orientate relationship marketing around the customer, because our concern is the 'ongoing sale', into which products and services are fused.

Quality gaps

Our basic concept of quality is simply the match between what customers expect and what they experience. This is perceived quality.[4] Any mismatch between these two is a 'quality gap'. As **perceived quality** is always a judgement by the customer, whatever the customer thinks is reality, is reality. However, customer service word-of-mouth information, past personal experiences, advertising and promotion, all mediate the acceptability of the offering, by influencing customer expectations. In effect, quality is whatever the customer says it is.

Defining quality in this way meets any 'customer orientation' test, but is it sufficiently robust to guide marketing decisions? There are two operational problem areas. Firstly, 'expectations' must be understood to mean what the customer thinks 'should' happen, not what the customer expects 'will' happen! Otherwise, the absurd implication would be that when consumers expect bad service and receive it they will be happy! Some companies seem to operate this way but it is not a safe position to take if quality is the goal. Secondly, the quality concept is not a single variable in itself but a function of both customer perceptions and the firm's resources and activities. The quality perceived by customers is the same **in kind** perceived by the firm providing it. The evidence remains the same. Only the perspective changes. Any quality gap is a mix of facts and judgements so it is important to remember that each party is ignorant to some extent of the other's intentions.

Research by Parasuraman and his colleagues,[5] conceptualizes four kinds of quality gaps or potential breaks in the relationship linkages, which lead to quality shortfalls. Because quality has been difficult to control it has been 'left to operations' by too many marketing managers, and perhaps we should add, left to chance by too many marketing academics. The fact that this research specifically focused on **service quality** by no means discounts its broader relevance. Gap **Type 1** occurs when managers do not know what customers expect; **Type 2** is an absence (for whatever reason) of managerial commitment to correcting what customers expect; **Type 3** is variability in the performance of what customers expect (this research study focused on contact personnel); and **Type 4** occurs when external communications about the offering increase customer expectations and in consequence, decrease perceived quality. These four gaps lead to a fifth gap which is in fact an aggregate of them all, i.e. the gap between quality expected and quality perceived to have been received. We shall revisit the idea of gap analysis in Chapter 4.

Understanding quality dimensions

Market research should define the key dimensions of quality within each and every market situation. The most widely reported set of **generic** dimensions is that of Berry, Parasuraman, and Zeithaml. While their focus was specifically service quality their analytical framework can be viewed as an 'extended' all-industries model, if only for the insights that it provides. Berry and his colleagues[6] captured the important influences on consumers' expectations and perceptions of delivered service within a ten-dimensional framework. With further refinement and testing this has been shortened to a five-dimensional set, as described below:[7]

- **Reliability** – ability to perform the promised service dependably, accurately and consistently. This means doing it right, over a period of time.
- **Responsiveness** – prompt service and willingness to help customers. Speed and flexibility are involved here.
- **Assurance** – knowledge and courtesy of staff and their ability to inspire trust and confidence.
- **Empathy** – caring, individualized attention to customers.
- **Tangibles** – physical facilities, equipment, staff appearance, i.e., the physical evidence of the service which conveys both functional and symbolic meaning.

Clearly some of these dimensions relate directly to human performance and staff contact with the customers. Empathy and assurance fit into this category at first glance. Responsiveness and reliability also seem to be the direct result of human performance and certainly, in high customer contact industries, customers would relate the outcomes to the perceived performance of people in the company. But is this customer perception correct, even in the so-called 'service' industries?

Without in any way minimizing the importance of high contact skills, staff can only perform up to the potential of the support they get from the total operating system. A tradesman is only as good as his tools, as the old saying goes. What is often overlooked is that reliable and responsive service is underpinned by the reliability and responsiveness of the firm's systems and processes, and the way in which the work environment is designed to facilitate the work task at hand. We might pause to think just how reassuring and empathetic an airline customer service officer would remain if his or her flight information screen was erratically malfunctioning!

We can see why things go right or wrong for the supplier, by constructing a hypothetical **quality map** of the customers' perceptual world (see Figure 3.2). Where each axis intersects, as at point 1, what the customer experiences of the firm's offer can be assumed to be exactly what was expected. There is no 'quality gap' at this point, only conformance to customer expectations. If the offer is experienced over time as unique and of value beyond expectations, the whole map moves a notch in perceptual space (this is shown at points 2 and 3 and by the direction of the arrows). Every other positioning is a quality gap, a waste of opportunity or resources, positively or negatively positioned as a variation from the intersect point.

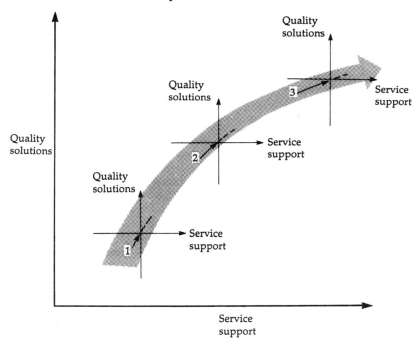

Figure 3.2 *Repositioning quality in the customers' perceptual world*

A word of clarification about the use of terms is needed here. What is **unique** and of **value** is in conventional marketing terms a successful innovation, a source of competitive advantage. And finally, what is of **value** in an offer is what meets customer expectations, even if that value is not unique in competitive terms.

Back now to our **quality map**. On the longitudinal axis we locate any quality characteristics which are instrumental to **quality solutions**. By this we mean all solutions to customer problems which are of value to customers. A solution which is perceived to be of unique value by customers extends the firm's offering **beyond** expectations, contributing to a shift in the customers' perceptual world. On the latitudinal axis, we locate any quality characteristics which facilitate or give support to the solution. We call this **service support**.[8] Support, which is perceived to be of unique value by customers also extends the firm's offer beyond customer expectations, and contributes to a shift in the customers' perceptual world.

In buying a motor vehicle and equally in the use of that vehicle after purchase, the **quality solutions** are represented for example by performance capability, reliability and durability, according to particular market requirements. These are like core competencies which underpin the total offering. The **service support** is represented by presale information, vehicle test drives, financing options, care and attention from the sales person during the sale negotiation, and aftersales support in terms of warranty, accessories and repair services. These extend the risk reducing and relationship supporting elements of the total offering.

Marketing has of course always set its sights on providing customers with what they need. Traditional thinking has been to use technology to do it better than the competition and economies of scale to keep costs (and prices) down. However, constantly updating technology still means using basically the same technology that is available to your competitors, and more volume capacity can lead to underutilization and higher costs, instead of lower. The way out of the commodity trap is to pursue quality as a competitive strategy, in our terms by offering quality solutions and service support of unique value for the customer.

Of course, the general characteristics of quality solutions and service support vary industry to industry and indeed, person to person because we are talking about the customer's perceptual world. In medical care for example, quality solutions tend to involve both the efficacy of individual drugs to produce intended effects, and the correct selection of the right drug and information as to correct dosage. These are highly sensitive core competencies sought by customers. Service support in this case involves issues of availabilty, home service or surgery extended hours, emergency services, and the reassurance of personal well-being, and the right balance of professionalism and empathy.

The **service support** dimension is critical for relationship marketing, because this is where an ongoing relationship link with the customer can be designed in and managed. This includes all those interactive transactions before, during and after the sale which **connect** the firm and the customer at specific times and places. Not only advice, information and functional delivery qualities but care and attention. It is worth remembering that service support can be represented symbolically through design, decor and ambience at the customer interface, corporate wardrobe, corporate graphics, logos, and all kinds of advertising messages, in fact all the way to the style of notepaper and envelopes.

We do not want to leave the impression that we advocate long-term **service support** as a competitive strategy independent of **quality solutions**. The competitive positioning of IMB PCs in the 1980s illustrates why. Right from the first launch the market signalled that it wanted IBM **reliability** and was willing to pay a premium for it. IBM captured market share quickly because customers knew that if problems arose, they would quickly be resolved. This was a case of unique value on the **service support** dimension. However, in a changing world IBM is now facing competition from DEC, Apple and others who are developing **quality solutions** around such unique values as 'interconnectivity' and 'user friendliness'.

IBM had built its reputation around providing the best service in its chosen markets around the world but in some markets, this led to a myopic relationship with client managers of in-house MIS systems at the expense of other intra-company client needs and interests. IBM is locked into service support but it still must take care that it does not miss out on shifts in its markets which require innovative change and technical progress on the quality solutions dimension.

Relationship marketing strategies, as we said earlier in this chapter, always seek to change the market demands in favour of a particular firm by providing unique value, sustainable over time. The quality solutions dimension **underpins** relationship marketing strategies and the service support dimension **extends** them. Short-term success might be gained by developing quality on one dimensional axis or the other, but both must connect strategically for long-run competitive advantage.

We are reminded of an old Japanese poem quoted by Deming in his book, *Out of the Crisis.*[9]

> Is it the bell that rings,
> Is it the hammer that rings,
> Or is it the meeting of the two that rings?

The problem is that quality solutions and service support dimensions have no connections to departmental divisions which would suggest some neat internal allocation of responsibility for quality. This is particularly the case in service industries, where production, delivery and consumption can occur at the same time. Making the connections between the activities of departmental divisions and customer perceived quality is the job of quality management.

Quality management

The best known quality management philosophy is total quality management (TQM). TQM is 'total', because it is concerned with all work processes and the way they can be improved to better meet customer needs. Quality definitions provided by TQM 'gurus' tend to locate quality within the company as a set of 'target values' so that work can be scheduled continuously in an orderly manner but without losing sight of customer requirements, which of course keep changing.

Some well-known TQM definitions of quality follow and have been bracketed in groups, to illustrate the particular emphasis they give:

- **Conform to specifications**
  The traditional production orientation to quality is 'conformance to specifications'. This used to be adequate in stable markets but ongoing acceptance of a firm's offering means that 'specs' need to be constantly changing. As the market is constantly changing, what is unique and valued yesterday will be a quality gap today. Merely conforming to specifications means you will be always one step behind.
- **Do it right**
  A better definition is 'fitness for use'.[10] This recognizes that quality is about efficient 'solutions' and continuous improvement. If you can improve the efficiency of the solution you will have an offer to place in the market which is of uniform quality. But is this enough? Will you anticipate the diversity of customers' requirements and support customers in implementing your solutions?
- **Do the right thing**
  Effective support of customers' needs requires some understanding of what the customer is trying to do with your offering. Does it effectively fit their requirements? Being responsive and flexible are key issues here. This could mean 'conformance to requirements'[11] or 'meeting the requirements',[12] so long as the customer is the author of those requirements.
- **Delight the customer**
  Deming has used the phrase 'delight customer' to describe quality going beyond the expected. Part of the 'delight' is **reliability**, something that works and is consistent over time, which we call 'fitness in use'.[13]

One of the most remarkable features of total quality management (TQM) is the way in which it has drawn practising managers from many parts of an organization to work together across traditional functional boundaries to improve quality and productivity.[14] This points up a rather simple yet dramatic conclusion that has not yet been properly brought to attention. It is this: **quality has become an integrating concept between production orientation and marketing orientation.**[15] Marketing has always lacked a method of making operational the connections between what the customer wants on the one hand and the activities of a firm, on the other. Quality management is the missing link.[16]

The effects (over time) should become visible in improved productivity (through elimination of waste) and improved sales (through building a loyal customer base). A harmony of purpose worth aiming at!

Through quality management we can find a structure for planning, improving and controlling the kinds of internal activities that will keep customers happy. Knowing what the customer expects is central to quality **planning** (more of this in terms of research methodologies in Chapter 4). Knowing what compensatory changes to make and how to do it is quality **improvement** (see Chapter 5). Establishing what internal checks and audits work best is quality **control** (see Chapter 6). Knowing where to start is no problem. Relationship marketing guides us to the customer activity patterns called the **customer value chain**.[17]

Customer value chain

We can define the concept of customer value chain as a series (or linkage) of actions a customer takes in specific contexts with the aim of producing value for that customer. This might be as basic as a visit to the bank (to get a loan) or preparing a meal (to satisfy hunger and to give pleasure). From this point of view, a firm's offering is input into the customer value chain. The behavioural patterns of customers which control or modify the way in which a firm's output is actually used are represented by links in the chain. For example, a bank savings account may be input into a customer value chain as a bill paying device, an investment for a 'rainy day' or a day-to-day savings account, according to how the customer goes about managing money and the priorities which are given value. It is not at all helpful to say that the customer is confused about how the savings account is meant to be used but it is helpful to know how the customer makes use of it. Mapping out what value a customer draws from the firm's offering is to begin to understand how and why it fits into that customer's value chain. The aim is always to identify what a customer is **trying to do** with the firm's offering at a particular time and place before jumping to any conclusions about what is valued and why.

The customer value chain concept shows us that making a unique offer may be a waste of money if that offer does not fit beneficially into the activities, sequences and links in the customer value chain. This is the particular meaning of **fitness in use** that we described earlier. The customer value chain is really a **path-goal** sequence of activities. Failure to meet the requirements in any part of the customer journey might be critical or relatively unimportant but if customers expect food to be 'salt free', you had better be able to deliver. If customers expect 'loans approved within 24 hours', you had better be able to do that too.

One convalescent hospital surveyed its patients' views of treatment and care as a series of time- and place-related events. They were expecting to find a range of performance issues that would require fairly large funds allocations to fix. Much to their surprise the most important complaint and the service which was least well performed according to the hospital patients was making a good cup of tea. The patients wanted tea made in a china pot (no tea bags) and served in china cups. This may be an extreme example, but who would have guessed this to be at the heart of improving the quality of the relationship.

The value a firm creates for its customers is a function of the **alignment** it can achieve between the **firm's** value chain and the **customer's** value chain. If internal organizational activities are not 'adding value' for the customer, they must represent non-value costs. Quality management therefore is about adjusting the way a firm traditionally manages its own functions, so as to increase value to the customer and reduce its own waste. What is involved?

Cross-functional work flows

Consider first a sole trader. The activities he or she performs on behalf of a customer are sequenced and integrated without the need for any command structure or functional differentiation within the 'organization'. The whole design, production, delivery, and personal service is integrated within one head. Once our sole trader succeeds with his or her quality offering and the firm grows in staff, problems of coordinating work activities arise, which require functional specialization and some kind of hierarchical command and control. This is fine for a while, but as the size of the firm increases, and the vertical controls are strengthened, the integration of work activities between people and across departments usually receives less corrective attention. The cost of quality is swollen by the sum total of all these mismatched activities which invoke delays and higher level 'fire fighting' decisions (see Figure 3.3).

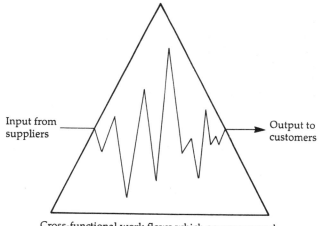

Input from suppliers

Output to customers

Cross-functional work flows which go unmanaged invite delays and 'high-level' fire fighting activity

Figure 3.3 *The cross-functional quality mismatch*

So it is that one person's **output** becomes mismatched with another person's **input** needs and there is a quality gap. To the extent that one department's output is mismatched with another department's input needs, there is another quality gap. The essence of many quality gap problems will be found **between** departments rather more than **within** departments. Failure to manage work flow, laterally across the organization, has a way of multiplying costs and quality failures all along the firm's value chain (see Figure 3.4).

One key task of quality management is to identify and examine the most critical cross-functional work flows and remove any blockages, thereby reducing the cost of achieving quality. Reducing or minimizing blockages in the work flows should begin 'upstream' in the value chain, at

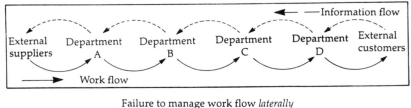

Failure to manage work flow *laterally*
across the organization has a way of
multiplying costs and quality failures

Figure 3.4 *Cross-functional work flows*

the design stage. In this way quality can be 'built in'. Yet even with access
to market information about customer wants and expectations, integrating this information into the design process has been a vexing task for
many companies. The customer 'voice' can be easily lost, resulting in a
final offering which falls short of the 'delight the customer' quality
orientation mentioned earlier.

The main technical challenge in quality management today is focused
on the design stage. One powerful integrative technique is called quality
function deployment (QFD).[18] This is a technique for translating customer requirements (the true quality characteristics) into design requirements (counterpart characteristics). The QFD methodology is not
complex conceptually but requires careful attention to detail in the
building up of a series of charts which show how customer requirements
and design requirements come together. QFD is not an exclusive
manufacturing design tool. Its valuable discipline is that by listening for
the customer's 'voice' 'upstream' at the design stage in the value chain,
activity 'downstream' can be aligned correctly.

How else could one begin an examination of cross-functional work
flow? You could start by locating a generally agreed problem area within
some work activity. Every work activity is part of a **process** and every
process is a link in the value chain. Even better, start with a single
customer concern that has been signalled from customer complaints or
from a market research study. Either way, the idea is to trace a sequence
of activities 'upstream' back to their original sources of input. Some of
these processes may appear to be totally without coordination or control,
or appear to be outside the control of the firm, or of a particular
department or division within it. That in itself is a basis for including them
in any examination.

The rationale for this kind of investigation is that all work activities
eventually connect 'downstream' through the value chain to the end
customer. The important issue is whether these activities add value to the
firm and to the customer (or merely add cost). Any investigation needs to
differentiate between the two. The way we begin is using a technique
called **flow charting** or **blue printing**, which is described in Chapter 6.

Internal customers and internal suppliers

The concept of **internal customers** and **internal suppliers** fits naturally with flow-charting techniques. The people who are involved in particular tasks identified by flow charting are 'internal suppliers' and those who next follow that identified process are 'internal customers'. Therefore everybody within the firm is both a customer and has customers.

Tracing these links **within** the firm from their starting point with the external customer, represents real opportunities for quality improvement. By carefully defining the ways customers use the firm's offering, large or small modifications can be made within the firm in terms of job designs, work environments, work processes, and training, to mention some key areas for diagnostic review (see Figure 3.5). What we see is how internal suppliers and internal customers each supply the other, invisibly connected, but nonetheless connected in terms of the input–output links in the value chain.

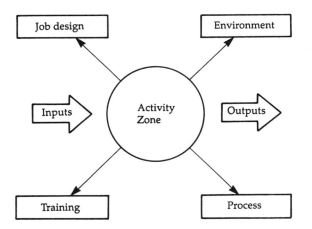

Figure 3.5 *Diagnostic model*

Success in reshaping external markets requires the involvement of marketing in the reshaping of internal markets. The networking of these internal relationships is called **internal marketing**. This phrase can be used to describe any form of marketing within an organization which focuses attention on the internal activities that need to be changed in order that marketing plans may be implemented.[19] For us, internal marketing involves creating an organizational climate where cross-functional quality improvement can be sponsored and worked on by the **people** whose job **processes** are involved. The internal marketing task might further extend to empowering and enabling the internal customers and internal suppliers to get together. That is why in Chapter 1 we expanded the elements of the traditional marketing mix.

One method of review of internal markets is 'department purpose analysis' (DPA) which has as its objective the clarification of buyer–supplier links within the organization (although external customers and suppliers need not in principle be excluded). The approach aims first to get a better understanding of the importance and performance of various activities within a particular work area which might be contributing to an internal quality gap. The department then identifies by working with its internal customers and internal suppliers the key opportunities for improvement. Small problems are best tackled first to build mutual confidence through results.[20]

The first step in dealing with any quality 'problem' between internal customers and internal suppliers is to recognize right away that as an internal customer you will not get far in 'blaming' the problem on your internal supplier. The relationship marketing approach is to look for **opportunities**, rather than problems. This way you can avoid personal conflict with your supplier! In any event, it is more likely that you will gain their cooperation for improving the **process** rather than improving their **people** involved in the process. This is practical advice which seems to work because everybody lives to tackle the next task, and the one after that!

A useful diagnostic tool which can be used here to explore improvement opportunities is the so-called **fishbone**, also called an Ishikawa diagram after its inventor, Dr Kaoru Ishikawa in Japan. This is described in Chapter 6.

Supplier partnerships

The firm and its 'downstream' quality is linked 'upstream' through the firm's value chain to its external suppliers. Building bridges with external suppliers is 'upstream' relationship marketing. Buyer–supplier relationships grounded in a commitment to quality improvement are becoming increasingly common. The first step is to arrange a meeting with the supplier to exchange information concerning your quality and reliability concerns. This person-to-person exchange is critical and should be supported by examples of failed parts, delivery delays, etc. As discussed in Chapter 1, dealing with suppliers as 'partners' opens up the possibility of tackling on a collaborative basis chronic quality problems, like reliability and timeliness, or working to eliminate incoming inspections.

IBM's communication products division in Raleigh monitors and manages its suppliers' quality efforts monthly. Those whose performance is found unacceptable are further reviewed by procurement quality engineers. Actions might include meetings with a particular supplier's management, reviewing the problems and visiting the site. Every effort is made to work with suppliers willing to improve quality, however, IBM does not continue to do business with suppliers who cannot or will not meet quality requirements.[21]

Supplier partnerships involve a fundamental change in attitude for all parties.[22] The idea of sharing mutual goals and sharing some of the risks, in order to participate in the rewards, is a little nerve rattling for managers who are used to working in an adversarial basis. A shift in attitudes can be gradual. As trust develops, efficiencies gained can be 'locked' into the way of doing business.

Supplier partnerships are a long-term commitment, one in which marketing has a role to play, particularly in supplying reliable demand/ sales forecasts. This is a critical area in relationship marketing. It has to be managed. In one company reported in a research study, the purchasing department regularly took marketing's forecasts and contracted for the required components with 'pre-qualified' suppliers. However, demand often exceeded supply by more than 100 per cent, which meant that the purchasing department had to regularly make urgent reorders. Unfortunately the reorders were seldom available in time from the prequalified sources and had to be placed wherever they could be met. This increased both costs and the variability of quality, and the firm's reputation and market share were badly shaken.

Where a firm's inputs are highly irregular, staff are forced to adapt procedures or to make allowances in other ways for things going wrong. For example, overstocking at the supply end might be a solution to the problem of stock-outs but it adds to inventory costs and does not face up to correcting the causes of the variability. One approach to tracking the movement of materials is called 'just-in-time' (JIT). Under JIT systems, single sourcing of materials is encouraged, plus more frequent deliveries in smaller qualities. However, JIT will not work effectively without supportive company-wide quality management practices.

The variability of a process is built in

Our examination of the value chain has shown how processes are linked (output to input), and that there are opportunities for the examination of these linkages, with a view to quality improvement. Outputs that are out-of-tolerance become out-of-tolerance inputs!

Quality is also at the mercy of variability built into the process. This too has to be managed. It certainly will not correct itself. Very often, no one really knows why a routine procedure was established the way it was, or the way jobs are organized, or the design of the physical work environment itself. It often doesn't occur to people that things could be done another way. If a quality problem (representing a quality gap) were easy to fix, would it not have been fixed already? What at first seems impossible to change is often found to be possible when the assumptions being made about the nature and purpose of the underlying process are made visible. A case of too close to the trees to see the woods.

Every work process generates outputs which in some way fall short of perfection and uniformity. All processes contain sources of variability and these differences may be large, or small beyond measurement. Variability can be reduced but it can never be entirely eliminated. The goal is to reduce these variations in quality, so long as the value being added exceeds the total cost of achieving it. We can also understand the relationship between costs and value from the opposite angle, that is to say, waste in all kinds of business activity can be brought under control by minimizing process variability. Eliminating 'waste' means eliminating cost that does not add value. This sounds like a traditional accounting approach and it is, except for one absolutely critical difference – you must focus on process variation, and reduce that. Organizations seeking to eliminate waste by cutting costs per se will almost certainly cut value, without ever knowing how or why.

Process variation is generated and passed along the whole chain of internal customers and suppliers to the final customer. Indeed, one eminent Japanese statistition, Genichi Taguchi, says that there is an incremental economic 'loss' for each deviation from customer 'target requirements', which has a flow-on effect to society as a whole.[23]

In this cycle of events, marketing has a pivotal position. Any major error in sales estimates, has a knock-on effect through the whole organization from supply to distribution. This kind of process variability should be monitored statistically not to find the 'culprit' but so that efforts can be made (continuously) to improve the frequency and adaptability of sales signals. Another form of variability that is a marketing responsibility is customer complaints. Many organizations take care in handling customers who complain, but it is possible to go further, monitoring the key categories of complaints statistically and diagnosing the causes for corrective action. Another sensitive if seldom pursued marketing statistic is a customer loss/retention measure. If patterns of repurchasing by customers begin to show variability, that might tell you something about the total offering, in terms of the variability of quality and service.

There are two kinds of process variability. These can be identified using statistical control methods.[24] First there are **assignable causes** of variation which can be traced to a particular process, setting or input, that is, in some special way related to materials, equipment, information, methods, environmental characteristics, people or job tasks. Second, there are **random sources** of variation, which are common to the process, that is, inseparable from the process itself.

There is an ingrained tendency for management to blame the 'performer' rather than the process, yet the bulk of performance problems are built into the process itself and are therefore the responsibility of management. Deming has estimated that 94 per cent of quality problems and opportunities are the responsibility of management. Whatever the figure, only in a minority of cases are decisions for introducing improvements within the authority of non-managerial workers.

As quality management techniques extend out from the factory floor to the purchasing department on the one hand, and distribution, and marketing on the other, 'people' dimensions become all the more important. In service industries, where the 'product is the people' as the customer often perceives it, the intangibility of key processes combines on occasion with relative statistical illiteracy among staff. This focuses the need for clear communication and collaboration in new ways. There is a role here for marketing, in liaison with operations and personnel managers, to get the quality planning cycle right. Marketing's internal role extends to staff climate surveys, internal (staff) communications, and collaborating in the design of the staff training packages.

This three-way department relationship would greatly ease the entry of quality management into any organization. While statistical process control is the traditional manufacturing entry point, it has tended to be resisted in non-manufacturing divisions. Another entry point is through 'motivating' the staff which unfortunately has tended to produce expensive short-run programmes for customer service training or 'customer care'. A third approach takes **people** and **processes** as interrelated dynamic elements in a service – quality drive for **'continuous improvement'**. We will now briefly discuss this notion of continuous improvement and extend the discussion more fully in Chapter 5.

Continuous improvement

The challenge of survival in the 1990s in volatile markets demands a management orientation which accepts that getting and keeping customers requires continuous improvement and innovation. The choice management must make is whether to drive workers harder at their assigned tasks, or whether to invite them to **participate** in generating new ways of improving the performance system. The first way treats people as 'prisoners' of the process and the second invites people to be agents of the process – a distinct and separate contribution for which their experience **within** the process makes them ideally suited.

All work is process. As previously discussed, sets of processes are connected as value chains. No matter what we do at work we are involved in these processes, indeed enmeshed in processes, as much as a worker in charge of a metal press, an airline pilot, or a bank manager.

Deming, Juran and others have found that the overwhelming bulk of the variation in the outcomes of processes can be attributed to the way the processes are designed to operate and are maintained. Invariably, they found that the process is the villain, not the worker. The opportunity area therefore is to review the policies, premises, procedures, machines and job structures which support (or hinder) the quality of work performance. There are limits to the standardization of processes of course, but these will be discovered by flow charting the relationship between various work activities, and by attempting to reduce the variability of the key processes.[25]

Quality as a competitive strategy certainly challenges our traditional understanding of the relationship between staff performance and the performance of the organization as a totality. For example, at first glance we tend to attribute the quality of 'front-line' service to the strengths or weaknesses of service staff. This is a natural enough perception but it is nonetheless only a partial observation. What constitutes 'performance' is the sum of the performance processes of which staff are the agents. Certainly 'front-line' service staff must perform well and need education in customer service skills. This is a separate and important marketing function.[26] However, efforts to improve 'front-line' service performance by improving staff 'customer service' training will add cost, not value, unless the design of work activities, the environment in which service is delivered, and the processes involved are all targeted for improvement, part of a continuous diagnostic review.

Managerial knowledge, the knowledge of accumulated experience, is seldom sufficiently broad or deep to sustain an ongoing diagnostic review of work processes in changing markets. What is it then that needs to happen to start the wheel of quality improvement turning? It comes down to knowledge generation and knowledge sharing **within** organizations, participation in improvement, up, down, and across organizations. Restore pride of workmanship, Deming would say.

Purification of effort

The 19th-century craftsperson knew his or her skill well. It was developed over time through the sweat of action, observation and imitation. Knowledge gained by action, gave workers mastery to 'act-on' the resources. Such 'know how' was an integration of many things. With diversity, complexity and size, came the routinization of work, the splintering and channelling of knowledge and skills, with 'efficiency' as the driving force and the pathway to profit. This has been aptly called the 'purification of effort' in the management of work.[27]

What has been gained is considerable, but what has been lost is the craftsperson's integration of work knowledge and that natural ability to 'act-on' the resources without guidance. Knowledge is now implicitly associated with the role of the manager who has become responsible for analysing and organizing work tasks, planning and controlling the outputs.

The 'purification of effort' was central to the agenda of the proponents of scientific management. Among the first and certainly the most famous was Frederick Taylor (1856–1917). His focus was to improve task design with assessments by 'expert' time studies, and later, time and motion studies. Taylor insisted that it was management's responsibility to organize, control and design work tasks and activities, so that workers could perform more efficiently.[28] And so 'purification of effort' built more and more mechanisms focused to supply managers and planners with data necessary for evaluation and improvement.[29]

Many management practices have evolved from Taylor's philosophy, such as work study, management by objectives and incentive pay schemes. More extreme examples of Taylorism fit with the view that there is absolutely 'one best way' to do any particular work task (and therefore that is the most economic way of proceeding in any situation). Also, that people are motivated almost solely by financial rewards (ignoring the broader range of social effects which impact on motivation and job satisfaction).

The Achilles' heel of Taylorism, is that it assumes that all **knowledge** is created and legitimized by management. So it is that **data** are channelled to managers for their appraisal, diagnosis and decision, to each according to their rank and experience. The dilemma for modern managers is how to generate enough knowledge (as distinct from the data) in time to improve or innovate, or merely survive! We may all do our best, but likely as not, we remain 'prisoners' of Taylor's iron cage.

Prisoners of the process

As 'prisoners' of the process we act within the organizational barriers. What is now required is to 'break out' of our routinized systems and organize the knowledge generation for quality improvement as a quite separate diagnostic process. It is a simple step in managerial policy to establish and support a permanent **quality review structure**, but an evolutionary one. It opens the way for staff at all levels to participate in the improvement of quality by generating ideas for that improvement – continuously (see Figure 3.6).

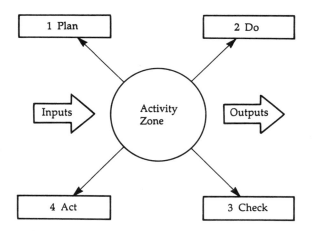

Figure 3.6 *Managing for continuous improvement*

An early concept of 'continuous improvement', was pioneered by Deming and taken to Japan in the 1950s. The Japanese style of 'continuous improvement' is sometimes called *Kaizen*, which figuratively means 'from dust we make mountains', and in practice means giving attention to detail, the fit and the form.

Your staff will do their job well if they know exactly what that job is . . . and if they are given the resources. That is, people work **within** systems because the very forces that provide the encasements – the prison walls'– also provide the support that make them feel secure.[30] However, to step outside this system, that is to 'act-on' the system, requires a managerial framework of another kind. So, what at first often appears to be simply 'getting staff motivated to do quality work' turns out to be a continuous process for researching out the critical quality issues, introducing diagnostic 'problem solving' reviews, generating quality improvements, implementing system adjustments, reviewing training schedules and rewarding participants.

Quality as a competitive strategy aims at getting and keeping customers, but first we must discover and monitor the critical quality and service issues. Asking the customer what he or she expects is the subject of the next chapter.

References

1   Porter M. E. (1985). *Competitive Advantage: Creating and Sustaining Performance*. New York: Free Press.
2   See for example in banking, Ballantyne D. F. (1987). You have to twist the kaleidoscope to see things clearly. *International Journal of Bank Marketing* **5**, 1.
3   For a strategic guide in this area see Mathur S. S. (1988). How firms compete: a new classification of generic strategies. *Journal of General Management*. **14**, 1.
4   Berry L. L., Shostack G. L. and Upah G. D. (1983). *Emerging Perspectives on Services Marketing*. Chicago: American Marketing Association; Gronroos C. (1984). *Strategic Management and Marketing in the Service Sector*. Chartwell-Bratt.
5   Parasuraman A., Zeithaml V. A. and Berry L. L. (1985). A conceptual model of service quality and its implications for future research. *Journal of Marketing*. **49**, Fall.
6   Berry L. L., Parasuraman A. and Zeithaml V (1988). The service-quality puzzle. *Business Horizons*. July/August.
7   Parasuraman A., Zeithaml V. A. and Berry L. (1988). SERVQUAL: a multiple item scale for measuring consumer perceptions of service quality. *Journal of Retailing*. **64**, 1, Spring, pp. 12–40.
8   A service quality model has been developed by Gronroos which **separates** objective technical outcomes from subjective functional processes. This is a well-known conceptualization, but making a division on ontological dimensions does not serve our purpose here. Interested readers should see Gronroos C. (1984). *Strategic Management and Marketing in the Service Sector*. Chartwell-Bratt.
9   Deming W. E. (1982, 1986). *Out of the Crisis*. Massachusetts Institute of Technology, p. 177.
10 Juran J. M. (1989). *Juran on Leadership for Quality*. The Free Press, p. 15.
11 Crosby P. B. (1979). *Quality is Free*. McGraw-Hill, p. 45.
12 Oakland J. S. (1989). *Total Quality Management*. Oxford: Heinemann Professional Series, p. 3.
13 Ballantyne D. F. (1990). Turning the wheel of quality improvement – continuously. *International Journal of Bank Marketing*. **8**, 2.

14 See for example Juran J. M. (1989). *Juran on Leadership for Quality*. The Free Press; Deming W. E. (1982, 1986). *Out of the Crisis*. Cambridge, MA: Massachusetts Institute of Technology; Crosby P. B. (1979). *Quality is Free*. McGraw-Hill; Fiegenbaum A. V. (1970). *Total Quality Control: Engineering and Management*. McGraw-Hill.

15 Gummesson E. (1988). Service quality and product quality combined. *Review of Business*. **9**, 3, Winter.

16 For a different but supportive approach to the subject of organization and integration, see Heskett J. L. (1988). Lessons in the service sector. In *Managing Services* (Lovelock C. H. ed.), Prentice Hall International. He suggests a series of integrative links between marketing and operating in planning phases and operating phases, aimed at improving quality within a 'strategic service vision'.

17 Porter M. E., *op. cit.*, p. 130.

18 For an operational description of quality function deployment, see Burn G. R. (1990). Quality function deployment. In *Managing Quality* (Dale B. G and Plunkett J. J., eds) Phillip Allan/Simon and Schuster; or for a more conceptual treatment, see Hauser J. R. and Clausing D. (1988). The House of Quality. *Harvard Business Review*. May-June, pp. 63–73.

19 See for example Berry L. L. (1984). Services marketing is different. In *Services Marketing* (Lovelock C. H., ed) Prentice-Hall. Gronroos C. (1984). *Strategic Management and Marketing in the Service Sector*. Chartwell-Bratt; and Piercy N. and Morgan N. (1991). Internal Marketing. *Long Range Planning*. **22**, 2, April.

20 *For a more detailed DPA description, see Oakland J. S., Total Quality Management, op. cit.*, pp. 30–35.

21 Burt D. N. (1989). Managing product quality through strategic purchasing. *Sloan Management Review*. **39**, Spring.

22 See for example Leenders M. R. and Blenkhorn D. L. (1988). *Reverse Marketing*. The Free Press.

23 There are similarities and differences between Taguchi methodologies and say, the Deming approach. For a preliminary introduction to Taguchi methods and design of experiments, see Scherkenback W. W. (1986). *The Deming Route to Quality and Productivity*. Mercury Press; and Disney J. and Bendell A. (1990). The potential for the application of Taguchi methods of quality control in British industry. In *Managing Quality* (Dale B. G. and Plunkett J. J. eds). Phillip Allan/ Simon and Schuster. See also Taguchi G. and Clausing D. (1990). Robust quality. *Harvard Business Review*. Jan-Feb, pp. 65–75.

24 See for example, Oakland J. S. (1988). *Statistical Process Control*. Heinemann.

25 For a good explanation of boundary crossing, customer-driven approaches to process redesign see Davenport T. H. and Short J. E. (1990). The new industrial engineering: information technology and business process redesign. *Sloan Management Review*. Summer, pp. 11–27.

26 See for example, Lash L. M. (1989). *The Complete Guide to Customer Service*. John Wiley and Sons; and Brown A. B. (1989). *Customer Care Management*. Heinemann.

27 Zuboff S. (1988). *In the Age of the Smart Machine*. Heinemann Professional Publishing, p. 40.

28 Kakabadse A., Ludlow R. and Vinnicombe S. (1988). *Working in Organizations*. Penguin Business Books, pp. 12–13.

29 Zuboff, *op. cit*, pp. 42–43.

30 Smith K. (1982). *Groups in Conflict (Prisons in Disguise)*. Kendall-Hunt, p. 12.

4. MONITORING SERVICE QUALITY PERFORMANCE

Central to the effective management of customer service within any organization has to be the measurement of service quality performance and the response of customers to that performance. Service quality improvement programmes which do not have clearly defined and **quantified** goals run a high risk of failure or at best of degenerating into cosmetic exercises where the only goals that are set are couched in terms such as 'improve', 'maximize', 'optimize' or even to be the 'best'. 'If you can't measure it, you can't manage it' must be the guiding maxim of any serious attempt at customer service management.

The purpose of this chapter is to set out some practical procedures and guide-lines that can be adopted to make the measurement of service performance a reality. However, it must be remembered that while the focus primarily will be on measuring and controlling service performance there is a similar requirement to employ a parallel approach in the production process generally through such techniques as quality function deployment (QFD) as briefly described in Chapter 3.

Quantifying service quality

In the previous chapter, service quality was defined as the ability of the organization to meet or exceed customer expectations. In this context customer expectations may be defined as the 'desires or wants of consumers, i.e. what they feel a service provider *should* offer rather than *would* offer'.[1] In an industrial marketing or business-to-business context the concept of expectations might be modified to encompass the idea of 'negotiated' expectation. In other words, service quality is measured in terms of the extent to which performance as perceived by the customer meets or exceeds agreed levels of service.

To complete the definition of service quality we must emphasize that the measure of performance is essentially a measure of **perceived** performance. In other words, it is the customers' perceptions of performance that count rather than the reality of performance. Indeed it can be argued that as far as service quality is concerned then 'perceptions **are** reality'.

We are now in a position to advance the basic measure of service quality:

$$\text{Service quality} = \frac{\text{perceived performance} \times 100}{\text{desired expectation}}$$

Under this formulation, anything less than 100 per cent is to be construed as a service failure.

From a marketing strategy point of view the service quality challenge can be put quite simply: to bring perceived performance and customer expectations into line.

Figure 4.1 presents a representation of a situation where expectations and perceived performance do not coincide. There are two possible responses by the organization to such a situation, not necessarily mutually exclusive. The first is to explore why perceived performance is low, is it because actual performance was low generally or is it because perceptions have been influenced by negative experiences in one aspect of performance, e.g. the difficulty of getting a satisfactory response to a telephone query even if the product was eventually delivered on time? The second response is to check that the customer expectation has been properly 'managed'. In other words, did the customer gain an expectation which was out of line with our own ability to perform? Sometimes this can happen because an overzealous salesperson makes a promise say on delivery, to help close the sale, but that promise is beyond the company's ability to keep. Or quite simply it may be that the customer has a level of expectation that exceeds our planned performance.

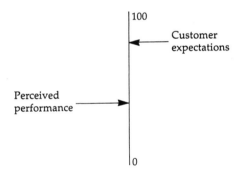

Figure 4.1 *A performance/expectation mismatch*

This latter issue highlights the need for organizations consciously to manage expectations. Service in a sense should be 'negotiated' or agreed in advance with customers so that there is no scope for misunderstanding what the organization intends to provide by way of service. This is an aspect of service management which will be returned to later.

As we briefly indicated in Chapter 3, research by Parasuraman et al. has indicated[2] that consumers' quality perceptions are influenced by a series of four distinct 'gaps' occurring in organizations (see Figure 4.2). These 'gaps' are:

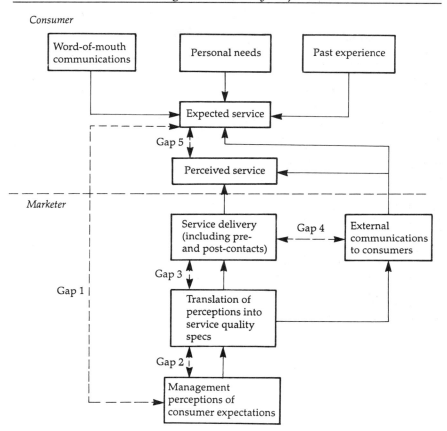

Figure 4.2 *Conceptual model of service quality*

Source: Parasuraman A., Zeithaml V. A. and Berry L. L. (1985). A conceptual model of service quality and its implications for future research. *Journal of Marketing*, **49**, Fall.

Gap 1   Difference between consumer expectations and management perceptions of consumer expectations.

Gap 2   Difference between management perceptions of consumer expectations and service quality specifications.

Gap 3   Difference between service quality specifications and the service actually delivered.

Gap 4   Difference between service delivery and what is communicated about the service to consumers.

In this model therefore the gap between the consumer expectations and perceptions (Gap 5 in Figure 4.2) is influenced by the four preceding gaps.

However, there is little chance of management acting in any meaningful way to close the gap between performance and expectations if these two key variables are not defined and measured. It thus becomes imperative to design and implement procedures for the monitoring of service performance against expectations.

Competitive benchmarking

One further point that needs to be made is that perceptions of service performance should be assessed relative to some appropriate **benchmark**. That benchmark could be the performance of competitors or even non-competitors. Indeed it is unwise to measure your performance only against competitors in that this can lead to a certain complacency of the sort that is expressed in the statement 'we are no worse than anyone else'. Benchmarking should attempt to provide a relative measure against the best practice relevant to the market place in which you compete.

The idea of benchmarking is aptly summarized by the Japanese term *dantotsu* which means the attempt to become the 'best of the best'.[3] It involves the continuous measurement of the company's products, services and practices against the standards of best competitors and the companies who are identified as industry leaders, resulting in continuous improvement in products and processes.

One of the earlier firms to adopt benchmarking was the Xerox Corporation who use it as a major tool in gaining competitive advantage. Xerox first started benchmarking in their manufacturing activity and it was focused on product quality and feature improvements. Following success in the manufacturing area, Xerox top management directed that benchmarking be performed by all cost centres and business units and by 1981 it was adopted company-wide. A key feature of the process was a high level of employee involvement which was the means by which benchmarking was implemented.

Initially there was some difficulty in performing benchmarking in departments such as repair service, maintenance, invoicing and collection and distribution until it was recognized that their 'product' was, in fact, a process. It was this process which needed to be articulated and compared with that used in external organizations. By looking at competitors' **processes** step-by-step and operation-by-operation, Xerox were able to identify best methods and practices in use by their competitors.

Now competitive benchmarking has come to be recognized as appropriate for any area of a company's operations. Figure 4.3 illustrates the wide range of areas where benchmarking can be undertaken including advertising, sales, R&D, customer and products, distribution, marketing, finance, plant and facilities, organizational aspects and planning.

William Gavin, executive vice president for Xerox Corporation has described how benchmarking works in his company:[4]

> Every department at Xerox benchmarks itself against its counterpart department at the best companies we compete with. We look at how they make a product, how much it costs them to make it, how they distribute it, market it, sell it and support it, how their organisation works, and what kind of technology they have. Then, we all go back and

figure out what it takes to be better than they are in each of those areas. In almost every case it means cutting costs . . . Cutting our inventory and our supplier base down to size was only one part of a larger plan to cut Xerox down to size. It was a plan to make the company leaner, more responsive to changing market conditions and, ultimately, more competitive. We came to call it the 'resizing' of Xerox. Since we began that resizing program in 1981, we've taken more than $500 million out of our cost base in manufacturing alone.

You can create benchmarks for practically any part of your operation. This list of potential benchmarking categories can help measure your operations against your competitor's.

Advertising
Expenditure
Themes

Sales
Terms
Sales force

- size
- structure
- training/experience
- compensation
- number of calls
- turnover rates

Sales literature
Proposals

- style
- structure
- pricing

Accountability
Cross selling

R&D
Patents
Staff
R&D $/sales
Government contracts

Customers/products
Sales/customer
Breadth of product line
Product quality
Average customer size

Distribution
Channels used
Middlemen

Marketing
Product/brand strategy
Market share
Pricing

Financials/costs
Profitability
Overhead
Return on assets
Return on equity
Net worth
Margins
Cash flow
Debt
Borrowing capacity

Plant/facility

- size
- capacity
- utilization
- equipment costs

Capital investments
Integration level
Quality control
Fixed and variable costs

Organization
Structure
Values
General goals
Expected growth
Decision-making level
Controls

Strategic plans
Short term
Long term
Core business/expansion or stability
Acquisitions

Figure 4.3 *Competitive benchmarking checklist*
Source: Strategic Intelligence Checklist. Cambridge, MA: Fuld & Co. Inc.

Initially, benchmarking activities were concentrated solely on competitors until it became clear that Xerox's objective in achieving superior performance in each business function was not being obtained by looking only at competitors' practices.

The objective of creating competitive advantage involves **outperforming** rather than matching the efforts of competitors. This, together with the obvious difficulties in gaining all the information required on competitors and their internal systems and processes led to a broader perspective on benchmarking being adopted. Thus benchmarking was expanded from a focus solely on competitors to a wider, but selective, focus on the products of top performing companies regardless of their industry sector.

Xerox have successfully used this broader perspective on benchmarking as a major element in increasing both quality and productivity. Collaborative cooperation between firms in **non-competing** industries offers significant opportunity in this regard. For example, in the Xerox logistics and distribution unit annual productivity has doubled as a result of benefits obtained from non-competitive collaborative benchmarking.

Today Xerox are a world role model for quality improvement with some 240 different functional areas of the company routinely involved in benchmarking against comparable areas. Gains can come from widely different industries. Figure 4.4 shows five practices relevant to improving productivity gains in Xerox that were identified from such widely disparate businesses as photographic film manufacturers and drug wholesalers.

Type of company	Practice
Drug wholesaler	Electronic ordering between store and distribution centre
Appliance manufacturer	Forklift handling of up to six appliances at once
Electrical components manufacturer	Automatic in-line weighing, bar-code labelling, and scanning of packages
Photographic film manufacturer	Self-directed warehouse work teams
Catalogue fulfilment service bureau	Recording of item dimension and weight to permit order-filling quality assurance based on calculated compared with actual weight

Figure 4.4 *Practices uncovered by Xerox via non-competitive benchmarking*
Source: Based on Tucker F. G., Zivan S. M. and Camp R. C. (1987). How to measure yourself against the best. *Harvard Business Review*, January-February.

Camp[5] has identified a number of benefits a company derives from benchmarking. These include:

- It enables the best practices from any industry to be creatively incorporated into the processes of the benchmarked function.
- It can provide stimulation and motivation to the professionals whose creativity is required to perform and implement benchmark findings.
- Benchmarking breaks down ingrained reluctance of operations to change. It has been found that people are more receptive to new ideas and their creative adoption when those ideas did not necessarily originate in their own industry.
- Benchmarking may also identify a technological breakthrough that

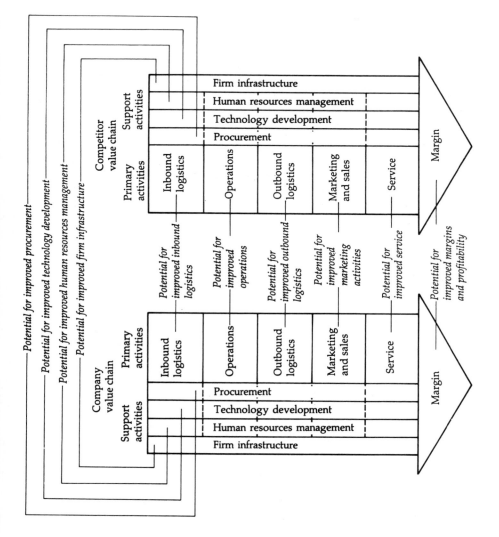

Figure 4.5 *Identifying improvements in value chain elements through competitive benchmarking*

would not have been recognized, and thus not applied, in one's own industry for some time to come, such as bar coding, originally adopted and proven in the grocery industry.

The value chain concept can be especially useful in benchmarking competitors. By systematically comparing **processes** within each element of the firm's value chain with those of competitors, areas for improvement can be identified. This is shown in Figure 4.5. Such systematic comparisons can make transparent areas where competitive advantage can be secured. For example, it may show where competitors are subcontracting activities out to third parties at prices lower than it would cost them to perform the activities themselves.

Service quality benchmarking

The benchmarking procedure that we advocate is to measure your organization's performance against both competitors and appropriate non-competitors. The purpose of measuring performance against competitors is to seek out opportunities for gaining competitive advantage through service leadership. Likewise the purpose of benchmarking against non-competitors is to identify opportunities for adopting leading-edge service strategies from outside the immediate industry or market in which you compete.

The approach to service benchmarking that we favour follows a five-stage process:

Step 1   Define the competitive arena, that is with whom are we compared by customers and with whom do we **want** to be compared?
Step 2   Identify the key components of customer service as seen by customers themselves.
Step 3   Establish the relative importance of those service components to customers.
Step 4   Identify company position on the key service components relative to competition.
Step 5   Analyse the data to see if service performance matches customers' service needs.

Figure 4.6. summarizes the five-step customer service audit process.

Step 1   Define the competitive arena

Given the basic proposition that service quality is potentially a powerful tool in the context of relationship marketing, it is important that the competitive context is clearly understood. Specifically the question is: with whom are we being compared by customers – both potential and actual? Furthermore, with whom do we want to be compared?

This definition of the competitive arena is not quite as easy as it sounds. With whom does an overnight document carrier compete? Other courier companies? Or fax machines or express mail? In making judgements of the technical service received from a supplier of word processors who

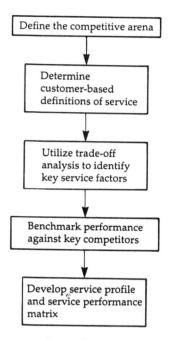

Figure 4.6 *The customer service audit*

does the office manager compare them with? Other word processor suppliers? Unlikely, because that office will probably only have one make of word processor. More likely the office manager will compare the service received with the service provided by the photo-copier supplier, the telecom engineer and other office service suppliers.

The point is that to be seen as an excellent company in the service context, the supplier must recognize that the real assessment takes place in the customer's mind against other comparable service encounters.

Thus when we talk about 'competitive' benchmarking the precise definition of the 'competition' needs to be given some thought. Our recommended approach is to utilize either 'focus group' discussions or individual depth interviews with representative customers to provide some insight into the extent of the real competitive arena. By asking respondents to talk first in general terms about service quality and then asking them to nominate good and bad examples of service from their recent experience, the discussion leader or interviewer can begin to probe the nature of the perceptual map of service quality that the customer utilizes when making judgements about the offer.

The first step in the benchmarking process can be coordinated, from a data-gathering point of view, with the next step.

Step 2   *Identifying the key components of customer service*

It is a common fault in marketing to fail to realize that customers do not always attach the same importance to product attributes as the vendor. The same principle applies to customer service. Which aspects of service are rated most highly by the customer? If a supplier places emphasis on stock availability, but the customer regards delivery reliability more highly, it may not be allocating its resources in a way likely to maximize sales. Alternatively, a company that realizes that its customers place a higher value on completeness of orders than they do on, say, regular scheduled deliveries could develop this knowledge to its advantage.

Therefore it is important to understand the factors that influence buyer behaviour and, in the context of customer service, which particular elements are seen by the customer to be the most important.

The first step in research of this type is to identify the relative source of influence on the purchase decision. If, for example, we are selling components to a manufacturer, who will make the decision on the source of supply? This is not always an easy question to answer as in many cases there will be several people involved. The purchasing manager of the company to which we are selling may only be acting as an agent for others within the firm. In other cases his influence will be much greater. Alternatively, if we are manufacturing products for sale through retail outlets, is the decision to stock made centrally by a retail chain or by individual store managers? The answers can often be supplied by the sales force. The sales representative should know from experience who are the decision makers.

Given that a clear indication of the source of decision-making power can be gained, the customer service researcher at least knows who to research. The question remains as to which elements of the vendor's total marketing offering have what effect on the purchase decision.

Ideally once the decision maker, or the decision-making unit has been identified an initial, small-scale research programme should be initiated based on personal interviews with a representative sample of buyers. The purpose of these interviews is to elicit, in the language of the customers, first the importance they attach to customer service vis-a-vis the other marketing mix elements such as price, product quality, promotion etc., and second, the specific importance they attach to the individual components of customer service. As we have suggested, from a research point of view, this data gathering could be combined with the previous stage.

The authors were involved in a customer service study to determine the elements of customer service in the market for a packaged grocery product and an initial series of personal interviews were conducted with senior buyers responsible for the purchase of that product in major retail outlets. As a result, a number of customer service elements were generated as follows:

Frequency of delivery
Time from order to delivery

Reliability of delivery
Emergency deliveries when required
Stock availability and continuity of supply
Orders filled completely
Advice on non-availability
Convenience of placing order
Acknowledgement of order
Accuracy of invoices
Quality of sales representation
In-store merchandising support
Regular calls by sales representatives
Manufacturer monitoring of retail stock levels
Credit terms offered

The importance of this initial step in measuring customer service is that relevant and meaningful measures of customer service are generated by the customers themselves. Once these dimensions are defined we can identify the relative importance of each one and the extent to which the customer is prepared to trade-off one aspect of service for another.

Step 3   Establishing the relative importance of customer service components

One way of discovering the importance a customer attaches to each element of customer service is to take the components generated by means of the process described in Step 1 and to ask a representative sample of customers to rank order them from the 'most important' to the 'least important'. In practice this is difficult, particularly with a large number of components and would not give any insight into the relative importance of each element. Alternatively a form of rating scale could be used. For example, the respondents could be asked to place a weight from 1 to 10 against each component according to how much importance they attached to each element. The problem here is that respondents will tend to rate most of the components as highly important, especially since those components were generated on the grounds of importance to customers anyway. A partial solution is to ask the respondent to allocate a total of 100 points among all the elements listed, according to perceived importance. However, this is a fairly daunting task for the respondent and can often result in an arbitrary allocation.

Fortunately, a relatively recent innovation in consumer research technology now enables us to evaluate very simply the implicit importance that a customer attaches to the separate elements of customer service. The technique is based around the concept of trade-off and can best be illustrated by an example from everyday life. In considering, say, the purchase of a new car we might desire specific attributes, e.g. performance in terms of speed and acceleration, economy in terms of petrol consumption, size in terms of passenger and luggage capacity and, of course, low price. However, it is unlikely that any one car will meet all of these requirements so we are forced to trade-off one or more of these attributes against the others.

The same is true of the customer faced with alternative options of distribution service. The buyer might be prepared to sacrifice a day or two on lead-time in order to gain delivery reliability, or to trade-off order completeness against improvements in order entry etc. Essentially the trade-off technique works by presenting the respondent with feasible combinations of customer service elements and asking for a rank order of preference for those combinations.

Let us take a simple example where a respondent is asked to choose between different levels of delivery reliability, order cycle time and credit terms. For the sake of example the following options are presented:

Delivery reliability	± 3 days
	± 1 day
	On time
Order cycle time	2 days
	3 days
	4 days
Credit terms	40 days
	30 days

The various trade-offs can be placed before the respondent as a series of matrices.

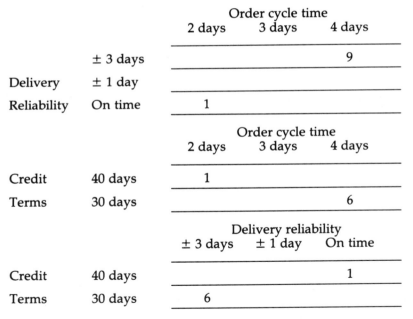

The idea is that the respondent should complete each matrix to illustrate his/her preference for service alternatives. Thus, with the first trade-off matrix between order cycle time and delivery reliability, it is presumed that the most preferred combination would be an order cycle time of two days with on-time delivery and the least preferred combination an order cycle time of four days with a delivery reliability of ± 3 days. But what about the other combinations? Here the respondent is asked to complete the matrix to show his/her own preferences. An example of a typical response is given below.

		Order cycle time		
		2 days	3 days	4 days
Delivery	± 3 days	6	8	9
Reliability	± 1 day	3	5	7
	On time	1	2	4

		Order cycle time		
		2 days	3 days	4 days
Credit	40 days	1	3	5
Terms	30 days	2	4	6

		Delivery reliability		
		± 3 days	± 1 day	On time
Credit	40 days	4	2	1
Terms	30 days	6	5	3

Using computer analysis the implicit 'importance weights' that underlie the initial preference rankings can be generated.[6] For the data in the above example the following weights emerge.

Service element		Importance weight
1 Delivery reliability	± 3 days	−0.480
	± 1 day	0
	On time	+0.480
2 Delivery time	2 days	+0.456
	3 days	0
	4 days	−0.456
3 Credit terms	40 days	+0.239
	30 days	−0.239

Thus for this respondent, delivery reliability would appear to be marginally more important than delivery time and both were in the region of twice as important as credit terms.

Information such as this can be most useful. First it provides us with an objective measure of the 'utility' that a customer or potential customer places on each aspect of service. This measure is more than a simple rank order or rough and ready importance score – it is a precise indication of the relative importance that the individual places on each service attribute. Second, by combining the weights against each attribute level we can identify preferred service combinations.

A further benefit provided by this type of information is that it enables us to distinguish the responses between types of customers – a most important consideration when examining the possibilities for differentiating the service offering by market segment – indeed it is this latter prospect of market segmentation on the basis of service preferences which is perhaps the most exciting aspect of the trade-off technique.

Many companies fail to recognize that there are frequently substantial differences in the service preferences of different customer types and hence miss the opportunity for developing service segmentation strategies – a powerful form of benefit segmentation.

The airlines have demonstrated how successful service segmentation can be when they recognized the different service needs of the business traveller – leading to the creation of the Business Class or Club Class product. Computer companies like Digital offer a variety of service maintenance and support contracts to customers, depending on their requirements.

Using trade-off analysis we can identify groups of customers sharing common service preferences. Our experience with this technique suggests that it can often reveal substantial market segments with service needs that are not fully catered for by existing offers.

Step 4   Identifying company position on key components of service relative to competition

Now we know from the previous two steps the key components of customer service and their relative importance, the next question is: 'How do my customers rate me on these components compared to the competition?'

The previous steps were accomplished using relatively small samples and in effect they serve as a 'pilot' study to provide the basis for a larger scale survey of the company's customers. The answer to the question of comparative service performance can best be achieved by means of a postal questionnaire, the sample for which should be chosen to reflect the different types of customer. The main purpose of the questionnaire is to present the components of service as elicited in Step 1 and to ask the respondents to rate the company and its competitors on each of these elements in terms of their perceived performance. Figure 4.7 reproduces part of a typical questionnaire for use in service benchmarking. For each competing company in the market in question the respondent is asked to rate its performance on each of the relevant dimensions of service identified in Step 1. When the responses are aggregated by trade sector or market segment, patterns may well emerge. On each customer service element it is possible to see how each competing supplier compares in terms of each other.

How would you rate ABC on the following:
(Score from 1 to 5; 1 = very poor, 5 = excellent)

	Please circle
Order cycle time	1 2 3 4 5
Stock availability	1 2 3 4 5
Order size constraints	1 2 3 4 5
Ordering convenience	1 2 3 4 5
Frequency of delivery	1 2 3 4 5
Delivery reliability	1 2 3 4 5
Quality of documentation	1 2 3 4 5
Claims procedure	1 2 3 4 5
Order completeness	1 2 3 4 5
Technical support	1 2 3 4 5
Order status information	1 2 3 4 5

Figure 4.7 *Customer service benchmark questionnaire*

Other analyses can include regional breakdowns and analyses by size and type of customer. The usual statistical tests can be applied to identify if different scores on any dimensions have significance. To ensure an unbiased response to the questionnaire it is preferable if the survey can be carried out anonymously or via a third party such as a market research agency. Also, as in the previous steps, it is important to make sure that the people to whom the questionnaire is sent represent the decision-making structure within their concerns.

Management now has a customer service database on which it can make a number of crucial decisions regarding the design of more cost-

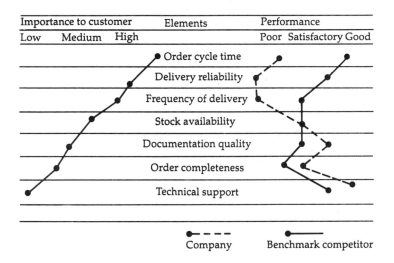

Figure 4.8 *Customer service profile*

effective customer service policies. Analysis of the data will enable service profiles for each competitor to be constructed and the results can be presented alongside the importance scores derived from the earlier trade-off analysis (Fig. 4.8).

Further profiles can be produced by disaggregating the data by customer type, market segment, region, etc. Competitive service profiles can provide additional insights if non-users or lapsed customers are also included in the survey. Companies who have conducted these types of competitive analyses find that they provide a clear guide for action. Often competitive profiles point to weaknesses that had not previously been recognized. Additional benefit can be derived from repeating these studies on a regular basis to monitor changes and trends.

Step 5   Comparing service performance with customers' service priorities

Using the data generated from the customer service audit we are in a position to contrast two key findings: first, what are the important dimensions of service, and second, how well is the company perceived to perform on those key dimensions?

A simple way of displaying this data is to represent the findings in the form of a service performance matrix. On one axis we measure the importance rating (usually on a scale of 1 to 5) and on the second axis is shown the actual perceived performance rating (also on a 1 to 5 scale). Figure 4.9 shows such a matrix.

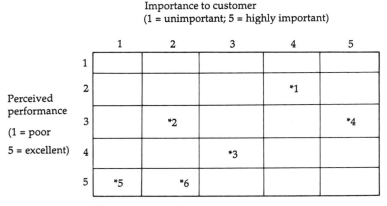

Key: *service attributes 1 - 6

Figure 4.9 *The service performance matrix*

In this hypothetical example we have shown the scores on six service elements jointly for importance and perceived performance. The six service elements might be taken to be:

1   Order cycle time

2   Order completeness
3   Documentation quality (e.g. invoices)
4   Delivery reliability
5   Technical support
6   Sales visits

The interpretation of this matrix is simple. It is clearly crucial that the company be seen to be performing well on those service dimensions that the customer deems to be important. Conversely it can be argued that if any particular service dimension is seen to be less important to the customer then high performance on that dimension amounts to 'service over-kill' or a misuse of resources.

Thus in this example the company appears to be underperforming on dimensions 1 and 4 – order cycle time and delivery reliability – and possibly overperforming on 5 – technical support and 6 – sales visits. Figure 4.10 generalizes this point.

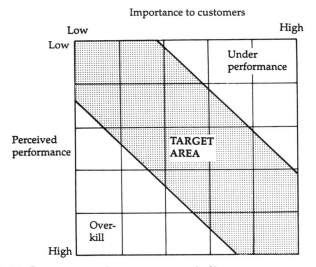

Figure 4.10 *Customer service management indicators*

Similar charts can be produced for individual market segments, sales areas, distribution channels or whatever by further analysis of the data that emerge from the customer service audit.

Smith and Prescott[7] have suggested that this analysis can be further extended by including competitive performance data. Thus the 'perceived performance' scale is modified to show 'relative' performance. In other words we express our performance as perceived by customers as a ratio of competitors' perceived performance. Figure 4.11 shows such a modified analysis in the form of a matrix. Three broad strategic positions emerge from this analysis:

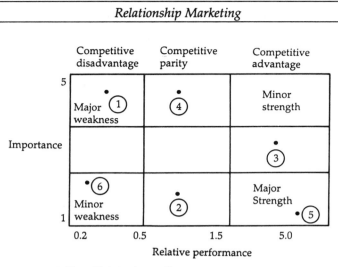

Key: *1-6 service attributes

Figure 4.11 *Competitive position matrix*

1 **Competitive advantage**
   Major strength (high importance, high relative performance)
   Minor strength (low importance, high relative performance)
2 **Competitive parity**
   Weaknesses and strengths match those of the competition.
3 **Competitive disadvantage**
   Major weakness (high importance, low relative performance)
   Minor weakness (low importance, low relative performance)

In the hypothetical example depicted in Figure 4.11, the company appears to have a major weakness in its order cycle time (1) and a minor weakness on sales visits (6). It has a potential advantage with the quality of its documentation (3) and its technical support (5) to a lesser extent. It has competitive parity on (4) and (2) – delivery reliability and order completeness.

Consumer research

While the preceding example related to a manufacturer supplying a distributor or stockist, exactly the same procedure could be applied to a consumer or service market. Thus in designing a competitive service package for an airport hotel, say, research could be conducted on similar lines. In such an instance it might be useful to begin with a focus group representative of the target market, say business travellers, and then to use the service criteria generated through that means as the basis for more detailed customer interviews.

The key point to remember in measuring and monitoring customer service performance is that the metric, or 'measuring rod' used must be customer relevant and normally that means that the measures must be generated directly from customers through research. A common mistake is to design customer service studies using **internally** derived standards (i.e. determined by management) and thus as a result, possibly drawing misleading conclusions.

However, it will be recalled from Chapter 3 that the research by Parasuraman et al. has suggested that there are a number of basic dimensions of service quality that can be generalized across markets. These are: reliability, responsiveness, assurance, empathy and tangibles.

These five dimensions were derived from extensive multi-market research and are in fact a reduction from ten service elements as shown with some examples in Figure 4.12.

Reliability involves consistency of performance dependability. It means that the firm performs the service right the first time. It also means that the firm honours its promises. Specifically it involves:

– accuracy in billing
– keeping records correctly
– performing the service at the designated time

Responsiveness concerns the willingness or readiness of employees to provide service. It involves timeliness of service:

– mailing a transaction slip immediately
– calling the customer back quickly
– giving prompt service (e.g. setting up appointments quickly)

Competence means possession of the required skills and knowledge to perform the service. It involves:

– knowledge and skill of the contact personnel
– knowledge and skill of operational support personnel
– research capability of the organization, e.g. securities brokerage firm

Access involves approachability and ease of contact. It means:

– the service is easily accessible by telephone (lines are not busy and they don't put you on 'hold')
– waiting time to receive service (e.g. at a bank) is not extensive
– convenient hours of operation
– convenient location of service facility

Courtesy involves politeness, respect, consideration and friendliness of contact personnel (including receptionists, telephone operators etc.). It includes:

– consideration for the consumer's property (e.g. no muddy shoes on the carpet)
– clean and neat appearance of public contact personnel

Communication means keeping customers informed in language they can understand and listening to them. It may mean that the company has to adjust its language for different consumers – increasing the level of sophistication with a well-educated customer and speaking simply and plainly with a novice. It involves:

– explaining the service itself
– explaining how much the service will cost
– explaining the trade-offs between service and cost
– assuring the consumer that a problem will be handled

Credibility involves trustworthiness, believability, honesty. It involves having the customer's best interests at heart. Contributing to credibility are:

- company name
- company reputation
- personal characteristics of the contact personnel
- the degree of hard sell involved in interactions with the customer

Security is the freedom from danger, risk, or doubt. It involves:

- physical safety (will I get mugged at the automatic teller machine?)
- financial security (does the company know where my stock certificate is?)
- confidentiality (are my dealings with the company private?)

Understanding/knowing the customer involves making the effort to understand the customer's needs. It involves:

- learning the customer's specific requirements
- providing individualized attention
- recognizing the regular customer

Tangibles include the physical evidence of the service:

- physical facilities
- appearance of personnel
- tools or equipment used to provide the service
- physical representations of the service such as a plastic credit card or a bank statement
- other customers in the service facility

Figure 4.12 *Determinants of service quality*

Thus it could be possible to conduct regular service audits using these ten generic factors as the basis for measuring service performance. However, a better approach would be to use the generic factors as the starting point and then to expand them, perhaps through focus group discussions or depth interviews, to make them more specific to the marketplace or industry in which the organization competes.

One valuable by-product of research into customers' service preferance is that it can reveal 'gaps' in the market where there is a real demand for specific service offers but where there is no current product available. Indeed it can be argued that there is a case for regular research which is focused not solely on measuring service performance but which also specifically seeks to identify service marketing opportunities.

Many of the techniques that have been developed in new product development (NPD)[8] can be used to great effect in researching the scope for new or extended service offers.

'Gap analysis', as it is sometimes referred to, is an umbrella term for a variety of techniques with a common aim – to seek out viable market segments with specific requirements that are not well catered for by existing offers.

A technique that has proved to be particularly powerful in the service research arena is known as 'perceptual mapping'. The idea behind this approach is that customers, whether acting for themselves or on behalf of organizations, utilize mental 'maps' which help them make comparisons and thus choices between competing offers. These maps are not unlike maps of countries which help us to 'position' one town or location in relation to another, except that in this case we are using maps to locate one product or offer against another. It must also be realized that whereas for a country map there is only one map with two dimensions (North–South, East–West), with a perceptual map different people may utilize different dimensions and there may be more than two dimensions!

Figure 4.13 provides an example of a perceptual map with multiple dimensions of the UK food retailing market. Construction of these maps is aided by the use of 'non-metric scaling' techniques[9] which, taking data from consumer or user surveys reflecting respondents' judgements on perceived similarity between existing products or services, enable 'ideal points' to be identified. Using maps such as these can often reveal hidden opportunities for developing more attractive service packages.

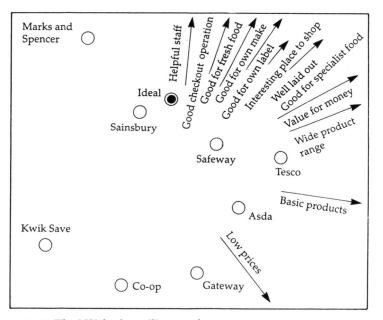

Figure 4.13 *The UK food retailing market*
> Source: Davies G. J. and Brooks J. M. (1989). *Positioning strategy in retailing*. London: Paul Chapman Publishing

Internal customer service surveys

Increasingly, organizations are coming to recognize that there is a direct relationship between the attitude towards customer service held by employees of the organization and the actual service performance of that organization. Not surprisingly they are discovering that when a positive customer service 'climate' exists within the company there is a greater likelihood that a higher quality service will result. Even more to the point, when negative feelings exist within the organization towards customers, then almost certainly service will suffer.

Recognizing that attitude change is a necessary precursor to behaviour change, we strongly recommend that part of the process of monitoring service performance should be an internal customer service survey.

This internal survey is similar in many respects to the external survey that we have previously described. The rationale of the survey is to measure the attitudes towards service of the key players in the service encounter. As well as monitoring attitudes it is also instructive to identify how our own people define service and what they consider the key dimensions of service to be. Our experience suggests that often there can be quite a wide divergence between the definitions of service adopted internally and those used by customers themselves.

Who should be surveyed in such an internal study? In a sense, the wider the sample the better. However, it is essential that all those responsible for an input to the 'service encounter' be included in the survey – not just the 'front-line' people like bank clerks or delivery drivers, but those in the warehouse or order processing department who have no direct contact with customers, but indirectly can have a major impact on customer service.

It is particularly important to ensure that the 'opinion leaders' within the organization are recognized and their views on service included in the study. As we all know from experience, within every organization there are complex networks of interactions and communications. These networks overlap each other and are linked by a limited number of people who are in more than one network. As such, these people may have considerable influence on the way that ideas and values are communicated around the organization. Also important are those people whose views carry greater weight because they have achieved greater 'legitimacy' than their colleagues.

Clearly it is important to involve these key people in any process of culture or climate change. Identifying them, however, may not always be that easy! While formal techniques to analyse networks do exist it may be possible to ascertain opinion leadership within the organization through observation.

Insight can also be gained from comparing the views of management towards service with those of other employees. Schneider[10] reported that often a divergence of service goals between management and work force can lead to a deterioration in service as perceived by customers. The same research demonstrated that customers perceive high-quality service when the service orientation of managers and employees converge, i.e. when everybody in the organization is 'singing to the same hymn sheet' as far as service goals are concerned.

We read and hear a lot about 'corporate culture' these days and it is now widely recognized that culture is a major determinant of the degree of customer orientation within a company, an issue to which we return in Chapter 6. It is therefore of some importance to gain a measure of what the inherent values and norms are across the business – again recognizing that these may not be shared at all levels.

Various methods have been advocated for gauging corporate culture but the approach we advocate focuses specifically on measuring customer orientation.

Quality improvement and customer care programmes are now a common feature across a wide range of organizations. However, the success or failure of these programmes will be determined in large part by the ability of the organization to identify the key customer service factors and to monitor competitive performance on those factors.

In today's competitive market place there is a clear advantage to be gained by a recognition of the factors that influence customer demand. Competitive and non-competitive benchmarking, combined with trade-off analysis, is a highly practical way to identify the 'order winning criteria' that underlie the customer's choice of supplier.

References

1 Parasuraman A., Zeithaml V. A., and Berry L. L. (1988). SERVQUAL: a multiple-item scale for measuring consumer perceptions of service quality. *Journal of Retailing*. **64**, 1, Spring.
2 Parasuraman A., Zeithaml V. A., and Berry L. L. (1985). A conceptual model of service quality and its implications for future research. *Journal of Marketing*. **49**, Fall.
3 Camp R. E. (1989). *Benchmarking: The Search for Industry Best Practices that lead to Superior Performance*. New York: ASQC Quality Press.
4 Gavin W. F. (1984). Competitive benchmarking. *Review of Business*. **6**, 3, pp. 9–12.
5 Camp R. E., *op. cit.*
6 For a more detailed discussion of trade-off analysis see Johnson R. M. (1974). Trade-off analysis of consumer values. *Journal of Marketing Research*. **XI**, May.
7 Smith David C. and Prescott John E. (1987). Couple competitive analysis to sales force decisions. *Industrial Marketing Management*. **16**, pp. 55–61.
8 Cooper R. G. (1987). *Winning at New Products*. Gage Publishing Co.
9 See for example, Green P. E., Carmone F. J. and Smith S. M. (1989). *Multidimensional Scaling*. Allyn & Bacon.
10 Schneider B. (1980). The service organization: climate is crucial. *Organizational Dynamics*. Autumn, American Management Association.

5. THE TRANSITION TO QUALITY LEADERSHIP

In this chapter setting up a quality improvement process is described 'from the inside out'. Quality improvement goes hand in hand with developing 'customer orientation' within the organization and our aim is to dispell the myth that marketing can ignore the former, while being involved in the latter. We also explore the issue of 'commitment', and introduce seven quality traps. Finally the important question – how do you know when you are succeeding? Some possible answers are offered.

We have said that quality is what makes the firm's offer unique and brings customers back for more. 'Real' quality is **perceived quality**, a judgement by the customer. Most companies, however, do not have good measures of perceived quality. As a result, many have not yet understood how quality can be the key to long-term competitive advantage.

So now we are left with an inescapable conclusion. Somebody has to start the wheel turning. Managing the change processes is strategic. Getting started is critical. If marketing can get involved in quality improvement, it will bridge the gap between **product orientation**, and **market orientation**. What is really at stake is an 'organizational transition' which embraces quality improvement, as a way of life.

Strategic intent

Most companies have corporate mission statements that emphasize customer orientation or customer service, as their guiding direction. We have described some of these in Chapter 2. Unfortunately, the reality of business life frequently falls short of these noble sentiments.

The marketer believes he or she is customer driven. Yet few companies really understand their customers. Many companies who do invest in market research do not focus on the service support issues. To make matters worse, even when good research is available, many companies are defeated by the task of converting that research into plans, design activities, and internal process changes.

With symptoms of failure all around us, clearly many marketing activities are no more than tactical. The big plans often fail to get off the ground because of inertia within the organization. When everything seems to be going crazy and there is no time for anything new, it is likely that within the organization there is no **alignment** of strategy around a central guiding idea which has broad appeal, no superordinate goal which guides departments and individuals in their actions and activities.

One of Australia's leading quality department stores is 'David Jones'. The managing director, Rod Mewing, recently rediscovered the original store credo written by the founding father, Charles Lloyd Jones. The credo set out the principles by which the company is still managed today. It said, 'If I were to define the quality of this company in one word, that word for me would be **service**. Treat customers as you would like to be treated.' A successful vision outlives the tangible form in which it is expressed and the visionary leader who first put it together.[1]

One reason why companies find it so hard to anticipate competitor's moves is that they tend to look to the evidence of competition, once it has surfaced, and respond to that. Competing **against** your competitors reactively is not the way to become fast and flexible. Competing for your customer requires strategic vision, a commitment to quality and innovation.[2]

To say that a company needs **strategic vision** may sound ambiguous or even trite. Yet what is required is a guiding wisdom, one which is likely to be shared by an influential proportion of staff. We believe that a quality improvement goal must be part of strategic vision. Relationship marketing demands it.

Quality as a 'mind set' serves the interests of shareholders, staff, and the customers, with a logic that is acceptable to each of these stakeholders. The quality improvement process brings cost reductions over time, when staff participate in that process. Quality goes up as non-value wastes and time-related costs come down. The beneficiaries are the customers, staff and shareholders, because expectations are not in tension with each other.

Peter Drucker, veteran management guru, has said that the first task of a leader is to define the company's mission. This is fine, so long as we remember that it is the leader's vision that gives rise to the mission in the first place. If you do not know where you are going, it will not matter which way you go! Of course, day-to-day work pressures overwhelm any strategic vision that is not diffused through the organization, codified in the form of a mission statement and monitored in terms of survey results. Strategic vision dies when it is not implemented as strategy, that is, when it is not actioned.

It is the **values** which support the strategic vision that give it such motive force. For example, the following values underpin the discussion on quality dimensions in Chapter 3. They were not brought to the surface specifically then, and now is the time to do so:

- Everybody serves a customer, everybody supplies a customer
- People work **in** the system, people work **on** the system
- All work systems exhibit variability
- Fix the system, not the people
- Quality improvement is continuous improvement, a way of life

The job of a manager is to improve the system and to invite staff to participate in that improvement process. These values are the essence of quality management, yet they run against the grain of much traditional management thinking.

In modern deregulated markets, you either attempt to guide your business destiny, or let destiny have its way and learn through the pain. The tendency has been to believe that top management has all the answers. Top management in turn, hesitate to admit they do not, for fear of demoralizing lower level employees. The result of this has been a cleavage between strategy setting and strategy implementation. Strategy formulation becomes an elitist activity separated from implementation. Under such structural conditions, there is no room for open challenge or discussion, up and down the organization. As a result, plans often fall short of expectations.[3]

When plans become undiscussable, even their 'undiscussability' can become undiscussable too! Where there is no room for participation, difficulties in getting things done become labelled 'communication problems'. In such underled and overmanaged situations, middle management is seen as part of the problem, or victim, according to your hierarchical perspective. In any event, tensions and dissatisfactions become institutionalized. On the other hand, when top management have confidence in their ability to share information in the change process, and encourage participation within that process, managers down the line gain the courage to commit themselves to new strategies. Then there is **fusion** between 'what' to do, the 'why' of it all and 'how' to do it. This to us is close to the heart of strategic intent.[4]

Commitment

Programmes for quality improvement often fall short of the initial enthusiastic expectations because it has not been recognized that something more is required beyond setting up structures for planning, organizing and controlling. There is also a tendency for top management to think that a decision to proceed is a sufficient signal of commitment, and that all that is required is to communicate that commitment down through the hierarchy of the organization.

Commitment is an act of leadership. In implementing quality improvement, the commitment of 'head office' or the CEO is a vexing issue. Overall, staff regard a 'commitment' to quality as taking business precedent over all else. Any act or talk which is out of line with the quality commitment negates or devalues that commitment. This is an awesome responsibility for management. In quality improvement it is often felt that staff must do all the changing. In truth it is management that must change first! Staff will be watching which 'signals' are going out – are they congruent with the quality commitment? Are they being treated seriously? What other change processes seem to be competing for the limelight?

In one organization, the move to quality improvement involved problem solving teams. These teams worked on specific problems in three monthly cycles. At the end of each cycle people were thanked, and a special 'presentation day' was organized for the discussion of proposals.

The 'presentation day' event was popular with staff. Soon, however, a difficult question rose to the surface – why did the company staff suggestion scheme offer a cash reward for good suggestions, when the problem solving teams went through their voluntary and time-consuming process without the prospect of a cash reward? This is an example of the unintended incongruity that can be expected to surface, even in the best run programmes. The solution involves **disengaging the logic** that connects the evidence. In this case, the company had recently set up a profit sharing scheme and was able to authentically demonstrate the logic of **transferring** rewards which previously existed for staff suggestion scheme contributions away from that scheme to the new profit sharing scheme.

Mixed signals to staff of course pop up everywhere, from the staff point of view. They always surface at some stage in a programme of 'quality improvement'. These mixed messages have social, cultural and symbolic importance and do need to be treated seriously. For this reason, the issue of authentic 'commitment' is likely to surface at the most inconvenient times. Staff morale and energy are at stake. 'Commitment' needs to be acted out, rather than talked out. It really is a case of actions speaking louder than words.

At this point, you may be wondering why so much attention is being given to the strategic intent and commitment issues underlying quality improvement processes. The traditional – or control orientated –management approach would restrict employee input to a relatively narrow agenda, whereas we are advocating an expansion of staff input in problem solving and ideas generation. We are talking about improving work processes, from inbound supply to sales and service, so as to eliminate bottlenecks and inefficiencies. More than this, to improve the quality of the offering demands a **market orientation** and the involvement of staff in why and how information is generated and used. This requires a shift in responsibility so that quality starts to become the concern of everybody and, in time, the **self-directed** responsibility of everybody.

At issue here are two incompatible views of what management can reasonably expect of workers and the kind of partnership they can share with them. One is based on imposing **control** to achieve compliance. The other based on eliciting **commitment**. The shift is not as radical as it may seem at first glance. A transitional approach is suggested.[5] The cornerstone of the transitional stage is the **voluntary** participation of employees in problem-solving groups.

If a real commitment to quality involves organizational change, then marketing must change too. A common error, especially in mature organizations, is to make only token changes and rely on internal and external 'communications' to achieve effects. Alternatively, or in conjunction with 'communications', management tries a succession of technique-orientated changes to achieve quality effects. None of this is wrong. It is just not sufficient. This is particularly evident in service industries, where the realization comes early that an improvement in customer service involves changing the way work is organized and the way managers must 'manage' the activities of the business.

Where quality change programmes are well intentioned, and not merely 'this year's marketing promotion', a third approach emerges from our case studies as a possibility. This approach treats people and processes as interrelated service-quality drivers with continuous improvement as the long-term goal. This latter approach was briefly mentioned and recommended in Chapter 3. This is the path-goal approach to **quality leadership**. We will examine this in more detail now.

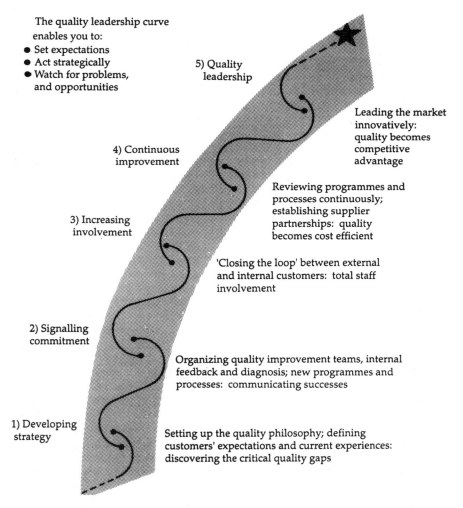

The quality leadership curve
enables you to:
● Set expectations
● Act strategically
● Watch for problems,
   and opportunities

5) Quality
   leadership

Leading the market
innovatively:
quality becomes
competitive
advantage

4) Continuous
   improvement

Reviewing programmes and
processes continuously;
establishing supplier
partnerships: quality
becomes cost efficient

3) Increasing
   involvement

'Closing the loop' between external
and internal customers: total staff
involvement

2) Signalling
   commitment

Organizing quality improvement teams, internal
feedback and diagnosis; new programmes and
processes: communicating successes

1) Developing
   strategy

Setting up the quality philosophy; defining
customers' expectations and current experiences:
discovering the critical quality gaps

Figure 5.1 *Quality leadership curve*

Leading the change

At this point, we introduce our quality leadership curve (see Figure 5.1). This model enables you to set your expectations on the journey to quality, to act strategically, and to watch for problems and opportunities on the way. The 'curve' is not based on statistical analyses, but it does fit with our experience and research with companies who are taking quality improvement seriously as a company-wide strategy. It is for this reason that we have designated 'quality leadership' as the ultimate goal of the quality improvement process. Of course quality leadership is a moving target. It is a relative concept, and it has no fixed point. However, there are a series of leadership steps, or more correctly **transitions**, towards the quality goal. Each phase has its own special characteristics and there is likely to be some degree of 'turbulence' before breaking through from one phase to the next. These turbulence zones are shown in Figure 5.1 at the intersect between the linked S-curves.

Quality leadership could be any company's **strategic intent**, when success is measured against customer expectations, within defined target markets. Just what this might entail will always be vague at the outset. Commitment to a precise goal at an early stage could lead to an incorrect choice. In the way that we wish to describe it, 'quality leadership' is a qualitative target. Having said that, there are steps to take, and these will involve transitions in the way things are normally done. This is a process of 'learning by doing'. These steps can be logically planned to advantage, individual projects set up and completed, and motivational and organizational structures put in place. All this can be achieved in terms of commitment to a superordinate quality leadership goal.

So far, so good, but it is worth pausing for a moment to ask whether a strategy for quality leadership involves change processes which are revolutionary, or logically incremental. The quality curve suggests an 'evolutionary' outcome, but the form of that outcome can only be seen with hindsight. The steps on the way are certainly 'incremental'. They vary in their exact nature according to environmental contexts and also according to social and political dimensions of **managing** the quality improvement process which may require sporadic 'revolutionary' inputs. The 'revolutionary' and 'incremental' viewpoints do not mean that a choice must be made between one and the other.

It was James Quinn who introduced the concept of 'logical incrementalism' to corporate strategic planning in the late 1970s. Following Quinn, we recognize that the quality goal can be achieved by multiple means and that it may be politically unwise for management to set in concrete a particular set of means too early in the quality improvement process. Incremental changes generate new knowledge and the application of that knowledge leads to new incremental change processes. This is not a way of 'muddling through' but it is a way of staying open to new information and reaching for sources of information up and down the organization.[6]

Moving up the quality leadership curve is a logical process not withstanding that the quality goal is ambiguously defined. The apparent paradox in all this is resolved if we keep in mind that the quality goal is predicated on the sovereignty of the consumer, and their shifting expectations. Exactly what that means must be discovered and redis-covered anew in each market. This is very puzzling at first for many managers, trained and socialized to perform best when the logical path is a straight line. In terms of the chess board, what is required is not so much the thrusting movement of a **rook**, or the tangential approach of a **bishop**, or the step by step approach of the **pawn**. It is the way of the **knight** that makes progress in quality improvement – two moves forward, one to the side. And from the perspective of the **knight**, there is no such thing as a backwards move! There can be no one way to quality leadership.

People and process

In relationship marketing, there is a recursive relationship between the people (who are involved in work processes) and the processes (which involve people). Each is the key to learning about the other. Each is the key to the effectiveness of the other. This involves a shift towards inviting the support and participation of people to work on **improving** the way processes are designed and organized.

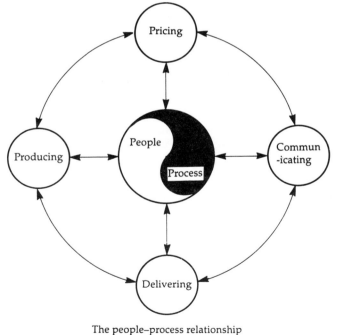

The people–process relationship
is the driving force for quality in
all organizational activities

Figure 5.2 *The service-quality drivers*

Under these conditions, the people–process relationship within the organization becomes the internal driving force for quality leadership (see Figure 5.2). We call these **service-quality drivers** because they energize the structure of all activities connected with the planning, improving and controlling of quality solutions and service support. These activities also take functional forms which in our model we have categorized as producing, pricing, communicating and delivering. These four functions, when aligned strategically, give total quality to the firm's total offering. Managed separately they remain different **perspectives** of the total organizational activity. Relationship marketing should recognize that quality is something other than the sum of the parts when viewed through customers' eyes.

Achieving quality improvement through the service-quality drivers points up a dilemma for marketing managers, in terms of their influence and authority. How can marketing possibly achieve satisfaction for customers when it has incomplete control over the quality making activities and hence total quality outputs? The other part of the 'bind' is to ask how can marketing lead or influence the development of a formal process for company-wide change, unless top management is committed to quality improvement? Difficult one way, impossible the next? There is an answer, and it has two parts:

- **Set up a 'pilot' quality improvement programme in one department or division.** In other words, the head of the department or a division must throw a protective umbrella over the project, as far as possible, and all that we have said about commitment, participation of staff, quality measurement and feedback techniques, applies as before.
- **Form an alliance with another department(s) and proceed on that basis.** Again, this is not a company-wide proposal, but the power base is now shared between two or more organizational units. This has the advantage of providing multiple perspectives, sources for cooperation and collaboration, and protection against becoming isolated within the company through the pursuit of 'counter-cultural' activities.

Doing things differently is, as any manager knows, unlikely to be applauded unless the project succeeds, and even then there is room for doubt. So our recommendation to every CEO is always to back the 'revolution' with his or her active involvement. Otherwise, keep the aims of the programme within bounds as a 'pilot'. It is more effective to work within the resilience of the existing culture in order to mount a pilot quality improvement programme than to 'hit the wall' head on. Marketing 'intrapreneurs' can stretch the cultural 'elastic' only so far, unless their efforts are legitimized by higher level authority. It is not easy to challenge and overturn the system of beliefs and assumptions operating within a company because they are part of an internally supportive and consistent web of belief.[7]

Major company-wide changes are more likely to be successful in the context of a company crisis, whether real or imaginary. When marketing

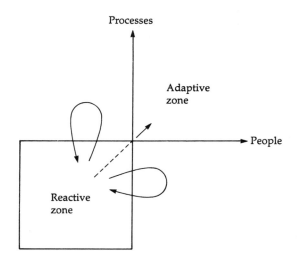

- If steps are taken to improve work processes but the old habits are still reinforced, then organizational innovation is stifled

- If people are encouraged to open up communications but key issues stay 'undiscussable', then organizational learning is stifled

- Each transformational driver involves the other ... from work practices to labour relations ... each contains the evidence of the other•

Figure 5.3 *Organizational transitions*

can take the lead in quality improvement or support the initiative of others, their customer orientation and strategic vision will give meaning and purpose to organizational activity which may otherwise be seen to be 'outside the square', that is, outside the realm of conventional thinking. An 'outbreak of excellence' in one department, or in a group of collaborating departments, may be constrained by cultural limits but at the same time it still sends powerful signals through the organization about new ways and means of achieving better results.

Relationship marketing emphasizes the involvement of the marketing department with its **internal market** of customers and suppliers, because, in the end, quality improvement is a collaborative internal activity, even if the effects are experienced externally.[8] What is most difficult to keep in mind is that the transition to quality leadership needs both social skills and technical skills. This is of course another way of saying **people** and **processes**.

Resistance points in the change process

Quality leadership involves a radical shift (over time) in the way people work with each other, and the responsibility they take for that work. Whereas the technical skills can be taught (indeed imposed), the social skills have to be experienced (felt). Organizational transformations are achieved only when activity along both axes moves together (see Figure 5.3). Getting the equilibrium right is a matter of judgement. In fact, it would be more accurate to use the phrase 'dynamic tension' instead of 'equilibrium'. This more closely suggests the psychological, social and political currents involved, not to mention plain old habits. If steps are taken to improve work processes, but the old habits are still reinforced, then organizational innovation is stifled. If people are encouraged to open up communications, but key issues stay 'undiscussable', then organizational learning is stifled. Each transformational process needs the other because each gives evidence of validity of the other.

We can put this another way. When task-building activities move ahead of relationship-building activities, it creates disequilibrium. The change process is halted, or pushed into reverse. The idea is to 'pull' people through, not 'push'. In other words, the motive force belongs to the people involved. When the process moves to 'push mode', by mistake or by coercion, resistance can be expected.

There will always be resistance points in the change process, because inevitably there is confusion about ends and means. The way **forward** is to revisit the last transition point on the quality curve and clear the pathway between this rear point and the forward advance point. Not everybody travels the road to quality at the same pace.

We have conceptualized four phases of organizational commitment to quality (see Figure 5.4). The process starts with those people who are already committed and therefore most active. They derive their legitimacy and support from the senior executive in charge of the quality improvement process. As discussed earlier, if this person is not the CEO, then the ambitions and scale of the change process should be kept within the elasticity of the corporate culture, at least for the pilot programme.

It is important that this **vanguard** group be identified early as change agents for the process as a whole. After all, change is political and those people most committed to the process are going to need support, and training in persuasion and influence. Not surprisingly, the target for their persuasions and influence **includes** the management group!

The job of the vanguard is to create a **ferment**, by which we mean to stimulate the involvement of those people who intuitively understand the quality message and who have the influence to help bring it about. These are 'opinion leaders' certainly, but they may at first be quite different people to those normally associated with leading opinion. Moving around the circle clockwise, **followers** of course follow, and **stabilizers** provide very necessary analytical skills by which means quality improvements are routinized and institutionalized. There is no fixed point at which one could say that 'critical mass' is achieved and that

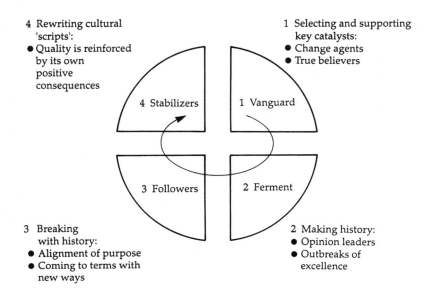

4 Rewriting cultural
  'scripts':
● Quality is reinforced
  by its own
  positive
  consequences

1 Selecting and supporting
  key catalysts:
● Change agents
● True believers

4 Stabilizers   1 Vanguard

3 Followers   2 Ferment

3 Breaking
  with history:
● Alignment of purpose
● Coming to terms with
  new ways

2 Making history:
● Opinion leaders
● Outbreaks of
  excellence

Figure 5.4 *Four phases of organizational commitment to quality*

the organization has changed. This is partly because there is no end to the continuous improvement towards quality, so there is no particular end to change. However, the idea of 'critical mass' intuitively fits stages 2–3 on the quality curve.

While it is important to 'get everybody involved', this takes time. As a result, those people (usually volunteers at first) who are most likely to create a ferment, should be allowed front running. Such people usually find their way into problem solving groups or quality improvement teams as facilitators. The job of facilitator is to provide resources to their group and keep 'political' blockages out of communications. Blockages usually belong to the process of change rather than to the individual actors. This is not always true, but it is the only way progress can be made. For example if there is a political blockage in department X, finding a person to blame will not help. Finding a process solution will.

Quality networks as structural installations

The key to managing change is to create quality networks as structural supports or 'safety nets' which allow staff to move from what they know (based on past experience) to what is unknowable (the future which is always imminent). The job of leader is to carry people from one temporal state to the next.

We recommend that small groups work on quality improvement and that the role of leader shift between members of a group, according to the talents of the group, and the task or maintenance needs of the group from time to time. Leadership, or the lack of it, is usually recognized by the 'followers' before the 'leader' catches on. According to Bennis, the 'training' issue is not how to train leaders, but how to create an environment in which people can grow into leaders quickly and with as much mature insight as possible.[9]

When small groups are established for problem solving or quality improvement, they are usually structured within informal networks that cross hierarchical lines. Where there are group facilitators, their role is normally connected to the strategic process, involving all groups, rather than to the task content of particular groups. In effect, the **network structure** is legitimized by top management.

These quality networks are sometimes called quality circles (if all the members are volunteers), quality improvement teams (where membership may be voluntary or invited), diagnostic review groups, quality leadership groups or the familiar task force (where members are appointed). With the possible exception of the last mentioned group, all the groups exist within the formal organizational structure and yet are not bounded by it.

As these groups operate **cross-functionally**, they have no direct hierarchical reporting lines. As informal networks, they have **informal** reporting lines, through to a quality coordinator, quality manager, customer service executive, 'year 2001' project coordinator, or whatever. Existing outside the organizational system and yet within it, they have freedom to act in generating idea and knowledge, but no special freedoms within the organizational structure in terms of decision-making authority. It is this pluralistic relationship, outside and within the organization, that gives scope to internal marketing and flexibility to quality management processes, hence their effectiveness in challenging the way things get done. In practice, the effect of this is not so much to 'change the culture' but to empower pre-existing **subcultures** within the organization. Freeing up these channels is useful in itself.

Work processes can be reorganized in any number of ways, but one way or another, the job of quality networks is to **turn the wheel of quality improvement**, around and around, breaking new ground with each turn (see Figure 5.5). Here we are talking about ways and means of looking inside the 'quality gap', and diagnostically reviewing the problems and opportunities revealed there.

The **diagnostic review** phase describes the process of making observations about the capability of a work process on the evidence available, and relating this to possible causes of failure, or opportunities for improvement, which can then be dealt with. Using **cross-functional** or **non-hierarchical** work groups as part of the diagnostic review phase leads to better solutions and quicker actions, which in turn improve customer support. Technical solutions need to take account of the existing social relations between people working on the current job. There is no one best way.

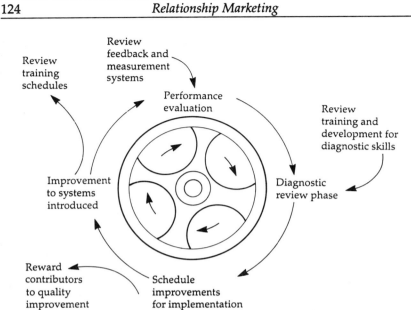

Figure 5.5 *Turning the wheel of improvement – continuously*

The role of facilitators

The role of facilitators in the quality network is to work with each small group (usually four to eight staff members) and create a learning climate to enhance the exchange of ideas, recognize the value of individual skills, and the way members take in information from each other and make decisions on it. There are two modes of facilitating small groups. The first is usually called 'task orientation' and the second is called 'process orientation'.[10]

Task orientation is something we are all familiar with. The 'task' may be a general direction for exploratory work or a detailed definition of a goal to be achieved. If the goal is ambiguous, a time deadline is usually set. If the goal is very precise and the task is complex, then the deadline might be more open-ended. Beyond this, there will be freedom for groups to approach the task in any number of ways.

Process orientation on the other hand, is not something that we know well from our family learning experience or schooling. The 'process' is about how things are done and the way people work for their achievement. Through experience and training, a facilitator can 'surface' any perceptions among the group which are contradictory or incongruent for any reason, providing these issues relate to the performance of the work group. This is not some kind of psychological investigation but a way of keeping work groups open to their expressed purpose. When 'undiscussable' issues can be talked about, energy is released. This saves time and a certain amount of anxiety.[11]

To be a facilitator, means to be able to shift your gaze between 'task' and 'process'. As Weisbord says, 'When work stalls, determine what is not being talked about – the gap between word and deed, the all too human shortfall between aspiration and action. You must shift your attention the way a pilot scans the instruments – from compass to altimeter to airspeed indicator – to keep task and process synchronized.'[12]

When facilitators concentrate on the task goals to the exclusion of the process issues, the group inevitably runs into 'the wall', a condition analogous to the biological seize-up that long-distance runners reach when all systems are challenged at once. 'The wall' in this case is a resistance point where the 'shock of the new' creates a retreat to past certainties, even when breakthrough is imminent.[13]

Communications

The traditional response to resistance is to 'get the communications right', make the message clear up and down the organization, 'sell it to the troops', and leave no doubt about what is intended. We agree. However, the problem remains that people have their own way of perceiving, their own way of understanding and putting value on messages. We all have a preference for listening, learning and problem solving in ways which have been framed for us by language, family, life experience and culture.[14]

Many people are intuitively uncomfortable with the idea that there are multiple 'realities' which underpin effective communications. Of course it is not the 'reality' that counts, but the perception of it. Marketing people have a head start here in understanding what will or will not work. They should not be bulldozed into thinking a 'strong memo' will change hearts and minds. It won't. Authentic discussion could, however, be pushed underground, and who would know?

Company-wide, we need to **design** our way out of quality problems. We are not naturally good at this because we have not in business life developed the constructive and creative habits of thinking that are required for design. This is why quality networks work well to enable the pooling of ideas and problem solving approaches. With a few minds at work, the sum total of inputs start to organize itself into an outcome. In a sense, the solution becomes 'obvious'. This is not our 'natural' way of thinking things through because our traditional Aristotelian logic is based on judgement and analysis. In practice, this means that we develop fixed concepts rather too easily. Sometimes these concepts become 'truths' with a life of their own, in disregard of changing contexts and changing historical circumstances.

Making history – breaking with history

All work is process, a series of linked activities in the value chain. In Chapter 3 we saw how as 'prisoners' of the process we stay inside the familiar patterns rather than 'act-on' them to change them. How can we possibly 'break out' of such routinized culture-bound systems?

What is needed is a framework for reviewing work processes, a cycle of continuous improvement. There are a number of alternative approaches. The case studies in Part Two of this book provide examples. They all involve 'turning the wheel' of continuous improvement. This means continuously reassessing the historic role of managers in the planning, organizing and controlling of work. It also means diffusing responsibility for **knowledge generation** so that staff at all levels can contribute to the process of continuous improvement by knowledge sharing. The decision authority of managers rests on **knowledge application** and need not be affected. In this way, there is more knowledge for managers to work with and a better informed workforce.[15]

This is a short transformational step to make, but one that is pivotal. It is a strategic step because it has a profound effect on internal communications and managerial styles, and challenges the corporate culture. Those in the vanguard of change will experience the enervating sense of making history, and in so doing, breaking with history.

There is more to it than this of course. Each company must establish coherence of strategy, structure, people and processes, in their own time, and place. We commend the case studies in Part Two to you.

Seven quality traps

In managing change, most of what needs to be done is invisible from the outside, hidden from sight. The part that is clearly visible can be wrongly interpreted as the whole of the action. This is what we mean by a 'quality trap'. Here are seven common quality traps.

Trap one

'We will cascade our commitment down to the troops. That should do it'

Internal marketing messages are going to be rejected by many staff unless the communications have a coherent logic which fits the evidence of their past experience. Just as with advertising, internal marketing communications work best when they are designed to 'preach to the converted.' Message making is a difficult job when it attempts to get people to change their minds. Messages work best when they reinforce how people already feel and think.

People do not so much resist change, they resist **being** changed, especially when the implications of the change are beyond their grasp. When internal marketing communications attempt to change people's minds, these messages can work as signals of strategic intent. People are often willing to suspend 'disbelief' while they wait for some demonstrable action which confirms the truth of the message. Their attitude is 'you've told me, now show me . . .' This is particularly so at middle-management level. They need to know that 'commitment' has substance before they can effectively cascade the message down. Middle management will be asking themselves what effect the change programme will have on their own roles and responsibilities. Unless commitment is **demonstrated** from the top, middle management may well go through the motions and then make sure that nothing happens.

As a safe planning dictum, expect staff (sometimes a majority of staff) to hear 'mixed messages' in all major communication from the top. In other words, 'they are saying this, but . . .'

Organizational defensive routines can cause a serious block in communications because they are effectively 'undiscussable'.[16] The quality trap really opens up if the CEO fails to realize the potentially ambiguous effects that apparently direct and clear communications can have in terms of established decision making processes and the alignment of organizational power. Communication without action as supporting evidence (both real and symbolic) is empty rhetoric.

Trap two
'We must invest in more training'

The most common mistake is to jump directly into intensive training. In marketing terms the questions that should be asked (and often are not) are:

- Who is my target audience?
- What are their expectations?
- What knowledge do they need now?
- What skills do they need now?
- How can we monitor the learning process?

The investment in training is wasted if too much training is provided for too many people too soon. These issues concern **scale**. On the other hand, training in skills is necessary so that **individuals** can adjust to changing work contexts. This kind of learning has been called 'single loop learning', especially where the intention is that organizational performance remains stable within organizational norms. The strategic issue, however, concerns **scope**. The pathway to continuous quality improvement challenges the patterns of operations and the very organizational norms which have previously defined effective performance. This second kind of learning is called 'double loop learning'.[17]

If this must be called 'training', then what is needed is a new process in training for line managers and specialists which allows them access across functional borders for information, and works to integrate solutions to problems which transcend the usual departmental blocks. The ability to codify what is learned over time and retain the knowledge through the organization is what is needed. This is a cyclical process, and one special representation of it is the 'quality wheel' presented on page 124. Another is the service quality management feedback and measurement systems presented on page 146. If the organization cannot teach itself to learn, which is the intention of 'double loop learning', then investment in training is a never-ending story. A cost-effective business proposal would be to invest in learning how people learn, then develop the training.

Trap three
'We intend to build a strong culture as a priority'

Just as the culture of a nation is shaped and sustained by deeply held values and beliefs, so too in the world in business. Changing the 'culture' of a particular company is a task of great subtlety. It is possible for example to change surface appearances without changing the culture at all, by changing the marketing artefacts such as logo, signage, mission statements, 'corporate wardrobe', and the design of the stationery. Giving a company a superficial change of identity, in itself, will have no significant or lasting cultural impact.

Yet corporate cultures do change. It is a question of intention and action. It starts with a vision of what the company might be, discussed earlier in this chapter as **strategic intent**. Having said that, you cannot take direct action to change cultures. Soft goals need hard plans. What is necessary is a series of coherent actions which confirm the strategic intention. It comes down to doing things in new ways, communicating the effects, and using some events symbolically to shine light on the meaning of those new ways.

The leaders of organizations have a major impact on corporate culture because they alter the way companies initiate and respond to opportunities and threats. Just as brand values must be congruent with brand image, so must corporate values be congruent with corporate aspirations. What kind of culture is desirable? One that suits the purpose, competencies, and market opportunities of the company. There is a lot of nonsense written about corporate culture and we certainly do not want to suggest that there are prescriptive rules for engineering its change. We recommend Schein as a guide through the maze.[18]

Trap four

'We want to get everybody involved'

Getting everybody involved sounds fine. It is a question of time-scale. Many companies give the impression of wanting to get it over and done with. People in organizations are so focused on the daily problems to be sorted out and on the downside risk of not doing so, they end up shutting out messages which signal opportunities and possibilities all around them. There is often virtue in starting small. In that way commitment can be built, confirmed by action programmes and the results broadcast across the organization. This provides a signal to others that the commitment has integrity. More and more people become involved in each recurring cycle of activity. The movement through the involvement phases of **vanguard, ferment, followers and stabilizers**, was described on page 122.

It is an exercise in futility to attempt to get people actively involved, if they cannot be supported within a quality network of committed people and by training resources. Our view is that involvement should be **task** focused but **process** lead. By that we mean people volunteer or are selected to work on the 'vital few' work processes which will create maximum impact.[19] Certainly, detailed planning must precede any communications to staff. It is here that **internal marketing** can function as a facilitating arm of quality management.[20]

Trap five

'We will introduce quality circles and see what happens'

A quality circle is a volunteer group of work-force members who have undergone training for the purpose of solving work-related problems.[21] The circle concept evolved in Japan in the early 1960s as a support for the quality management techniques which had been introduced there by Deming and Juran in 1950 and 1954 respectively. Historically, circles are an adjunct to a more broadly based quality management approach. Quality circles differ from other participative groups such as quality improvement teams or diagnostic review groups in that they are always volunteer-based and usually select their own problems for diagnosis. It would be fair to say that their great advantage is in dealing with the assignable (special) causes of variation which were discussed in Chapter 4. Because the participants are always close to the problem area, they are able to contribute valuable solutions to the 10,000 little issues that in aggregate make a difference. Because the main focus of such groups is assignable/special causes, they are able to effectively 'drain the swamp' so that the real characteristics of a process are revealed for statistical control, or monitoring in other ways.

So far so good. Difficulties arise when circles unsupported by management and they do not have access to valid customer data which guide the choice of problems for diagnosis. A closely related problem is that if quality circle networks are not connected to the organization's heirarchy through a quality planning group or steering committee, they tend to 'float off' the organizational chart.

There are probably good reasons for introducing quality circles in some companies as a pilot venture towards a more broad-based quality improvement process. Without a champion, however, they will surely die. When quality circles demonstrate a better way of managing, and lead to a more substantial quality commitment, they serve as a catalyst. However, it is unwise to launch a quality circle programme to 'see what happens'. It will only make the launch of a full-scale initiative at some future time more difficult.

Trap six

'We can't improve service unless we set standards'

Only the customer can 'set' service standards. Therefore, how the customers' standards are signalled and interpreted by the company is the central issue. It is no good setting operational standards which have no meaning to the customer. This is illustrated in the ANZ Bank Case Study (see Part Two). It is characteristic of an authoritarian approach to quality improvement to move quickly to standard setting as a prerequisite for improving service. There are better ways. The first step is to identify which work processes are connected with the 'vital few' customer service characteristics that are of critical concern to the customer.

One technique sometimes used is quality function deployment (see p. 78).

What are also needed are clear process definitions, usually achieved by flow charting (p. 137). What is usually revealed at this point is that critical processes have no clear ownership patterns. In other words, nobody is in charge! Who **owns** the process? This is next to be resolved (see Figure 5.6). This might involve negotiation with key departments, perhaps using a departmental purpose analysis technique (see p. 80). Linking the 'vital few' critical service issues to key processes is a matter of judgement and wisdom.

Through a process of linking and matching, a **target value** might be generated after careful consideration as representing the ideal state of a particular process characteristic. This is the **standard** at which to aim, but it is by no means the standard by which performance of the process in its current state can be measured. Of course, intermediate goals can be set as 'standards' and these relate to periods of time and certain operating conditions.[22]

The setting of service standards is not a prerequisite for diagnosis of

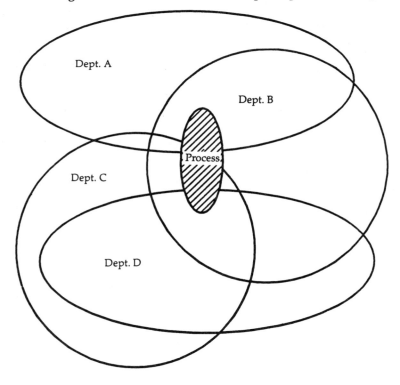

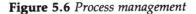

Who owns the process? Who recognizes
the quality improvement opportunity?

Figure 5.6 *Process management*

assignable causes of variation or random effects operating in the process (see Chapter 3, page 82). The quality goal is really the elimination of variation against a target value. Setting standards for 'front-line' service quality and managing against those standards can work in service industries where there is very little process back-up for front-line service staff. When, however, people are part of the process, the **total process** is the service experienced by the customer.

Some people say that it is what gets measured, gets done. This is a useful structural approach but it is the quality of the measurement systems on which attention should be focused. Otherwise, standards can distort the true direction of enquiry. What is wanted is not so much feedback about performance against standards, but **feed forward** which effectively channels a sense of commitment and teamwork to quality improvement.

Trap seven

'Our bottom line tells us when we are succeeding'

There is no one solitary way of measuring the score and what is useful is a range of external and internal feedback mechanisms which enable a 'fix' on quality. One example of a suite of quality management feedback mechanisms for retail banking can be found in Chapter 6 (page 146). Another more generic list of strategic audits and surveys, which broadly fits the 'six markets' model in Chapter 1, is shown here (see Figure 5.7).

Quality improvement can actually **reduce** the cost of quality. It is a question of eliminating waste in resources and time without reducing value to the customer (see Figure 5.8).

Primary focus	Secondary focus	
1 Strategic intent	1.1	Mission statement
	1.2	Philosophy statement
2 Strategic audits and surveys	2.1	Staff markets (internal climate monitor)
	2.2	Customer markets analysis (critical service issues)
	2.3	Potential markets analysis (non-users)
	2.4	Competitors (benchmarking)
	2.5	Non-competitors (benchmarking)
	2.6	Suppliers (co-partnership opportunities)
	2.7	New product markets (product development)
3 Strategy formulation/ realignment	3.1	Strategic direction
	3.2	Market selection
	3.3	Revisit mission statement in 1.1
	3.4	Revisit philosophy statement in 1.2

Figure 5.7 *The strategic scanning process for quality leadership*

Time is a powerful dimension of success in quality improvement. This has been the Japanese experience. The strategic imperative is not to set up projects at great speed, rather it is to set the sights on the quality leadership goal, take small steps, check the outcomes and effects as you go then take more decisive action according to the evidence from internal and external sources of feedback. Turning the quality wheel in this way is slow at first but produces results, which have all the appearance of 'fast and flexible' action, when viewed from your competitor's watch tower.

The final score is of course traditionally profits or surplus, expressed in numbers and set in an historical cost accounting framework. This is an important convention, but it is still only one dimension.[23]

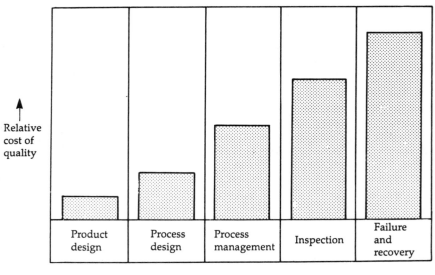

Production stage ⟶

Figure 5.8 *How to reduce quality costs*

References

1 *Marketing.* (1989). Australia, p. 10.
2 Ohmae K. (1988). Getting back to strategy. *Harvard Business Review.* Nov-Dec, pp. 149–156.
3 Hamel G. and Prahalad C. K. (1989). Strategic intent. *Harvard Business Review.* May-June. The authors are among the first to look behind the process of strategic planning and ask what is served by the dichotomy between strategy formulation and implementation. They suggest that an **elitist** view of management tends to disenfranchise most of the organization.

4 Hamel G. and Prahalad C. K., *ibid*.
5 For an excellent elaboration of the issues involved, see Walton R. E. (1985). From control to commitment in the workplace. *Harvard Business Review*. March-April.
6 See Quinn J. B. (1989). Strategic change: logical incrementalism. *Sloan Management Review* SMR Classic Reprint, Summer. Logical incrementalism according to Quinn demands conscious process management. It is not uncoordinated activity. It allows the executive to (p. 55) 'bind together the contributions of rational systematic analyses, political and power theories, and organizational behaviour concepts. It helps executives achieve cohesion and identity with new directions'.
7 For a systems-based explanatory model of the cultural web of an organization, see Johnson G. (1988). Rethinking incrementalism. *Strategic Management Journal*. **9**, pp. 75–91.
8 For an interesting analysis of the evolution of service marketing and the applicability of service concepts to the industrial sector, see Gummesson E. (1985). Applying service concepts in the industrial sector – towards a new concept of marketing. In *Service Marketing – Nordic School Perspectives* (Grönroos C. and Gummesson E. eds), Grönoos and Gummesson.
9 Bennis W. (1989). *On Becoming a Leader*. Addison-Wesley.
10 The dichotomy between task and process orientations was first elaborated by the social psychologist, Kurt Lewin, who contributed much of the groundwork to organizational development theories (OD) in the 1940s.
11 The organizational development processes for moving from the old to the new are discussed in Weisbord M. R. (1987). Toward third wave managing and consulting. *Organizational Dynamiccs*. Winter pp. 5–24.
12 Weisbord M. R. *ibid.*, p. 10.
13 See for example, Tannenbaum R., Margulies N., Massarik F. (1985). *Human Systems Development*. Jossey-Bass.
14 Ian Mitroff offers a Jungian based psychosocial model for interpreting the world and making decisions on that evidence. See Mitroff I. L. (1983). *Stakeholders of the Organizational Mind*. London: Jossey-Bass. In similar vein, Myers and Briggs have an empirically grounded survey instrument called the **Myers-Briggs Type Indicator**, copyright, 1957.
15 See also Ballantyne D. F. (1990). Turning the wheel of quality improvement. *International Journal of Bank Marketing*. **8**, 2. The ANZ Bank case-study material which appears in Part Two was first elaborated in this journal.
16 For a discussion on the logic embedded in mixed messages, and how to avoid the pitfalls, see Argyris C. (1986). Reinforcing organizational defensive routines: an unintended human resources activity. *Human Resource Management*. **25**, 4, pp. 541–555.
17 The subject of *organizational learning* is an evolving one. For an

introduction to the topic, see Garratt B. (1987). *The Learning Organization*. Fontana. For 'single loop learning', see Bateson G. (1972). *Steps to an Ecology of Mind*. Ballantine; and for 'double loop learning' see Argyris C. and Schön D. (1978). *Organizational Learning: A Theory of Action Perspective*. Addison Wesley.

18 Schein E. H. (1985). *Organizational Culture and Leadership*. Jossey-Bass.

19 Under the Pareto principle, a 'vital few' of work processes will account for most of the quality defects. This is a phrase coined by Joe Juran, see for example Juran J. M. (1989). *Juran on Leadership for Quality, an Executive Handbook*. The Free Press, p. 150.

20 Ways and means of overcoming barriers to create involvement is discussed in Pace L. and McMullen T. B. (1988). What is true involvement? *Journal for Quality and Participation*. **11**, 3, pp. 36–38.

21 Juran J. M. 1989, *op. cit.*, p. 360.

22 For a useful description of standard setting in service industries, see Kacker R. N. (1988). Quality planning for service industries. *Quality Progress*, August, pp. 39–42.

23 For an account of how Japanese management accounting systems have played a major role in integrating new business strategies, see Morgan M. J. and Weerakon S. H. (1989). Japanese management accounting: its contribution to the Japanese economic miracle. *Management Accounting*. June, pp. 40–43.

6. *MANAGING RELATIONSHIP MARKETING*

Quality leadership does not happen by chance, it has to be carefully planned and its implementation formally organized. Much of what we read or hear about service and quality suggests that it 'all comes from people'. However, there is more to service than motivated employees – they have to be given the tools and the procedures to carry out the service mission.

The challenge of relationship marketing is to bring the three 'circles' of service, quality and marketing much more closely into alignment. At the moment for many organizations there is little linkage or integrated management of the three crucial elements. In a way it is like spotlights on a stage: each of the three areas may well be given attention but on a separate and individual basis. Thus three spotlights fall on the stage as in Figure 6.1. Relationship marketing brings all three into a much closer concurrence as in Figure 6.2 where all three spotlights focus on the same place as nearly as possible.

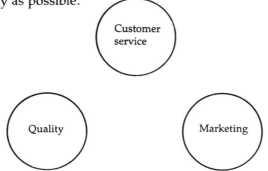

Figure 6.1 *Relationship marketing – unaligned*

Throughout this book we have emphasized the need for the development of formalized and structured processes whereby consistent levels of desired service quality can be achieved. Because of the central role of the delivery system in customer service management it makes sense to begin this chapter with a discussion of the way that such systems can be designed and managed.

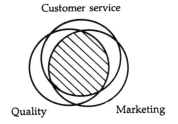

Figure 6.2 *Relationship marketing – central focus*

The service delivery system

When we talk about service delivery systems we are essentially concerned with the **logistics of service**. Conventionally, logistics has usually been associated with the movement of **physical** materials and products, yet in reality it is equally valid as an approach to the management of service systems.

In structuring a logistics system for service delivery the objective is to achieve a cost-effective yet consistent output. That output being a defined service level. It is only by looking in detail at each stage in the process whereby inputs are converted into service output, and particularly at the interfaces between those stages, that the most cost-effective delivery systems can be designed. The problem with so many delivery systems is that they are not really managed as **systems**. Rather they are a fragmented and uncoordinated series of activities; often with each activity being separately managed and controlled with little attempt at integration.

In those organizations where service delivery systems are haphazard and poorly managed then typically service failures will be high. One reason for this loss of quality is that no one person in the chain is responsible for overall performance, indeed managers are rarely aware of cause and effect. A further source of quality failure is that in loosely coordinated systems, inconsistency of output tends to be high. For example, if a service delivery system has ten stages and if a failure or mistake occurs at each stage on one in a hundred occasions, then 11 per cent of the final output will be affected (i.e. $1 - (1-0.01)^{10}$). Thus we may find that errors in the order-entry stage, which may by themselves appear insignificant, can quickly be compounded by errors in the warehouse or in the accounts department or wherever. A major challenge for service management therefore is to overcome the fragmented nature of most service delivery systems to ensure a consistent quality output.

It is probably no coincidence that the companies most frequently cited as service leaders – organizations like McDonalds, Disney, IBM – are also those that pay careful attention to the design and management of the delivery system and who have installed integrated processes and procedures to ensure consistent outputs.

How might an organization go about designing cost-effective, high-quality delivery systems?

Flow charting the service delivery system

In the same way that manufacturing systems can be analysed and modelled to improve operating performance, so too can the service delivery system.

A basic starting point in the process is what has come to be known as the service 'blue-print'. Essentially this is a flow chart or systems analysis of the entire process for the delivery of each aspect of the service package. Shostack[1] describes the procedures involved in blueprinting:

- The first step in blueprinting is to diagram all the components of a service so that the service can be clearly and objectively seen.
- The next important task in blueprinting is the identification of fail points – that is, the areas most likely to cause execution or consistency problems.
- Setting execution standards is the third critical part of the blueprint. These represent the main quality targets for the service. Execution standards not only define the costs of a service, they also define the performance criteria and tolerances for the completion of each service step.
- Finally, the manager must identify all of the evidence of the service that is available to the customer. Each item that is visible to the customer represents an encounter point, during which interaction with the service will occur.

What Shostack describes as the 'encounter point' has also been termed 'moments of truth' by Carlzon[2] the President of Scandinavian Airlines. These moments of truth are the critical events or 'risk points' in the service delivery system where the customer comes 'face to face' with the service process.

The identification and management of the moments of truth is vital if quality service is to be achieved with the highest possible consistency. Each moment of truth is an opportunity for the service provider to demonstrate the quality of service or, alternatively, to fail and hence to reduce the customer's perception of quality. British Airways is one service provider that has consciously adopted this approach in redesigning its products. When 'Club World' – its Business Class – was relaunched, British Airways sought to **increase** the moments of truth. The idea being that, given their confidence in the quality of their service, this would enhance the overall perception of service quality in the eyes of the customer. For example, previously meals had been served on one large tray, now each course is served separately and hence the moments of truth have increased.

The challenge to the designer of service delivery systems is to seek to create a linked system of carefully managed and controlled moments of truth where nothing is left to chance but everything is planned. This may sound a little mechanistic but quality, as in manufacturing, has to be

designed into the process and thus the process itself must be controlled. In fact, providing the proper level of structured support through carefully designed and managed procedures actually helps the personnel involved in the moments of truth to perform their job better. Hence they will feel better about their own performance and a self-reinforcing cycle of quality improvement will most likely be achieved.

The aim of flow charting is to break the flow of activities within a defined process down into logical steps and sequences. The flow chart itself is a diagram which shows a series of events that occur from beginning to end, keeping in mind of course that the end of one process (output) is the beginning of another (input). The flow chart is made up of symbols that help identify what type of action occurs at each step of the process. Inevitably **variability** is built into the process due to the effects of human judgement, random unpredictability or assignable causes.

Building up a flow chart requires a basic tool kit, which is nothing more than a set of symbols for describing key steps in any work process (see Figure 6.3). The flow chart is really a picture of the steps in the interaction

Activity	Description
☐	*Inspection* A checking function
○	*Operation* Indicates the main steps in a process. It involves the addition of information to a paper or a handling operation, such as stapling, folding, sorting, collating, assembling, filing and so on
D	*Delay* This symbol means that there is a time delay in the process
◨	*Combined activity* When two activities are performed at the same time, or at the same work station
⇒	*Travel* Travelling occurs when something is moved from one place to another
▽	*Storage /filing* This symbol is used when a form or document is filed or stored for a period of time

A flow chart is a diagram which shows a series of events that occur in a process from beginning to end, made up of symbols that help to identify what type of action occurs at each step in the process. The table defines each symbol used to draw a flow chart.

Figure 6.3 *What is a flow chart?*

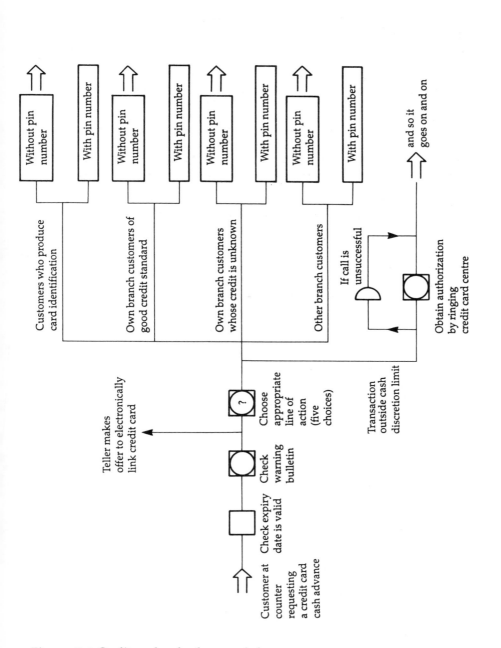

Figure 6.4 *Credit card cash advance – before*

between people, materials, equipment, information, methods and environment, within a particular process of linked processes. The mapping out of the steps brings to light any inefficiencies (time or resources) in any process linkages. The places where the steps can be simplified (with saving of customer's time and the firm's time and resources) often become 'obvious' once they are committed to paper in this way.

An example (see Figures 6.4 and 6.5) shows the 'before' and 'after' flow charting of a process for credit card cash advance at a retail bank. In the 'before' example, bank tellers were required to choose one of five procedures according to the type of card and the policy discretion for certain cash amounts allowed to the particular teller. Cash advances outside the teller's discretion had to be authorized by the credit card centre via a phone call. Flow charting this process showed up right away just how complex the process was and why tellers had great difficulty in 'carrying out laid down procedures'. The procedures were inherently mistake-prone. What was even more important was that the authorization call to the credit card centre incurred a fee for service charged back to the bank, that is, not a transfer cost but a real cost. Furthermore, delays for authorization were common which increased the call time and the ability of the teller to deal with the transaction efficiently. While the teller waited for authorization, customer service was delayed as new customers entered the bank and were forced to wait their turn.

The solution proved to be quite simple once the problem was signalled to the bank's data processing department. A relatively simple programme rewrite would enable the tellers' electronic terminals to be connected on-line to the credit card customer database. Effective 'authorization' could then be obtained at the teller's workstation without costly phone calls and without all the delays. Approval to make the changes was obtained quickly because the flow chart highlighted the problem and the solution opportunities with more impact than a departmental report. The bank saved almost one million pounds in call costs in the first year, plus time saved by tellers and flow-on efficiencies. Some larger branches were even able to reduce the number of telephone hand sets which gave an additional saving on telephone rentals!

The reason these changes had not been designed-in before is simple. From the perspective of data processing alone, the cost of the programme rewrite could not be justified because the benefits were not clear. When the cross-functional work flow was charted, thereby linking the customer value chain to the firm's value chain, the connection for the first time could be made between the waiting time from the customer's point of view, the critical time wasted from the teller's point of view and the hidden costs.

Flow charting can be made more powerful by introducing **time lines** (to show the elapsed time for discrete stages in a process) and to show how the customer is involved in the process, either waiting (dead time), participating (active time), or non-participating (absent time). Research and design teams and manufacturing management have used flow

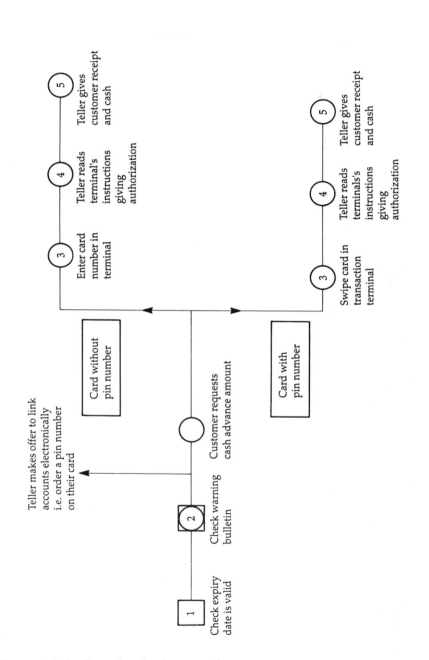

Figure 6.5 *Credit card cash advance – after*

design and control methods for years. What they often lack (and marketing input must provide) is the data on quality gaps and customer's expectations.

Flow charting may not seem very much like a traditional marketing activity, yet these approaches have potential for designing-in value for customers of a kind that exceeds the cost to the firm. Indeed, the cost of quality falls in overall terms as suboptimality is addressed with a programme of total quality improvement. Every work activity is part of a process and every process is a link in the value chain. When we view work as processes we begin to understand how the quality of the output is largely determined by the quality of what is designed in.

Service quality management

The impact that quality improvement programmes have had in manufacturing industry is well documented. However, as we have previously argued the concept of quality goes far beyond the product itself to embrace the entire relationship between the organization and its customers. This is the principle of total quality management (TQM) and indeed from the customers' point of view it is the **only** relevant measure of quality. It has been suggested that nine out of ten quality failures relate not to product quality but to failures **after** the end of the production line. Thus delivery delays, documentation errors, unhelpful sales people and so on actually contribute more to the customers' perception of quality than the inherent functional quality of the product itself.

The interesting thing is that the same concepts and techniques of quality management that work in the factory can also be highly effective in developing improved quality in the service delivery system.

How can a service quality management process be implemented?

The first step is to utilize the customer survey data generated along the lines described in Chapter 4 to identify critical service issues. It is no use seeking generalized improvements or to rely on exhortatory messages from senior management if the organization is serious about service improvements. Once we understand what the issues are we can define measurable improvement targets such as 'to improve the retention rate of customers from 70 per cent to 80 per cent', 'to reduce the time taken to process claims from eight working days to five working days', 'to increase the on-time delivery rate from 95 per cent to 97 per cent' and so on.

Diagnosis of the critical service issues is best achieved by the people involved in the work processes and thus a first step might be to organize a series of task forces which preferably cut across departmental lines and reflect the 'lines of flow' reflected in the service blueprints which should previously have been mapped.

To guide these task forces in their target setting, one excellent and practical device is to look at each step in the delivery system and to identify the internal or external customer that is being served at that point. Every activity in the delivery system must have a purpose to justify its continued existence. Likewise every person must also be able to define who they serve. As Albrecht and Zemke have said: 'If you are not serving the customer, you had better be serving someone who is!'[3]

Once these internal or external customers have been identified they – the customers – should be asked to agree to required service outputs. In other words it is the customers who define the service improvement goals.

A useful diagnostic tool which can be used here to explore improvement opportunities in service delivery systems is the so-called **fishbone**, also called an Ishikawa diagram after its inventor, Dr Ishikawa.

The fishbone is a way of structuring a particular work process by representing all the probable cause and effect relationships in a simple diagram. The 'effect' is really the problem in the process being studied and is represented by the pointed end of the central backbone of the 'fish'. The various fishbones are used as a way of structuring thoughts about the causal elements and each main 'bone' represents a particular category of causal elements. Once people get the hang of the creative use of the fishbone as a diagnostic tool, they are soon looking at the causal elements in greater detail and finding subsidiary factors that need investigation. These are written in as 'tiny bones' connected to main causal elements. The example given in Figure 6.6 shows how a fishbone diagram can be used to diagnose the cause of flight departure delays at an airport.

Once a particular problem is mapped out in this way (and we emphasize again that this is a creative approach), any particular factor that seems promising for whatever reason can be looked into. A second stage in using the fishbone is to shift the emphasis from **problem analysis** to **solution analysis**. This time, the solution opportunity is entered in at the head of the fishbone as the 'effect' being studied and the diagram then becomes a set of categorized factors which potentially contribute to the solution. The fishbone technique is fun to use and marketing managers should find plenty of applications within their sphere. Remember that cause and effect relationships identified on the fishbone are **possible** cause–effect relationships. Only data will point to **actual** causes. There are as many uses for the fishbone in marketing applications as there are on the factory floor. The relationship marketing objective here is to encourage and participate in the use of quality management techniques across the organization. It is through common methods that the organization learns to speak a common language, and cross-functional quality barriers start to fall away.

The service management process can be assisted by creating a high level of visibility for the achievement of results. Making quality happen must be seen as the driving force within the organization and as something that receives acclaim and reward. Internal newsletters, seminars and incentive programmes are all ways in which the enthusiasm for quality can be encouraged within the organization.

One company, previously described, that has been at the forefront of developing service quality improvement programmes is Rank Xerox. One of the pioneering steps they have taken is to link senior executives' pay

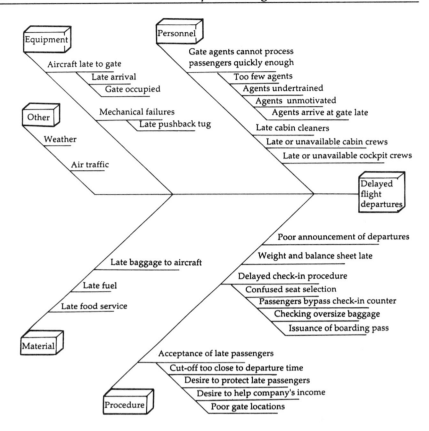

Figure 6.6 *Causes of flight departure delays*

Source: Wyckhoff D. (1984) New tools for achieving service quality. *Cornell Hotel and Restaurant Administration Quarterly*. November, 78–91.

with the achievement of service targets. Every manager at Rank Xerox' head office has, for some years, had their bonus linked to a quantified index of customer satisfaction. This index is compiled by objective, externally generated survey research which measures such things as satisfaction with the technical service received as well as a customer loyalty rating based on the percentage of customers retained at the end of each year.

Service quality control

In both service and manufacturing quality, the aim should be to design quality into the process rather than to 'inspect it into the output'. The challenge for service quality management is that the production and delivery of service often occurs at the same time. There is little opportunity for production inspection **before** delivery.

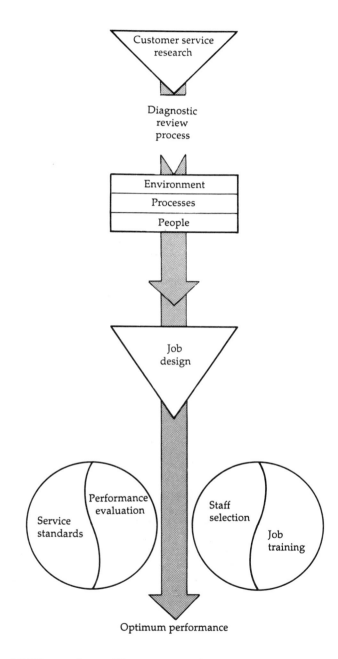

Figure 6.7 *The service quality management process*

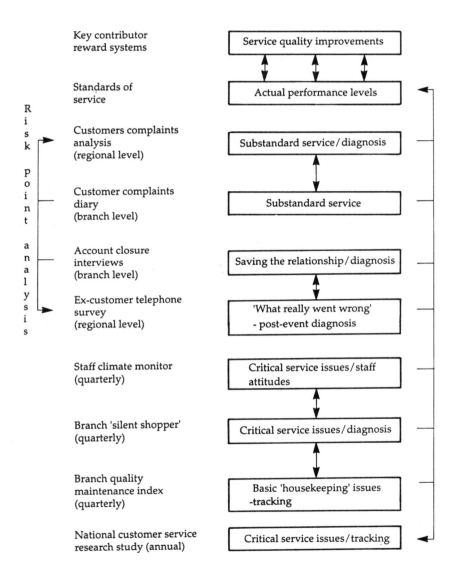

Figure 6.8 *Service quality management feedback and measurement systems*
Source: Ballantyne D. F. (1990). Turning the wheel of quality improvement continuously, *International Journal of Bank Marketing*, **8**, 2

Certainly within the service encounter, for example the interaction of a bank and its customers, the service is produced **and** delivered interactively from the customer's point of view. The focus of quality standard setting therefore shifts to the customer. How the customer's 'standards' are dealt with in the service encounter becomes the central issue.

Behind the 'face' of the service encounter lies the interdependent service support territories of environment, work processes and job design. Setting statistical controls to measure variances in these territories only makes sense providing they are clearly connected to the 'production' of service. In other words the measures needed must be customer focused and not operationally focused.

A step-by-step research approach is necessary; one that is congruent with the paradigm for service quality management that is proposed in Figure 6.7. This step-by-step research approach is highlighted in Figure 6.8 taking the example of a retail bank.

In this model we suggest that the service quality management process moves logically from a benchmark customer service research study to diagnosis of the service issues (from the customer research) and a staff attitude survey (or climate monitor) to setting up a range of 'risk point' feedback systems and, last of all, progressive introduction – and review – of service quality performance measures.

These service quality performance measures have four principal functions as follows.

Benchmark research and diagnosis

No one person or department within an organization can uniquely fix a particular critical service issue. The 'solution' is often a mix of changes that cross departmental boundaries. Service 'problems' are only in some part a situation which can be resolved by action in a single department.

The first task therefore is to structure a review of critical service issues based on customer service research and the use of inter-departmental teams for identifying major (chronic) quality problems and achieving significant improvement (breakthrough). This has the advantage in that the process can involve a review of both departmental and non-departmental related issues by interdepartmental teams.

Staff climate monitor

Measure what service issues are important from the point of view of staff as a monitor on the internal 'climate' and as counterpoint to the external customer service research study. The techniques for conducting an internal customer service survey were described in Chapter 4 and essentially the purpose of the exercise is to audit the service philosophy and motivation, department by department.

'Risk point' feedback systems

Develop and introduce various forms of 'risk point' analysis for monitoring 'risk points' in customer service processes and delivery (e.g. monitor and analyse reasons for account closures and the concerns or complaints received from current customers).

Measure quality performance

Measure outstanding service performance against preset desired levels derived from analysis of information gained from the steps above (i.e. with baselines set for measuring excellent performance rather than minimum performance).

It is possible to 'short-circuit' this four-stage process by setting 'operations' standards for control of service performance **minima** e.g.:

- The number of times the phone rings before it is answered.
- The number of people permitted to be left waiting in a queue at a bank before the next teller is called to serve at the counter.

There are dangers in the 'short circuit' approach. It focuses on symptoms, not service solutions. Obviously no one person can both answer the telephone and serve customers at the counter. Everybody knows that this dilemma sometimes occurs but diagnostically speaking, it signals a job design issue more often than a 'people' problem.

Setting service standards

A crucial element in the service quality control process is the setting of appropriate service standards. These standards should be outward looking and customer based rather than narrow, internal measures of performance. Ideally they would be derived through the use of customer service surveys of the type described in Chapter 4.

Berry[4] and his colleagues have argued that a common failing in organizations is poorly defined and misunderstood service standards. This leads, they claim, to 'service role ambiguity' the causes of which may include:

- No service standards exist.
- Too many service standards exist resulting in a loss of priorities.
- Poorly communicated service standards.
- Service standards unconnected to the performance measurement, appraisal and reward systems.

A useful framework to utilize in constructing the key service standards against which performance can be measured is that provided by La Londe and Zinszer.[5] They suggested that customer service can be decomposed into three component areas:

- The pre-transaction element
- The transaction element
- The post-transaction element

Examples of the types of service dimensions that might be contained under each heading are given in Figure 6.9.

Pre-transaction elements

For example:

- Written customer service policy
  (Is it communicated internally or externally, is it understood, is it specific and quantified where possible?)
- Accessibility
  (Are we easy to contact/do business with? Is there a single point of contact?)
- Organization structure
  (Is there a customer service management structure in place? What level of control do they have over their service process?)
- System flexibility
  (Can we adapt our service delivery systems to meet particular customer needs?)

Transaction elements

For example:

- Order cycle time
  ((What is the elapsed time from order to delivery? What is the reliability/variation?)
- Inventory availability
  (What percentage of demand for each item can be met from stock?)
- Order fill rate
  (What proportion of orders are completely filled within the stated lead-time?)
- Order status information
  (How long does it take us to respond to a query with the required information? Do we inform the customer of problems or do they contact us?)

Post-transaction elements

For example:

- Availability of spares
  (What are the in-stock levels of service parts?)
- Call out time
  (How long does it take for the engineer to arrive and what is the 'first call fix rate'?)
- Product tracing/warranty
  (Can we identify the location of individual products once purchased? Can we maintain/extend the warranty to customers' expected levels?)
- Customer complaints, claims etc.
  (How promptly do we deal with complaints and returns? Do we measure customer satisfaction with our response?)

Figure 6.9 *The components of customer service*

While this simple framework originally was devised to define the customer service process we would argue that it can be extended to encompass the entire relationship marketing concept.

As we have emphasized throughout this book, customer service is multifaceted and so therefore the control systems must also be multi-dimensional. A further requirement is that the target service levels specified on each dimension must be quantified. This begs the question: 'What is the appropriate level of service?' Again our preferred response to this question is to turn to the customers. The research methodology described in Chapter 4 enables the organization to identify the relative importance attached to each service dimension and then to 'benchmark' the level of achievement necessary to be regarded as excellent on all aspects (using both competitors' and non-competitors' performance levels as the baseline).

However, it must be recognized that, while we wish to be perceived as 'excellent' in performance across all the key dimensions of service quality, not all customers justify or indeed require the same levels of service. In the same way that airlines offer different classes of service (i.e. First, Business and Economy) according to need and ability to pay, so too should all organizations that seek profit maximization carefully examine the cost benefit of their service strategy.

Whenever possible the opportunity to develop 'tailor-made' service packages should be exploited, particularly to key accounts, based on 'negotiated' service levels. The idea here is that no two customers are alike, either in terms of their requirements or, specifically, in terms of their profitability to the supplier. One UK-based company in the consumer electronics field identified that while three of their major customers were roughly equivalent in terms of their annual sales value, there were considerable differences in the costs generated by each. For example, one customer required delivery to each of his 300+ retail outlets, while the other took delivery at one central warehouse. Similarly, one company paid within thirty days of receiving the invoice, the others took nearer to forty days to pay. Again, one of the three was found to place twice as many 'emergency' orders as the others. Careful analysis of the true costs showed that the profitability of the three customers differed by over 20 per cent yet each customer received the same value-related discounts and the same level of customer service.[6]

It has long been recognized that the so-called 80/20 rule or 'Pareto's Law' holds when it comes to the profitability of customers. In other words, most companies might expect something like 80 per cent of their total profit to come from only 20 per cent of their customers. Closer analysis of this data also reveals another 80/20 distribution. This time that 80 per cent of the total costs of providing customer service are accounted for by only 20 per cent of the customers and also, more importantly, those 20 per cent are not the same customers that appear in the top 20 per cent by profitability.

Access to this type of information enables management to better target service resources and to focus on areas of maximum opportunity for profit improvement. This is not necessarily to suggest that unprofitable customers should have lower levels of service but rather that means should be found to make them **more** profitable.

Customer order management

One common feature that seems to underlie the approach to business adopted by those companies which are generally noted for their service excellence is their approach to **order management**. Typically these companies recognize orders as the life-blood of the company and hence give the greatest priority to the way in which an order is handled from the moment it arrives until the time it is delivered – and beyond.

In developing an order management system we are in effect seeking to link the ongoing process of generating and receiving orders to the service delivery system.

A number of practical steps for improving customer order management processes are suggested below.

Eliminate the 'non-value-added' activities

In reviewing the existing order processing system each element and each link in the chain should be critically examined to identify the value that it creates and the cost that it adds. 'Value' in this context refers to customer value, meaning a benefit that will contribute to the total utility of the product or offer in the eyes of the customer – and hence their willingness to pay.

In many service processes it will be the case that a large proportion of the time spent will be non-value-added time. For example, delays in paperwork, time that is 'consumed' while a product sits as inventory in a warehouse, time spent on checking and rechecking and so forth. The target should be to eliminate all non-value-added activities.

The order processing system is a fabulous hunting ground to seek out and remove non-value-added activities. So often we find that no one has ever questioned the way in which paperwork is managed, or the sequence in which activities take place or indeed why those activities take place at all! Where possible the goal should be to look for opportunities to combine steps in the processes, to integrate separate groups of people performing adjacent tasks and to simplify processes by reducing paperwork and reports. It should always be remembered that a major part of the time consumed in meeting customer requirements is actually redundant and its elimination will improve the consistency and reliability of the delivered service thus enhancing its 'value' in the eyes of the customer.

Order fulfilment groups

Given that from a systems viewpoint the process of managing orders can be refined along the lines described above, what scope exists for improving the 'people architecture'?

Several companies have experimented with the idea of a cross-functional, cross-departmental team to take responsibility for the management of orders. This team has been termed an **'order fulfilment group'** by Digital, the computer company.

The idea behind such a group is that rather than having an organizational structure for order management where every activity is separated with responsibility for each activity fragmented around the organization, instead these activities should be grouped together both organizationally and physically.

In other words instead of seeing each step in the process as a discrete activity we cluster them together and bring the people involved together

(a) Traditional sequential order prossing system

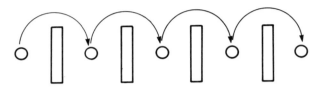

(b) Order management system with 'clustered' activities

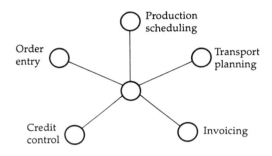

Figure 6.10 *Sequential and clustered approach*

as well – ideally in a single open-plan office. Thus the order fulfilment group might comprise commercial or sales office people, credit control and accounts, production scheduler and transport scheduler – indeed anyone involved in the crucial business processes of **converting an order into cash**.

Figure 6.10 contrasts the traditional approach with the suggested alternative. The effect that such groups can have is often dramatic. Because all the key people in the order fulfilment process are brought together and linked around a common entity – the order – they are better able to sort out problems and eliminate bottlenecks. Order cycle times can be dramatically reduced as team-work prevails over interdepartmental rivalry. New ways of dealing with problems emerge, more non value-added activities are eliminated and customer service problems – when they arise – can quickly be resolved, since all the key people are in close connection with each other.

Schonberger[7] gives a number of examples of how the concept of a manufacturing 'cell' – where linked actions are performed in parallel by multifunctional teams – can work just as effectively in order processing. One of the cases he quotes, Ahlstrom, a Finnish company, has reduced lead-times in order processing from one week to one day, and variation in lead-time has dropped from up to six weeks to one week. Another case was that of Nashua Corporation in North America, where order entry lead-time has been reduced from eight days to one hour, with a 40 per cent reduction in space and a 70 per cent reduction in customer claims.

This approach has been likened to a game of rugby rather than a relay race! What this means is that a team of closely integrated colleagues runs up the field together passing the ball as they run. In the relay race no one can run until they receive the baton from the preceding person in the chain. The end result is that this vital part of the service process can be speeded up while simultaneously improving the quality of the output, hence a major competitive advantage is achieved.

In a manufacturing context the customer order management system must be closely linked to production planning and the materials requirements plan. Ideally all the planning and scheduling activities in the organization relating to the order and its satisfaction should be brought together organizationally. Figure 6.11 illustrates the linkages.

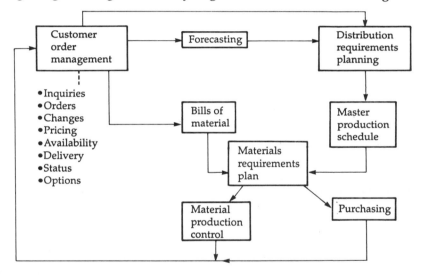

Figure 6.11 *Customer order management*

Customer communications systems

It will be clear from much of what we have described and detailed in this book that a vital part of the process of building enduring customer relationships hinges around communications. Specifically we are referring to the quality of communications between the supplier and its customers.

So many perceived quality failures are exacerbated, or even arise in the first place, because of poor customer communications. It is often the case that customer communications are not managed on a **proactive** basis but rather on a **reactive** basis. What this means is the supplier will tend to respond to stimuli from the customer e.g. queries, orders, complaints, rather than to have a managed customer communications programme. For example, in the managed communications environment, the customer would never have to enquire about the status of an order – the supplier would keep the customer informed on its progress at all stages. Likewise there would be 'no surprises' for the customer e.g. non-availability of stock would be immediately communicated, lead-times would be transparent and overall the customer would know exactly what to expect. Bearing in mind that a crucial part of the service management process is the meeting of customer expectations it will be understood that communications play a major role in the establishment of those expectations in the first place.

There are a variety of ways in which a customer communication system may be established ranging from telephone 'hot lines' to electronic data interchange. In practice it is not so much a single channel of communication but a number, all of which are managed and proactive. Figure 6.12 identifies some of the most effective ways of developing close and continuous communication linkages with the customer base and these are described below:

- *Field visits to customer sites by personnel*

    This can be a very effective means of both communicating with customers and improving internal motivation. The idea is that our

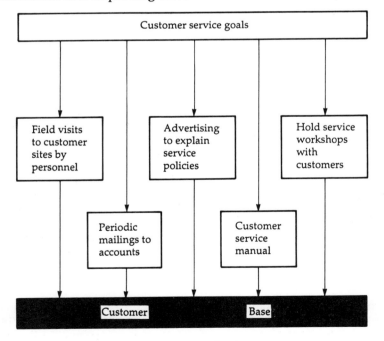

Figure 6.12 *Customer service communication process*

internal people who normally never see customers and often only know them as company names or account numbers, should visit customers from time to time. The effect can be even more powerful when personnel visit their 'opposite numbers'. So for instance people who are responsible for preparing invoices could visit the accounts department of the customer and meet those who have to process the invoice once received. Similarly people from the warehouse responsible for assembling and packing orders could visit those responsible at the customer's premises for receiving goods. As well as good customer relations, there will be frequent occasions where ideas for improvement in specific areas can be sparked off through these meetings.

- *Periodic mailing to customer accounts*

  These can take many forms but perhaps the most effective are customer service newsletters which are informative and report on changes in procedures or improvements in the service field. These need not be produced too often and should always be informative – the last thing the customer needs is still more 'junk mail'. On a more regular basis it can be helpful to the customer to receive fact sheets on products and end markets and an idea well worth considering is a customer service 'update' on availability and delivery which is regularly circulated to customers.

- *Advertising to explain service policies*

  An observable trend is the growing use by service-oriented companies of advertising to emphasize their service offer. Not only does this inform the would-be customer of the service package and establish a level of service expectations but it can also be a powerful marketing tool in its own right.

  Xerox is a company that has fought back against strong Japanese competition by emphasizing quality and service. Its recent advertisements underline this point (see Figure 6.13).

  It is not just potential customers to whom these advertisements should be directed but also **existing** customers. Research has indicated that among the people who read advertisements in the greatest detail are those who have **recently bought the product**. Thus with advertisements for cars, for example, it will be found that the recent purchaser of the model featured in the ad. will be highly likely to read it – primarily to seek reassurance that he or she has made the right decision! Hence the importance of emphasizing the desire for a relationship through service in such communications.

- *Develop a customer service manual*

  We have emphasized several times the importance of managing the customers' expectations of service and one effective contribution to this process can be through the means of a customer service manual.

  A customer service manual might take many forms but essentially it

Figure 6.13 *Using service quality to sell*

is a document given to customers that defines the organization's customer service goals and details the procedures whereby business is transacted between the parties. Hence the manual would begin with quantified service objectives in terms of delivery lead-times, stock availability and so on, it would provide specimen copies of basic documents such as delivery notes, invoices, bills of lading etc. It would list key executives' names and telephone numbers (including home numbers) and provide details of 'hot line' services and order status enquiry systems. In fact every aspect of the formal relationship that is sought between the organization and its customers should be included in the manual.

The result can be a document of tremendous practical value as well as contributing to the customer's perception of the business as a service-oriented company.

- *Hold workshops with customers*

    There are many areas of mutual concern between buyers and suppliers and consequently there will be advantage in bringing teams together from both parties on a regular basis. These meetings are not confrontations but problem-solving workshops which seek to improve the quality of service provided.

    Rather like the customer visits proposed earlier much can be gained by bringing together, say, the commercial and accounts people in the supplying company with those responsible in the buying company for dealing with invoices and supplier originated documentation.

    In companies selling direct to end users e.g. a retailer or a service provider like a bank or airline such meetings might take the form of feedback sessions and customer service 'focus' groups where new opportunities for service enhancement are sought.

These are just a few of the ways in which the organization can develop continuing and open channels of communication with its customers. The key point to emphasize is that these communications must be planned and managed and not just left to chance.

Customer retention management

While it is frequently observed that the purpose of marketing is 'getting and keeping customers', there tends in practice to be more attention focused on the 'getting' and rather less on the 'keeping' and yet it may cost as much as five times more to get a new customer than it does to keep an existing one.

We briefly discussed the role of customer retention in a relationship strategy and it is worth emphasizing again the point that loyal customers who keep coming back are the most profitable type of customer. They tend to spend more and they may even act as our ambassadors through positive word of mouth. Obviously these satisfied customers involve very little sales and marketing expense and thus their true profitability at the

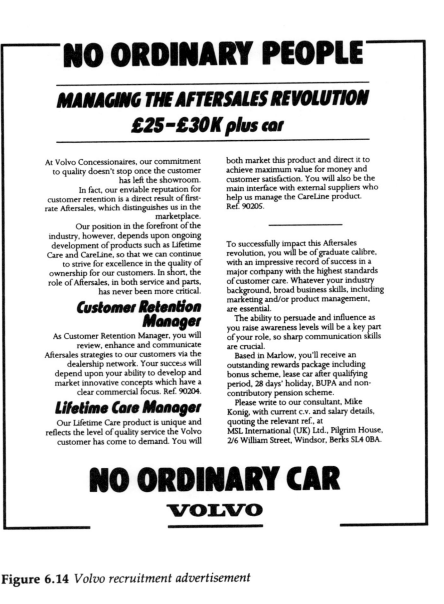

Figure 6.14 *Volvo recruitment advertisement*

margin can be very high. A recent recruitment advertisement in the UK for Volvo (see figure 6.14) indicates that they recognize the importance of customer retention by seeking to appoint someone to the role of 'Customer retention manager'!

The 'lifetime' value of a customer can be immense – although difficult perhaps to calculate. A successful chain of North American fast-food outlets, Domino's Pizzas, estimate that a regular customer is worth more than $5000 over ten years and hence the importance of holding on to them.[8] A question that managers should ask frequently is: 'What proportion of customers that we had a year ago are still with us and by how much has the value of their business in real terms increased?'

The type of chart that those concerned with building relationships in the market place should regularly have in front of them is depicted in Figure 6.15. To produce this data requires a breakdown, on at least a sample basis, of the customer base. Many companies already have access

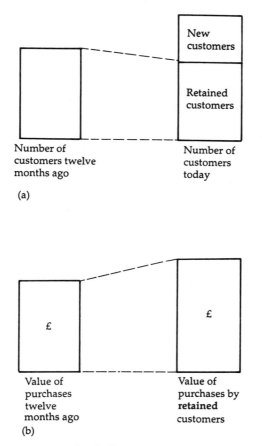

Figure 6.15 *Customer retention indicators*

to some of this information through consumer panels or through repeat purchase studies. Increasingly, organizations are coming to recognize the opportunities for using **database marketing** whereby the profiles of existing customers are analysed to correlate their demographic and other characteristics with their purchase patterns. The purpose of this is to seek to maintain the closest contact with their customers, often through direct marketing (e.g. personalized mail shots) and to build the relationship.

Database marketing has been made possible by developments in information technology which enable the organization to utilize multiple databases containing information on customers and their purchase behaviour in order better to target new customers and – just as importantly – to develop existing ones. It is now possible to integrate multiple customer files and sets of related data to identify the particular purchases and purchasing patterns of individual customers, to segment the customer base by any of a number of criteria, to deliver highly targeted marketing communications and, of course, to monitor the response.

One way to improve the customer retention rate is by seeking to analyse the causes of customer defection and in particular to focus on complaints. Various estimates have been made of the proportion of customers who, having experienced a service failure, proceed to complain. It would appear that the complaints received by any organization represents only the tip of the iceberg. In consumer markets (i.e. selling to the end user) it is thought that only one in twenty of customer complaints are communicated to the vendor and in industrial markets (i.e. business-to-business) it is still only one in five.

However, what we can say is that complaining customers are worth their weight in gold!

The reasoning behind this paradoxical statement is that it is only by listening and hearing that we can recognize failure and take corrective action. Customers should be encouraged to complain and it should be made easy for them to do so. Whether it be by including a reply-paid card for comments with a purchase, or a comments form in a hotel, or even the novel approach used by British Airways at Heathrow Airport where a facility exists for customers to record their comments on video. Whatever the business, companies should welcome the challenging customer and utilize the service failure as an opportunity to improve and even to impress the customer! This latter point is based on the fact that successful recovery from service failure can often have a substantial 'positive feedback' effect on the customer. Thus the airline customer with the missing luggage who is given immediate attention by senior management, and whose bags are personally delivered to the hotel, and who is offered immediate and generous refunds and who receives a letter of apology in every case, will almost certainly leave that particular service encounter more impressed than they were before.

The key to the 'service recovery' is that it should be the result of laid down, systematic procedures which are not left to individual employees' discretion. While employees should be encouraged to **exceed** the level of service specified, responding to customer complaints must never be discretionary.

The formal analysis of complaints in the aggregate can often provide useful data for service improvement programmes. The cost of a dissatisfied customer is huge in almost every case – not only the cost of putting things right but the possible cost of lost sales and the risk of negative word of mouth.

The market-facing organization

Making service happen is the ultimate challenge. While it is by no means easy to develop strategies for service that will lead to improved competitive performance, the hardest task is to put that strategy into action. How do we develop an organization that is capable of delivering high-quality service on a consistent, ongoing basis?

These days, most companies are familiar with the idea of 'mission statements' as an articulation of the vision of the business. As we explained in Chapter 2 the mission statement seeks to define the purpose of the business, its boundaries and its aspirations. It is now by no means uncommon for organizations to have such statements for the business as a whole and for key constituent components. What some companies have found is that there can be significant benefits to defining the **customer service mission** of the firm.

The purpose of the customer service mission statement is to give a clear indication of the basis whereby the business intends to build a position of advantage through closer customer relationships. Such statements are never easy to construct. There is always the danger that they will descend into vague 'motherhood' statements that give everyone a warm feeling but provide no guide-lines for action.

David Norton[9] has put forward a useful model to assist in this process of creating a shared vision which has particular relevance to an organization trying to sharpen its customer service focus. The model is summarized in Figure 6.16.

A key step in this model is the identification of the 'do wells'. In other words what does the organization have to do well to achieve the desired ends? The definition of these 'do wells' is best done by those who are closest to the customer – the front-line people and those who support them. An early step that British Airways took in their dramatic shift towards a service orientation was to empower the people, working through 'customer first teams' (i.e. service quality circles), to identify key areas where improvement was needed and then to implement that change.

These teams ideally should be multifunctional and able to bring a broad perspective to the issues in question. Most importantly they must be given the total support of top management so that they are motivated to bring forward proposals that they know will be actioned.

It is not sufficient to do as some companies have done and appoint a customer service manager and say to him or her: 'Service is now your

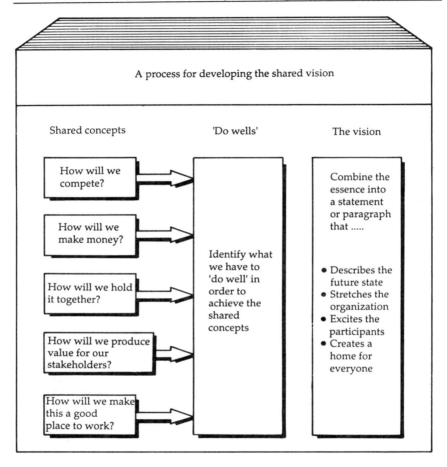

Figure 6.16 *A process for developing the shared vision*
           source Norton, 1988

responsibility – make it happen!' Service as we know is everyone's responsibility and hence the need for this to be reflected in the way we organize. It is questionable whether there should even be 'customer service managers' in any organization.

How do we focus the organization on customers and their service needs?

The basic problem with traditional organizations is that they are functionally focused not market focused. In other words they are compartmentalized around the basic business functions of production, finance, marketing, purchasing and so on. They are typically driven by seeking to optimize the use of **inputs** and hence are budget driven rather than seeking to optimize around **outputs** and thus be market driven.

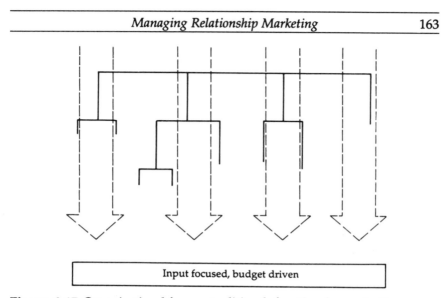

Input focused, budget driven

Figure 6.17 *Organizational focus – traditional, functional organization*

Given that 'shared vision' can be created and communicated – itself no easy task – how can these values be translated into action? In practice what is found is that the organizational structure of the firm will either help or hinder this process. Figures 6.17 and 6.18 contrasts two extreme organizational orientations. In the traditional functional organization responsibility for customer service, if it resides anywhere, will be seen as marketing's responsibility. The other functions will specialize in engineering, manufacturing or whatever and will not see a clear line linking them to the market place.

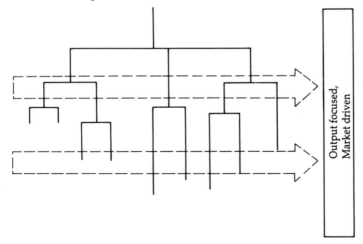

Output focused, Market driven

Figure 6.18 *Organizational focus – market-facing organization*

In the market-facing organization there is a greater attempt to draw key players together in multidisciplinary teams or groups that seek to marshal resources to achieve market-based objectives. The functions still exist but they are now seen as 'pools of resources' from which the market-facing teams draw their members.

It will be apparent that this concept is very close to the idea of a 'matrix' organization. Much has been written about the matrix organization and often it is suggested that authority can be shared between the functions and the missions. Our view is that such 'power sharing' rarely works and that it is only by developing an organization structure that is market facing (i.e. as in Figure 6.18) that a true customer orientation is likely to be achieved.

In considering the implementation of relationship marketing, the McKinsey and Co. 'Seven S' framework provides a powerful device for planning organizational change. The framework consists of seven elements: strategy, structure, systems, staff, style, skills and shared values. The framework and a description of each of these elements is given in Figure 6.19.

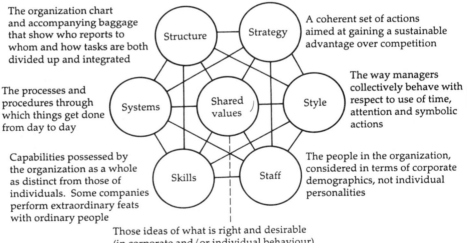

The organization chart and accompanying baggage that show who reports to whom and how tasks are both divided up and integrated

A coherent set of actions aimed at gaining a sustainable advantage over competition

The processes and procedures through which things get done from day to day

The way managers collectively behave with respect to use of time, attention and symbolic actions

Capabilities possessed by the organization as a whole as distinct from those of individuals. Some companies perform extraordinary feats with ordinary people

The people in the organization, considered in terms of corporate demographics, not individual personalities

Those ideas of what is right and desirable (in corporate and/or individual behaviour) which are typical of the organization and common to most of its members

Figure 6.19 *McKinsey & Co. framework*

The traditional view of an organization is that strategy is the starting point in implementing change and that from this strategy the type of organizational structure is implicit. From this organizational structure and strategy the types of systems necessary to carry out the strategy follow. The 'Seven S' model, by contrast, suggests that four additional elements – style, staff, skills and shared values – should be considered.

Strategy
- Integrated plan for development of marketing orientation
- Formalized definitions of markets and mission
- Detailed specification of marketing objectives
- Commitment to implementation

Shared values
- 'We will become a fully customer-driven organization'
- 'Customers come first'
- 'Marketing expenditures are an investment'
- 'Service is paramount'

Style
- Top management support for marketing through symbolic actions and commitment of time to marketing and customer-related activities
- Open communications between all functional groups and marketing staff
- Recognition and reward of customer/market-oriented behaviour

Systems
- Customer intelligence reports
- Competitor intelligence reports
- Marketing planning and control systems
- Remuneration and performance appraisal systems geared to support marketing orientation
- Financial reporting systems reflecting product line contribution and profitability

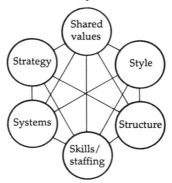

Skills/staffing
- Recruitment of an adequate number of people with requisite marketing skills
- Marketing training programs and facilities
- Knowledge of market
- Analytical skills in segmenting markets and identifying decision making units (DMU's)

Structure
- Simple structure based on markets/geography
- Key account sales structure to service most important customers
- Decentralized marketing staff to provide close and fast support to customers
- Staff rotation of non-marketing staff through customer contact positions

Figure 6.20 *Developing a relationship strategy*

The McKinsey research showed that while the average and poorer performing companies tended to place most emphasis on strategy, structure and systems, the top performing companies placed emphasis on all seven elements in the framework.

In this model the starting point is shared values. These should reflect the positive key aspects of the organization's culture. In a sense the shared values are the 'glue' that holds the organization together. The 'Seven S' model illustrates that organizational effectiveness and successful implementation of organizational change comes about through careful orchestration of the seven elements. McKinsey and Co. use the metaphor of a compass to suggest that each of these elements should be lined up, like compass needles pointing in the same direction, so that they support each other. The 'Seven S' framework, originally developed as a way of thinking broadly about the problem of effective organization is also an excellent tool for judging the achievability of a strategic implementation. Strategy implementation is not only a matter of getting the strategy and structure right, but of considering all the other elements in the 'Seven S' model. If the needles of the compass are aligned the company is purposefully organized to carry out the task; if not, each of the elements need to be looked at to see if it can be altered and realigned to achieve organizational integration. The 'Seven S' framework is an excellent way to check the strategic fit.

Waterman[10] raises a number of questions which need to be addressed in the context of checking strategic fit to achieve implementation. They are:

- Given a proposed strategy, do the other S's in the 'Seven S' framework support that strategy?
- How difficult is it to change each of the other S's?
- Does management have the will and patience to make these changes?

Let us imagine a major new strategic thrust for a company that involves a change from a product orientation to a marketing orientation. What is involved in implementation? Figure 6.20 provides a checklist under the headings of strategy, structure, systems, staff, style, skills and shared values, of the issues that need to be addressed. The example in this case is a generic one rather than one aimed at a specific company. The model can then be used to identify the positive attributes possessed, the negative attributes and the new required skills that need to be developed. A careful consideration of all of these seven S's can help ensure the successful implementation of the programme or the making of a decision that the desired degree of fit between the seven elements cannot be achieved given the culture of the organization. The examination of each of these elements draws our attention to the need to focus on the behavioural aspects of strategic plan implementation as well as the mechanistic ones.

Conclusion

In seeking to explore the possibilities for enhancing market place performance we have emphasized the 'relationship' as the intrinsic and core focus for the organization. This concept of relationship is broader than the traditional marketing orientation which tends to be biased towards a study of 'exchange' or 'transaction' relationships. We believe that true relationship marketing seeks to develop a set of shared internal values within the organization which are themselves of significance and importance to customers. Thus under our definition of relationship marketing, the culture and style of the organization is as important as the products and services that it offers.

We began this book by emphasizing that there were six markets that the firm must satisfy to ensure long-term competitive advantage. These were: customer markets, supplier markets, employee markets, influence markets, referral markets and internal markets. The internal market is the heart of the enterprise. Through motivated and customer-focused people sharing common goals and values we begin to achieve success. We have tried to show how such a process may be initiated and managed and to make Theodore Levitt's[11] words into a reality:

The purpose of a business is to create and *keep* a customer.

References

1   Shostack G. L. (1985). Planning the service encounter. *The Service Encounter* (John A. Czepiel *et al.*, ed.) Lexington Books.
2   Carlzon J. (1981). *Moments of Truth*. Ballinger Publishing Corp.
3   Albrecht K. and Zemke R. (1985). *Service America!* Dow Jones-Irwin.
4   Berry L. L., Zeithaml V. A., Parasuraman A. (1980). The imperatives for improving service quality. *Sloan Management Review*. Summer.
5   La Londe B. J. and Zinszer P. (1976). *Customer Service: Meaning & Measurement*. Chicago, NCPDM.
6   Christopher M. G. (1985). *The Strategy of Distribution Management*. Gower Press, 1985 and Heinemann Professional Publishing.
7   Schonberger R. J. (1990). *Building a Chain of Customers*. The Free Press.
8   Reichheld F. F. and Sasser, W. E. (1990). Zero defections: quality comes to services. *Harvard Business Review*. September-October.
9   Norton D. P. (1988). Breaking functional gridlock: the case for a mission-oriented organization. *Stage by Stage*. **8**, 2, Lexington, MA: Nolan, Norton & Company.
10 Waterman R. H. (1982). The seven elements of strategy fit. *Journal of Business Strategy*. **2**, 3, Winter.
11 Levitt T. (1983). *The Marketing Imagination*. Free Press.

PART TWO
Case Studies in Quality Leadership

One of the challenges of managing quality is to stay focused on the critical performance issues and allocate time and resources where effort counts most. Certainly customers are continually experiencing and evaluating the quality of offered solutions and service support, so they are continually 'adjusting' their perception of quality. Once the firm 'fixes' something, the priorities among other critical issues will naturally rearrange themselves.

In each of the case studies to follow, the reasons for getting to the starting point of quality improvement are quite different. Sometimes the pivotal 'crisis' is about survival, as in the case of Rank Xerox, Ilford and Johnson Matthey. Sometimes it is about new competition and deregulated services markets, as in the case of ANZ Bank. Sometimes it is about technology and time horizons within which to carve a leading position, as in the case of Datapaq.

Rank Xerox's multinational parent company Xerox Corp. in 1989 won the holy grail of quality in the USA, the **Malcolm Baldridge National Quality Award.** So when people like Derek Hornby, now chairman of Rank Xerox UK, say they spend most of their time at Xerox on quality, who would really doubt it?

These companies are all very different in size, location, industry, culture and history. Also, they are all at different stages of evolution towards quality leadership. What they do share in common is a predisposition or belief, which has been brought to the surface in our discussions. It's so obvious that it gets overlooked. It is this: **the quality of relationships with people outside the company (customers) depends on the quality of relationships between people inside the company (staff).** This is where **relationship marketing** shares common ground with quality management. This is why marketing managers must get involved in managing quality.

The case studies which follow do not necessarily make a case for a 'marketing' dominated quality improvement process. Rather, they make a case for marketing commitment and involvement. Each in their own time, and place.

CASE 1 *Just another Cambridge hi-tech company?*

Datapaq is one of 400-plus new high-tech companies that have in the past ten years located their activities in or around the Cambridge Science Park (UK). Many of these companies have already come and gone, by absorption or through failure. 'I don't want Datapaq to become just another Cambridge hi-tech company, another failure statistic,' says John Bates, Datapaq's founder and managing director, revealing his pride in their progress since the start-up five years ago and perhaps his horror at the amount of effort they had invested.

The company manufactures and distributes a range of integrated temperature data gathering and reporting systems for in-process quality control in the finishing industries. Datapaq's unique products are used in semicontinuous manufacturing processes, especially where the item to be monitored is hot, remote or in some way particularly difficult to access. These systems provide statistical process control for processes with cycle durations of the order of a few seconds in some applications to about 150 hours in others.

Like many entrepreneurial start-ups, the idea was developed over a dinner among friends. After early difficulties and disappointments in gaining venture capital finance, the embryonic Datapaq company began the long haul from prototype to production. With only a few dedicated hands to work on hardware and software development, eighty to one hundred-hour weeks were common in the first year. One or two people took to working thirty-six-hour shifts then sleeping on the office floor near the photo copier to keep warm before starting again.

Essentially, the strategy from the beginning was to take charge of marketing, product design and assembly, with the manufacture of components being subcontracted out. The strength of the early years was that everyone did a bit of everything. There was never enough time and the company unintentionally operated on a 'just-in-time basis'. For example, the story is told of one programmer who was still writing a Datapaq programme as he travelled to make a delivery of that programme to a customer in Denmark! While this was good for stock control it was also part of the early chaos.

More staff were hired, after the first three years, as much as budgets would allow. Even so, a problem arose in breaking down work into discrete areas because many tasks were closely interlinked and there were still too few people to allocate single jobs.

John Bates admits that getting the show on the road was a big effort and put a lot of strain on his directors and managers, whose commitment was enormous. But as he said to his managers at the end of these formative years, 'We can't yet afford to relax, we still have only two industries covered and we need at least six to build a sustainable business – that's still going to take some doing. If we lose the full momentum now we'll just stop in our tracks.'

Their efforts started to pay off in the fourth year and by the end of the fifth year, Datapaq had become the world leader for in-process monitoring in its chosen market niches. It was trading profitably, had absorbed all its start up costs and losses, and was employing almost forty people including most of the originals from the early years.

One characteristic that distinguishes Datapaq from many industrial and scientific instrumentation companies is its **market orientation**. At Datapaq the customer relationship comes first and the technology is then applied to that. The organization of the company reflects this philosophy by locating the key product decisions with a multiskilled marketing manager who is constantly in touch with the market.

Each Datapaq product is designed and given the service support necessary to become the industry standard in each market as soon as possible. Future success depends on their ability to provide unique high quality systems. To justify a premium price and at the same time make profits, Datapaq's directors recognized that they must deliver unique quality solutions to customers at the lowest possible cost to themselves, that is, the price premium on their offerings must exceed the additional costs of being uniquely valuable compared to competitor offerings.

The next steps

Some staff might have been forgiven for thinking that the time had come to rest a little after these formative years to enjoy the fruits and successes they had earned through maximum effort. It was not to be so. When they were a small multifunctional team, quality was implicit in everything they did, often with direct customer contact. With growth came functional specialization. Basically everybody was becoming more remote from the customers on a day-to-day basis. So as they entered their sixth year, John Bates dropped the 'quality brick' to his managers in these terms:

'We will develop and grow only by continuously improving the things we do and the way in which we do them. Our continued leadership depends on QUALITY. Our policy on quality must be total involvement and total commitment at all levels – doing it right as well as doing the right thing.'

Quality had become the new strategic issue at Datapaq. So far, reliability had been achieved at a cost by customizing critical parts of the product systems. This required high levels of inspection before the units were sent out the backdoor. There was also the issue of their responsiveness from prototype to production. Too many customer deadlines were met with only minutes to spare! They were achieving quality from the customers' point of view but it did not feel like quality from the inside. There was too much rushing about and as a consequence, too much waste. The other part of the quality problem was the need for new product development. Their continued success depended on it. They could not go through another prototype to production cycle again unless they sorted out the time and materials blockages that had somehow grown up with the evolution of the company.

When John Bates put these ideas to his management team there was some hesitancy at first. Yet another challenge! However, they all gave him their commitment because as someone said, if they started work on 'quality' now, they could head off the next crisis before it even began. All the key players were ready in place including a senior quality assurance engineer who had joined them earlier that year.

John Bates also knew that his entrepreneurial style of management would not serve the company's interests indefinitely 'As long as I am here, people won't use their talent to the full extent,' he told his directors. 'We all need to keep learning and to do that we will have to stay multifunctional. We need to be able to form all kinds of project teams at a moment's notice.'

The directors knew that they must stay flexible to keep their quality leadership. They did not want 'fuzzy' quality evangelism but on the other hand, as a youthful company, they did not want bureaucratic quality 'red tape'. They decided they needed some outside help to make a start with their quality leadership commitment. John Bates and his finance director approached a quality consultant who suggested a 'continuous improvement' approach. The benefit of this approach would be that the staff would be invited to participate in designing the changes which would affect their work. This would improve the multifunctional skills of those involved and improve information flows within the company. Standards would be set as critical processes were identified but it would be a step-by-step learning approach. This was agreed.

The quality consultant was invited to the next managers' meeting to meet the team and discuss the quality initiative. The managers also agreed to set aside half a day in the week following for a detailed discussion of strategies, plans, and methods of implementation. They also agreed to set up a full staff meeting for half a day during the week after that. This would be a familiarization workshop titled 'Planning for Quality Leadership'. At this point, the commitment was made concrete and ratified by the managers. There was naturally some anxiety about where it would all end.

The managers' briefing

The quality consultant began by defining quality as 'meeting customers' requirements'. He said that this was a marketing orientation as well as a production orientation. Everybody in the company could focus on one goal – the customers' requirements. By using people's talents to the full and by investigating and improving work processes continuously, competitive advantage **and** cost savings could be achieved.

The total **quality leadership philosophy** for Datapaq was discussed in these terms:

- Quality is a commitment to long-term relationships.
- Quality is customer focused.
- Quality is based on respect for people.
- No department or function is excluded.
- All employees may participate in improving quality.
- Quality improvement brings benefits to customers, staff and share-holders.

They could start with the external customer (buyers) or the internal customer (staff). The consultant explained that in quality management terms, everybody was a customer, connected through the **value chain**. This provoked further discussion about where to begin. Starting with the external customer would provide quality benchmarking for new product development and product modification. On the other hand, this would take time. The other way to go would be to look at the **cross-functional** work flows within Datapaq, make improvements and remove blockages. This might increase the effectiveness of what they were already achieving in terms of quality and market acceptance. They decided to begin with the second alternative first but to plan for the external quality benchmarking which could follow later. By taking this strategy they would be able to begin to involve staff in the quality improvement process right after the first staff **quality leadership workshop**. In this way staff would see that the words 'quality leadership' were not empty but a commitment with practical consequences. They (as staff) would be invited to take some responsibility for quality leadership opportunities in their own work practices, as internal customers and internal suppliers. As the consultant explained, quality is not working harder or faster, it is using information better.

Some managers at this point had doubts, and expressed them. One of the potential problems was in raising the expectations of staff to unrealistic levels. Another was that the role of the manager was less clear and that his or her authority might be threatened in some way by staff recommendations for changes. These points were talked through. Raising staff expectations could be avoided by making sure everybody understood the quality leadership philosophy. Also, if staff were asked to think of quality in terms of 'how can I improve this process for my customer and save money at the same time', they should be on the right track.

As to the loss of authority by managers, they agreed to set up a formal **diagnostic review process** (along the lines of the 'turning wheel' method mentioned in Chapter 5). In other words, quality leadership teams would be established to work through critical issues diagnostically and report back their findings and recommendations after a three-month interval. These feedback meetings would be in the form of presentations to all Datapaq staff. Arrangements would be made to make these 'presentation day' events something special. There might be three or four cycles of the diagnostic review process in any one year. The bottom line in terms of managers' authority was that staff would make recommendations and managers would still make decisions.

One interesting point that came out of the 'managers must manage' discussion was that managers would not be excluded from the quality leadership teams as their experience and knowledge would be absolutely critical.. The criteria for selection to a group would be first, self-nomination, and second, ability to contribute to the topic under study by virtue of experience or interest. As John Bates said, 'If managers manage quality improvement as a **process**, staff will begin to manage themselves.'

Guide-lines for the quality leadership teams were established as follows:

- Teams work on one problem/opportunity at a time
- Aim is to achieve incremental (step-by-step) quality improvements
- Cross-functional talents will produce cross-functional information flows
- Teams will be non-hierarchical
- Ideas will be generated by the team and anybody else they may wish to co-opt
- Meeting customer requirements is the overriding goal
- Saving money is the task objective
- Teams may disband after a three-month plan – do – review – report project cycle
- New information and learning should be broadcast through the company after each project cycle
- New process performance criteria to be established where appropriate (standard measures should only be set up to monitor critical issues)
- Recognize and value each team members' contribution.

One manager set the discussion going on the issue of 'measurement'. He had some knowledge of quality improvement programmes in other companies and they had tended to drift off into low-value, high-cost, time-consuming activities. He did not want to see Datapaq drift along in this way. His concern was dealt with at a number of levels. Firstly, the managers had already agreed to introduce quality benchmarks as a second phase of the quality leadership programme. These would provide market input. It would be possible within the **quality network** of quality leadership teams to set this task up as a team project. Secondly there were internal performance measures which would give early indications of improvements in the internal flow. These could include monitoring customer complaints, the ratio of returns to shipments per month, and the ratio of reworked systems to zero defective systems per month. Also, a simple staff 'morale' survey could be established as a basis for revealing any sensitive staff issues.

One of the first tasks would be to identify all the key points in the Datapaq value chain. For example, where does the process you are going to study start and stop? No work of this kind had been done before at Datapaq. When key processes had been identified, it would be correct to ask what are the inputs and suppliers to these processes? Who are the internal customers of these processes? Finally, what are the outputs in terms of products and services? They would almost certainly discover previously unaccounted for variability in all key processes because without formal quality management, nobody manages the cross-functional work flows. Setting up internal measures which connect to the end customers' requirements is something that would need to be checked time and time again during the evolution of their quality leadership programme.

It was becoming clear that rather than 'devolving' responsibility away from managers, the quality leadership commitment added new responsibility. The process of managing the process was something that was an executive responsibility so they agreed to set up an executive-level **quality planning group** to do just that. A group of four was appointed. Their first task was to coordinate the staff workshop scheduled for the next week. All the managers agreed that what they would hope for from this workshop was some understanding and staff enthusiasm for the aims of the programme. Also, a call would go out for volunteers for two or three quality leadership teams to work on tasks suggested by the quality planning group or perhaps even by the teams themselves. All this would sort itself out within the framework of the workshop.

Later when staff opened up their personalized letter sent under the signatures of the quality planning group inviting them to a 'Planning For Quality Leadership Workshop', they read:

> 'Quality is a journey,' say the Total Quality gurus. This is . . . a way of indicating that there is no absolute one best way of improving quality. Each business organization must find its own pathways. So our commitment to **quality** belongs to us. We must listen to advice but we choose the way to proceed 'towards achieving Quality Leadership in our industry'.

They were on their way. As one manager said with a smile, 'I've got my fingers crossed.'

Postscript

The Datapaq story shows that too rigid a set of rules for guiding a company through the early phases of quality improvement can be inappropriate. Obvious weaknesses must be dealt with first. The transition requires a combination of skills, perhaps the most important being the ability to tolerate uncertainty and ambiguity, both in external and internal markets. At the heart of it all is strong motivation and commitment. As John Bates says, 'I don't want Datapaq to become just another Cambridge Hi-Tech Company.'

CASE 2 *The shift to 'customer orientation' in retail banking*

Major revolutionary events are changing the nature of retail banking world-wide. They are grounded in new technology (information and delivery systems) and emergent consumer action in open market conditions (deregulation).

Far from being a local show or a passing fad, this time of turmoil is part and parcel of the broader questioning of present day society. It ties in directly with the concerns of our times about the quality of actions, including customers' expectations for service quality. It is a revolution that is strongly influencing corporate planning, marketing strategy, and at the heart of it all the meaning of service quality management.

To bring service quality into strategic focus, we need to look at how broader technological, environmental, psychological, social and economic realities influence the managerial view.

First, technology is extending the range of delivery systems and thereby the type of service branches. This is best understood as a transformation from fixed point-of-purchase branches to multiple point-of-performance zones reaching right into the home – with new configurations possible for both service quality and productivity.

Second, the customers' growing need for a sense of control is largely derived from social and cultural changes world-wide which can be described as a movement towards **consumer sovereignty**. Remote though the connection may seem, this has effect in the banking system as a desire for more relevant money managing options and for financial advice.

In this environment, banks have begun to act as a change agents; changing the agenda, changing the product configuration, changing the perception of customer service. Shifts in ground rules and established managerial beliefs are involved. Breaking free from traditional marketing thinking has been a long time coming.

The banks that do well in the 1990s will be those which rediscover the customer and start to manage customer service. What this actually means is quite complex. For example, the 'service encounter', the interaction between bank staff and customer, seems to be the obvious focus for service quality improvements. Yet **everybody** in retail banking is connected to the 'front line' as support for that very tangible encounter with the customer. Thus the design of environment, work processes and the way in which jobs are organized either supports or inhibits the quality of the service encounter.

Poor service quality is 'unselling'. It loses customers. Therefore, the banker's job is to manage the customer relationships at the front desk and the processing at the back desk. If quality is not 'built-in' to the delivery systems, variations in the process are experienced by customers as poor or inconsistent service at the front counter. Without a process for ongoing review of the process elements, there will be variance in quality due to common (random) causes and special (assignable) causes – as total quality management people put it.

Involving staff in the quality improvement process at ANZ Bank

When organizations set up a framework for staff diagnostic review groups (or quality improvement teams) the focus is sometimes on 'trouble shooting', sometimes on customer service improvement and rather less often on influencing changes in management–staff relations. With the support and encouragement of top management, ANZ Bank (ANZ Bank is one of the four major retail banks operating Australia-wide, and is Australia's largest international bank) began its 'Customer Care' programme with an intentional focus on all three aspects. In other words, the programme was in one sense 'top-down' but it could also be called a 'bottom-up' programme. Culture changing effects were moving up the hierarchy, in terms of a more participative and open style of management, at the same time as 'customer first' messages were moving down the management chain to branch staff. In this way the interests of management and staff as legitimate stakeholders in the organization moved with relative harmony of purpose; likewise the interests of shareholders as stakeholders were vested in the income.

In building diagnostic groups in the Retail/Branch Banking Division at ANZ Bank, the intention was to remove any focus on hierarchies, that is to flatten hierarchies out. Groups are composed of people from all levels including managers. 'Groupies', they call themselves. This flattening of hierarchy is confirmed by the absence of status titles in programme guides and in the programme itself. People seemed not to object to status as a surrogate for excellence – in fact they liked it. But they objected to status being used as a surrogate for power.

In ANZ groups, people talk about the concept of a 'natural' person, one who brings his or her whole self to the work. This is opposed to the role player, who brings to work only those personal values that 'fit' with what he or she feels comfortable; a secure fit within the organizational norms. This notion of the 'natural' person is a culture-challenging proposition. It unfreezes personal constraint and opens up the possibility of self-directed action, challenging the rigidity of the established culture.

Groups are set up in regional workshops of 'volunteers' i.e.: people preselected, invited, who accept. There is no coercion. Participants are bonded into small groups of four, in a workshop process involving sixteen to twenty people. Using group dynamics and small group bonding is the key developmental process. The small group bonding opens up the participants to a level of knowing about the group and themselves. This is a basis for self-development and learning, a platform from which personal growth can be pursued by each participant, within his or her small group, during and after the workshop.

This is very necessary as a support element for the work task ahead, where each 'groupie', must return to his or her branch and generate service quality changes, perhaps in the face of indifference, disbelief, or cynicism from some staff members.

The aim of each workshop is to reach higher order personal values which motivate, those beyond 'fame', 'status' or cash 'rewards'. The commitment of groups is therefore focused on a superordinate goal, which is to put the 'customer first' as a philosophy in practice. This is to be achieved after the workshop via practical service quality improvements.

The workshop process begins implicitly with personal 'value searching' because if the 'customer first' mission is largely congruent with individual personal values, there is motiv(ation) for action. The group process opens up possibilities of new and more effective ways of going about work on a day-by-day basis, something of **practical** value in itself. This also is a motiv(ation) for action.

A further value motive is the prospect of personal growth, something that many people have not considered. So adding up the opportunities for self-growth, practical and fulfilling approaches to work, and a focus on the customer, ANZ reaches out to every group member for their personal commitment to **action**.

Put another way, commitment to action starts with a **focus** on organizational goals which are congruent with personal values. A final incentive to action is a firm task **deadiine**. This is set for two to three months out from the workshop date and agreed to by participants at their workshop.

It is a diagnostic review process. There is a clear task focus in ANZ's approach and a specifically defined method. It consists of a set of methodological steps which enable service quality improvement, or **opportunities** for improvement, to be defined and examined on a fit-for-use basis.

Those who particularly value self-development, usually enjoy the programme and processes so much that they want to contribute to the self-development of others – another motivation for action. This would normally involve more workshops with a view to developing 'process' facilitation skills. The goal is that the person becomes capable of first, planning and organizing one complete cycle of the diagnostic review phase in their region, and at a second level, assisting in the facilitation of a workshop, and at a third level, 'full licence' facilitation in any aspect of the programme.

The workshop programmes emphasize creative approaches to diagnosing critical service issues rather more than rational logical approaches. The intention is to challenge the existing cultural norms. Creative problem solving approaches also enable a sense of fun to be maintained in a working environment. This is the climate which permits innovation and a coming to terms with the desirability of change, and managing change.

In the workshops, permission is given to openly discuss what would otherwise in the banking culture be 'undiscussable', which leads to a developing sense of trust and commitment. The process is one of empowering people who, day by day, work in an environment where attitudes and actions are fairly prescribed.

The construction of **networks** of people involved in the diagnostic review process is focused on a district (regional) level. People involved in the programme feel a bond of kinship, Australia-wide. These network relationships are maintained by information-sharing structures and by informal modes. There are network newsletters which are written and distributed on an Australia-wide basis to group facilitators and on a regional basis to group participants. These newsletters are the vehicles for explaining new techniques and information of value in the diagnostic review process.

Networks are the vehicles for supporting and developing the practical service quality improvement which is the task goal of the programme. The 'self-help' attitudes and experiences developed through creative problem solving techniques and the application of these to practical situations gives 'life' support to the network itself. In this way, the culture-challenging effects associated with diagnostic review groups are not easily extinguished.

Every ANZ diagnostic 'groupie' is conscious of the history of the programme, its origins, and his or her part in it. This is given tangible support at every opportunity, including well-presented programme guides, network directories (names, addresses and 'phone numbers) and certificates of merit. There are formal 'presentation' ceremonies to regional managers for discussing results achieved in service quality improvement. Other channels are used for passing on service quality improvements which have application on an Australia-wide basis.

There is a genuine sense of excitement and challenge about all this. Every diagnostic 'groupie' senses that they are working 'against the grain'. They know that the organization cannot change of itself and they accept some of the responsibility for initiating that change. The commitment to that responsibility is the beginning of personal development and the beginning of service quality improvement at grass-roots level, and the role modelling of a new kind of banking behaviour which fits ANZ's strategic focus.

In his or her work, involving culture change, the ANZ diagnostic 'groupie' is truly an invisible leader. As a change agent working toward practical improvement in service processes, the role as leader is quite visible. But it is the invisible aspect of leadership that counts in the long run. It is the kind of leadership that seeks out a more participative and less autocratic system of management. When 'groupies' take practical action in terms of diagnostic work, this influences changes in their relationship with their manager, indeed the relationship of that manager and the rest of the branch staff.

The same invisible process begins at regional level where the 'groupie' facilitator through his or her task-focused actions influences the relationship the regional manager has with his staff, and the relationship of the regional manager with his own branch managers.

Enthusiasm and task focus begin the diagnostic process. The practical outcome is the generation of ideas for improvement in service quality processes which in turn challenge the organization towards changing the **way** things are done, the **methods** which are used, and the **attitudes** that go with it.

ANZ could never achieve a retail 'customer-focused' transition from an operationally focused organizational culture with diagnostic review groups alone. What they have achieved are tangible results at the customer interface, and the value data is broadcast up and down the organization. The outcome of this is that more opportunities for strategic interventions into the organizational culture open up for legitimate action, at all levels of the organizational hierarchy.

And so the process goes on, continuously.

Motivation and performance

The experience at ANZ Bank over the past few years indicates that staff will do their job well if they know exactly what that job is . . . and if they are given the resources and a supportive organizational framework. To step outside the system, to change the system, requires a strongly supportive framework of another kind. Again, the experience of ANZ Bank provides some valuable insights here. Ideas for quality improvement are generated within staff 'networks' and at the same time, decisions on quality improvement remain the province of management, according to hierarchical authority.

One alternative to the ANZ Bank approach would be to ask staff to perform better, to 'do their best' in improving customer service. Even if adequate training and encouragement is provided, it is hard to avoid the conclusion that such methods are essentially 'coercive' and fail in the long run because they ignore the range of service quality defects already built into the performance system and its processes.

Another alternative to the ANZ approach would be to 'motivate' staff by setting firm service performance standards, at the outset. This is the 'what gets measured gets done' principle. If the call goes out to improve service quality by performing harder, staff might do it – for a while. However, if there are systemic defects, or blockages in the performance system, staff will of necessity try to subvert the system.

It is embarrassing but true that many financial institutions draw up lists of service standards, indeed often with the agreement of staff, which include specific performance levels which cannot be consistently achieved. The case of telephones which ring, say, more than three times, illustrates this. If staff are expected to meet an 'impossible' standard they will try to do it, but in the absence of any formal diagnostic approach to problem solving, they eventually will give up. Some people might then be tempted to reflect that 'this is the kind of staff problem that we see more and more today', and perhaps an observation of even more comfort would be 'we observe that our competitors are having similar problems'.

The choice management must make in introducing 'service standards' is whether to drive workers harder at their assigned tasks, or whether to invite them to **participate** in generating ways of improving the performance system. The first way treats people as prisoners of the system and the second invites people to be agents of the system – a distinct and separate contribution for which their experience within the system makes them ideally suited.

Rewards and motivation

As people become involved in the diagnostic review work at 'grass-roots' level, the challenge of spreading the philosophy of service takes on more focus at 'head-office level'. What at first may appear to be a simple process of 'getting staff involved' is in fact a cyclical review process which involves finding the critical service issues, introducing diagnostic review, assessing quality improvement ideas, implementing and codifying systems adjustments, reviewing training schedules and rewarding the participants.

Rewards are intended to lead behaviour in certain directions, or to reinforce existing behaviour. Under what customer service conditions do rewards actually motivate staff? As work performance is subject to random effects within any performance system, staff often wonder whether 'trying harder' is worth the effort. However, when the focus shifts to quality management and customer service improvements, then the contribution of an idea becomes a voluntary act, uniquely outside the system, behaviour that should be reinforced.

Theories on rewards motivation are anchored historically in the economic rationalism of the scientific management theorists and are often unhelpful. Notwithstanding, as Ed Schein has pointed out, top management can quickly get across their own priorities, values and assumptions by consistently linking rewards and punishments to the behaviour they want to encourage.

In other words, rather than directing discretionary remuneration to 'top performers' within the process, discretionary remuneration might be directed to performers who 'act-on' the process and suggest ways of improvement. In spite of the difficulty of judging the value of contributions, the right people are rewarded for turning the wheel of quality improvement. Vanguard management thinking is the 'positioning' of rewards for quality improvement linked to a formal diagnostic review process.

'Quality' is a motivator so long as the quality improvement process is seen to be customer orientated, an opportunity to test one's personal limits, and in so doing contribute to the organization's success. This three-way motivational outlook provides opportunity for personal growth and the shift in management style from traditional/ autocratic towards participative/ collaborative.

CASE 3 *Involving senior managers in the quality improvement process at Johnson Matthey*

The frequent complaint of those involved in implementing quality management techniques is that senior managers are not showing enough commitment. Even more damaging, the question of commitment is often top of the staff list of perceived roadblocks to progress in improving quality. This situation is coupled with a frustration on the part of the senior managers, who are exasperated that they seem never able to do enough to satisfy everybody!

Once staff have their attention focused on 'quality' they naturally become experts at recognizing 'non-quality'. Each senior manager becomes a role model for good, indifferent or bad quality. This, in turn, opens the way for employees to excuse their own performance inadequacies by seizing any 'quality' aberration of their managers, however trivial, and holding them up as an example of lack of commitment. As much as senior managers may despair, staff think 'commitment' means 'there is no other way'. So the congruence between ideas and actions really is the issue.

Johnson Matthey, for example, took the critical view that the issue was not senior management **commitment**, but senior management **involvement**. That is, the only correct signal is **doing** something.

Let us start their quality story at the beginning.

Johnson Matthey is a hi-tech conglomerate linked to the refining, marketing and fabricating of precious metals and a manufacturer of catalytic systems, speciality chemicals, pharmaceutical compounds and a range of electronic and other materials. The company has significant manufacturing operations – major research and development on four continents and a technology centre involving 200 high-calibre scientists.

In 1989, Johnson Matthey turned in its best profit for 150 years. It was not always so. Only four years earlier, one of their divisions had collapsed – and as with many major companies, it was this crisis that provided the catalyst for their quality improvement process to get underway. Not surprisingly, a new chief executive arrived who had been with a company that was 'doing quality'. The decision was taken that Johnson Matthey should view 'total quality' as part of their recovery strategy.

They produced a quality mission statement, had outside consultants to help set up a staff function at head office and divisional steering committees in the divisions. They elected a quality improvement team at each of forty-four business units. They were in business!

Operating business units were made accountable for the quality improvement process. Making quality a soft option at head office expense was not seen as an effective way of harnessing commitment, given the spread and diversity of their business interests. Each business unit was invited to organize and educate themselves. And it did happen. For a year everybody turned up on time, had lots of meetings, achieved many small, though important successes, and published lots of 'quality awareness' newsletters. Things looked good.

Under the surface, however, staff nurtured a feeling that senior managers were not quite 'committed'. They were making supportive noises about the process, without **doing** anything beyond the communication of their support.

For example, the constant flow of 'good news' contained in 'quality awareness' newsletters was at serious odds with the internal 'grapevine'. This was especially worrying, as many business units are each other's internal customers and suppliers. So the head office quality manager undertook a series of reviews, part of which involved drawing together groups of twenty to thirty people at random from various workplaces and talking in an open way about whether the quality initiative had changed their life. It often had, but along with the nice little success stories came bad news.

The critical questions centred around these themes

- Was the time spent justified? Everybody seemed to be 'constantly' in quality meetings of some sort!
- Was there too much flag waving? What about hard action and results.
- Is senior management really committed?

This last one especially was beginning to test the coherence of the whole quality improvement process. When the head office quality manager spoke with his colleagues in quality in other companies, he heard plenty of the same stories and concerns. It seemed that perceived lack of actual involvement in the process by senior managers tested its credibility.

It was after this that the quality manager took the steps that would lead to a shift in ownership away from the pioneering head office enthusiasts, into the hands of senior line managers in the business units, who had nominal accountability for it anyway. With Johnson Matthey top management support, the head office team started a series of regional workshops. In these, they brought together groups of around twenty people by region who were already involved in the process. These workshops, facilitated by their own in-company quality specialists, were asked to create their own agenda. For example . . . in our business unit, what are the roadblocks to . . . awareness . . . action, etc. Being from different business units, the participants were at different stages in their implementation of quality, so with that cross-flow of experience, they debated, brainstormed, and problem solved to reach their own unique set of recommendations. These recommendations were then presented by regional coordinators to their respective boards, and were accepted or modified. Either way, firm plans for implementation emerged at senior management level.

This process of dialogue convinced senior managers that they should be doing more visibly, and could do more without fear or confrontation by supporting significant recommendations from the regional workshops. These recommendations reflected, after all, the views and concerns of significant groups of employees from varied sites in their region.

Out of one of these workshops came the recommendations that eventually caused the quality improvement process to be clearly committed to the hands of senior line managers. Their involvement was ensured through the normal strategy planning processes, and adoption of these additional requirements.

- A quality plan was developed each year for each business unit, as part of the strategy planning process. This formal plan was to locate the crucial few quality issues which would generate the most customer satisfaction with the greatest cost savings.
- At division level, a division board member became responsible for the implementation of the plan for the current year and the formulation of next year's quality plan. He or she did this for one year, each board member thus having overlapping responsibility, on a rotating basis.

There was no longer need for a separate system of head office quality coordinators, essential though they had been in the early days. Now any quality activity, workshop etc., could be delegated down as a management-driven project. Another element emerging from regional workshops was a recommendation, adopted by the executive board, that the International Quality Standard – ISO 9000 – be a requirement, where technically appropriate, for all operating companies and business units. These accreditations were certainly not seen as the be-all and end-all of quality at Johnson Matthey, but ISO 9000 would eventually become the minimum ticket to establishing ongoing relationships with major customers. Overall, the regional workshops released groundswell support for the idea of targeting customer requirements for quality, rather than rest solely on internally generated specifications.

In this way, many of the earlier problems associated with 'commitment' dissolved. But these changes were not just changes in attitude. Changes in behaviour were prompted by changes in structure. The fact that the annual planning cycle at Johnson Matthey now demanded a quality plan, signed off by the division director, inclined senior managers to do what they say they would do in terms of commitment and involvement.

Congruency of plans and actions

At Johnson Matthey, quality is the means of closing the loop between getting customers and profitably keeping them. Their belief in the process led them to set up company-wide methods and educate their people to understand and accept them, so that they might better identify and progressively eliminate non-conforming events. Their view now is that whatever 'culture change' they may still have to achieve, it will come more naturally if their people get involved in solving quality-related problems as a requirement, and not as an option. It is a question of choosing the right timing, and context.

Sooner or later, and usually sooner, every quality improvement process strikes a crisis of confidence. However, when senior management understand that managing quality is really a better way of managing diversity and conflicting interests, and they renew their commitment through actions rather than words, the internal process soon gets up and running again, improving the way things get done. The element that differentiates the Johnson Matthey 'commitment' from many others is the formal quality component built into their planning process. Thus through quality, marketing and operations achieve more coherence in purpose, across the diversity of business interests and across the spread of regions.

The litmus test of a quality committed company is the constancy of senior management involvement in the quality improvement process, from the point of view of supervisors and staff. This is what Johnson Matthey have learnt.

CASE 4 *Achieving real culture change at Ilford*

Ilford has been in the photographic industry for over one hundred years. Their reputation is based on high-quality innovative black and white photographic products.

Not long ago in such a long history, they used to achieve high quality by inspecting out the bad from the good. They were proud of their extensive quality control facilities, but the down-side of such an approach was high costs. They were not yet conscious of the cost of quality that results when quality is 'inspected in'.

The photographic industry serves global markets, the main suppliers being the USA, Germany and Japan. Against this formidable competition, Ilford's uncompetitive cost structure was a major factor leading to an unglamorous market retreat during the 1960s and 1970s. Like any company in a quality and cost bind, Ilford tried to stem the tide. One after the other, or sometimes in clusters, initiatives were taken, aimed at turning the company around. These initiatives included:

- Productivity improvement programmes
- 'Consultants' who knew the cure
- Management by objectives
- Team building for non-existent teams
- Action-centred leadership programming
- Introduction of consultative committees in a cascade briefing system
- Reorganization, reorganization and reorganization
- Cost centres
- Profit centres
- Quality circles
  and every two or three years
- Productivity on lower volumes of sales, achieved by restructuring, retreat and staff lay-offs.

These initiatives would usually be introduced in a high-profile way, championed by top management, set up on a project basis, and led by a fast-track manager. Unfortunately the next external threat would hit before benefits of the last initiatives could be diagnosed, leaving the blunt instrument of cost cutting and redundancies as the only action possible to achieve short-term survival. The Ilford experience, which is common to many companies with old and famous brand names who find themselves in highly competitive markets, was the breeding ground for Ilford's special blend of 'management by cynicism'.

Management started to believe that whether you put a lot or a little into change programmes, the end result would likely as not be the same, so you had better take precautionary steps and get ready for the next cost cutting/numbers reduction exercise. Not surprisingly, 'productivity' was not a positive word at Ilford. What is more, after routine purges on 'productivity', initiatives for major change tended to slip down the list of management priorities as people got back to 'normal business', at least until the next threat appeared.

The problem of real change was compounded by the fact that historically, managers had not got to where they were by their skills in management. Also, top management were happy to support any proposed initiatives that might 'transform' the company, yet generally saw the initiatives as starting next level down, thus protecting the traditional system that got them to where they were. Although they did not know it at that time, this was the culture that Ilford's history had grown. This was the culture Ilford had to change.

In the early 1980s, major restructuring turned Ilford from loss making to profitability. With new people in key positions, they focused on what it would take for long-term survival in the highly competitive international photographic business. They decided to concentrate their efforts on 'black and white', and get that right. The same executives had heard of quality improvement programmes about that time. They worked up a proposal and began quietly in February 1985 with a diagnosis of the company, using two external quality consultants.

The outcome was a shock but not entirely a surprise. Management wisdom was that their difficulties resulted from poor technology, intransigent unions and poor workforce attitudes. However, the diagnosis showed the following:

- Roles, responsibilities, accountabilities unclear
- Procedures and information systems inadequate – repetition of mistakes
- Problem symptoms addressed – repetition of problem
- Error proofing not done due to pressure of other work
- Manufacturing processes were complex
- Communications inadequate
- Training minimal
- People were not regarded as assets
- 'Ivory tower' management style.

In other words, the problem was a management problem, specifically the **way** in which Ilford was being managed. This was an uncomfortable period and the management committee took several weeks to come to terms with the diagnosis. Since it meant that they were part of the problem, therefore to solve the problem they had to fundamentally change the way they were operating. Acceptance of this was an heroic step but vital to achieving the real change which followed. Once they had absorbed this, they moved quickly into the quality improvement process.

Over the next few months, the top 160 managers at Ilford (10 per cent of the workforce) were trained in quality management techniques, with particular emphasis on problem solving. They defined the strategy and structure for their own quality improvement process. Up until this time the management committee met monthly with a normal business agenda. They added a second monthly meeting devoted to quality improvement and so quality initiatives became an integral part of ongoing business, implemented through the line rather than as 'staff' projects.

After the success of the initial senior management training, Ilford's first big initiative and first mistake was to implement a 'problem trawl' through the company with the enthusiasm of their first success acting as their spur. The 4000 problems that they collected from staff suggestions nearly stopped them in their tracks! They simply could not see how to handle all this new workload and at the same time keep business going as normal. Ilford's senior management overcame this 'problem' by coming to terms with priorities. That is, it was clear that the total workload opportunity greatly exceeded available resource, so, they had found what **not** to do. The lesson learned came down to this. Saying 'no' in a difficult situation is hard, but saying 'yes' and not delivering on that promise is worse.

So they tackled prioritization like this:

- The management committee reviewed and agreed on their critical business objectives, plus some tasks that they had to achieve to meet short-term financial targets and some key longer term initiatives.
- They then listed and prioritized the staff suggestions against these essential tasks and objectives. They set up problem solving teams.
- Resources were then allocated strictly in accordance with the agreed priorities. This became their strategic plan. It was communicated through their business sections and used as a key implementation and control document at monthly management meetings.

This was a painful and difficult time. It took three months, but taught Ilford valuable lessons and was another step towards changing their management style. What emerged were three key points of organizational learning for the management committee:

- By working to one planned company-wide accord, rather than a collection of separate functional plans, resources are released. Waste (cost) results from conflict between departmental functions fed by well-meant personal interest.
- When the first responsibility is to company-wide business with functional responsibility next, moving resources between functions becomes easier. There is less 'blaming' and more understanding.
- It is easier to accept the rephasing or cancelling of 'important' projects when you can see the overall picture. Authentic communication pays dividends.

Achieving these working principles was a breakthrough. However, the time taken, almost three months, was perceived by the workforce as a sign that management was losing interest in the quality improvement process. Time had to be invested to get the programme back on the road. Still, managing priorities against the priority business targets they had set enabled them to run normal business and quality activities.

Once back in control they enjoyed the next few months of problem resolution. Success stories from problem solving teams filtered up to quarterly management meetings. Membership of teams was motivating and management recognized and thanked teams for their success. As someone said, 'We created an efficient fire brigade with the pleasure of a regular flow of fires.' However, what had not been achieved was depth in company-wide participation. If the handful of people driving the quality improvement process had stopped then so would quality improvement process! It was ironic that at the very point when considerable improvements from problem solving were being achieved, some senior managers started to become disillusioned with the approach to quality.

The key people involved stood back and analysed what they were doing. They realized that virtually all efforts in the first and second phases had been aimed at introducing problem solving tools and techniques. They had not tackled or understood the people dimension. So they set to addressing the following issues as their third phase:

- Functions/departments not customer orientated
- Poor communications
- Pockets of cynicism
- Lack of teamwork
- Fear of change
- Unachievable quality goals
- Priorities not clear and changed frequently
- Lack of training
- Organizational fit (round peg–square hole)
- Resistance to change
- Human resource policies and practice not linked to business objectives
- Poor individual performance

The management committee based their phase-three efforts heavily on TQM and Deming's philosophy in particular. They took care to translate it into Ilford language and their business environment. In essence they wanted to be able to explain to themselves and their staff that an Ilford manager manages, like this ' . . .'.

They put together a new three-day training programme. Top management started with themselves, and then the next level, ensuring always a cross-functional mix. The next level then trained their reporting managers, supported by one or two management committee members. This cascade approach was used for all 160 managers and they achieved considerable progress in team working, the recognition and removal of fear, breaking down functional barriers, and delegation.

They set out to reduce fear; fear of redundancy, individual embarrassment, admitting mistakes and admitting the possibility of saying 'no' to an impossible task. In Ilford now if you ask the question 'how are things going?' you will get an answer that is meaningful. The challenge, 'is that a TQM approach?' entered Ilford's language.

Then they entered the most difficult phase which was practising what they had been preaching. For example, starting from their business objectives they defined the roles and responsibilities for their functions, then departments. Overlaps and conflicts were resolved rather than ignored, gaps filled and as a separate step, individual roles and responsibilities were defined and agreed.

To try and underpin a total company-wide approach rather than allow quality initiatives to become narrow and functionalized, monthly evening meetings of departmental coordinators were held, supported by management committee members. This dealt with specific management issues with the objective of finding and agreeing the TQM way of dealing with them. The outcomes from these meetings were often incorporated into their company-wide method of working, part of 'the way we do things in Ilford'.

Despite the inevitable business pressures, management continued to meet monthly for half- and occasionally whole-day sessions grinding through the detail and above all ensuring consistency between business objectives and the new way of managing. The outcome of many months of work was amazing, cynicism receded and most importantly a critical mass of staff took on ownership of total quality management. The management committee role changed from driving to directing and supporting. This third stage of Ilford's quality improvement process had moved them from problem solving to installing and trying to operate TQM style, company-wide.

The majority of management now 'owned' the process. Management committee continued to meet monthly to evaluate progress and initiate and encourage initiatives. The benefits were tremendous and three years into the change process and they could show tangible and measurable results in many areas including:

- Productivity
- Yield
- Customer complaints
- Production consistency
- R&D projects on time
- Customer service levels

The intangible improvements were also great, the management committee worked as a team, delegation created time to do better planning, start their vendor programme, and increase routine customer contacts. They were becoming proactive rathr than reactive. At last, communication was starting to flow naturally across/between functions rather than up and down.

Then, at the very point when the benefits of TQM were so obvious, resistance to further initiatives again emerged. Too many people actually believed that they had 'achieved' TQM. 'It's in the woodwork, let's get on with business' was a famous statement made by one of the managers.

Clearly they had moved the company to significant new levels but this was simply another plateau. Yet the next level of change to **continuous improvement** was outside their reach.

Part of the problem was that they had no mechanism for assessing organizational change. They had lots of measurements for tangible factors, i.e. yields, productivity; but none for the way they were 'managing'. To overcome this, they implemented a TQM audit across the company. A small team produced a seventeen-point profile describing what a typical Ilford department might look like, three years on from their first start at implementation.

The results from this survey instrument showed significant variations between departments across the seventeen-point profile. The audit process itself as well as the results were then used as a springboard for further discussions and initiatives. These included:

- Departmental action programmes on a broad front driven by local management.
- Company support for statistical process control, with training and more internal consultants to support the continuous improvement.
- The use of ISO 9000 systems standard to unify their procedures and to bring training back into the work location rather than make it a separate 'experience'.

Progress as before was encouraged and monitored through their management committee, communication events, and management workshops.

It was during this fourth phase of the TQM process (coincidentally four years on) that many, but not all, department efforts started to come together, and rates of improvement accelerated. It was interesting that this was not so much a period of new initiatives but the systematic application of quality techniques piloted and refined over the last three to four years.

Organizational transitions

After such a courageous effort by many, many people at Ilford it would be nice to say that all goes well and they lived happily ever after. They had after all successfully transformed the company. They are achieving their business mission of leadership in black and white photography and successfully competing internationally. Their standards of quality, productivity, new product introductions and customer orientation are at levels today that would not have been possible before.

Yet in terms of culture change, they are still concerned about their 'plateau' mentality which causes people to say: 'We are doing well, so why do we have to keep pushing for improvement?' Some people are saying 'But we have solved all our problems.' By that they mean quite understandably that their department is under control and capable. They are working well, they are not fighting fires, they achieve the objectives of their department.

Real cultural change, however, would bring Ilford to the point where their people are working to achieve **their** task, achieving a **naturally** coherent fit with the **company goals.** Acceptance of this ideal concept is not difficult. Doing it requires an **unconscious** way of working, where it is natural for everyone to improve the way in which they do their tasks, continuously. This is not problem solving, this is seeking continuous improvement routinely as night follows day.

At Ilford the conscious understanding and achievement of **continuous improvement** is at the core of the management committee goals and their marketing and operations concepts. It doesn't matter what department you represent, the orientation is the same. The final shift from conscious to unconscious commitment is a shift into corporate culture. A tall order. You may ask how they could get 'there' sooner. Unfortunately, there is no absolute 'place' to get to unless implicit understanding and shared beliefs is a 'place'.

Certainly, if they had understood the process at the outset, they may well have saved time. But they would say at Ilford, that you have to **start** to learn! The fundamental people and process issues have to be faced, step by step, and the internal environment created and recreated anew, as people grow in strength and knowledge. Their commitment, courage and compassion speaks for itself.

The Ilford story reveals that total quality management for them is not so much a system of quality assurance, but a way of managing relationships profitably, a way of inviting staff participation in the decisions that effect them, and a way of developing pride in work with a clear customer orientation. In short, a way of building relationships inside and outside the company. Ilford may have succeeded more than they can know. Time will tell.

CASE 5 *From 'crisis' to quality leadership, at Rank Xerox*

Early in the 1980s, Rank Xerox and its multinational parent company, Xerox Corp., faced sharply declining market share and profits. The company had been the market leader in plain paper copiers – its staple product – but it was not prepared for the tide of competition coming from Japan. The survival strategy Xerox chose was quality improvement, both as a marketing goal and as a process for internal change. Quality as a competitive strategy has since revitalized Xerox's approach to marketing, human resource management, and operations, right across the world.

It took Rank Xerox some time to realize that they were facing a fundamental **product** challenge. During the late 1970s, they were at the end of a product cycle and their product range, in comparative terms, was badly differentiated in terms of functional benefits and price. At first they looked inwardly at their productivity and pricing strategies. For example, at the company's Mitcheldean plant, the principle Xerox manufacturing unit in Europe, they developed an overall productivity index based on product defects. The index was calculated as a percent per thousand against a base of all the company's manufactured products. This index was rather ingeniously weighted for complexity by taking into account the number of design drawings that were associated with each product – many thousands in the case of large copying machines or electronic printers.[1]

At the same time the approach to quality improvement that really galvanized action worldwide was the establishment of a market sensing process which Xerox called **competitive benchmarking**. Each functional area was held responsible to close the gap with the best world-class performer they could find in their particular function. Success within each function would then make Xerox, in aggregate, 'best of the best'.

As a point of convergence between marketing and operations, competitive benchmarking was to shake up every Xerox function and activity. The first benchmarking exercises compared Xerox from one end of the **value chain** to the other, against its Japanese rival, Canon. Benchmarking was a revelation. Xerox thought they had an operations problem but they found that they had a service support problem as well, from product quality to after-sales service to how long it took to answer a letter.

Other initial efforts to respond to the competitive crisis at various sites included a joint union/management initiative called **Quality of Work Life**. This was an employee involvement strategy modelled after Japanese quality circle concepts. This was the process by which Xerox people began to participate in influencing their work activities and work life. At the outset it was centred on the manufacturing work-force.

By 1983, Rank Xerox was making significant progress in Europe. Competitive benchmarking and employee involvement were beginning to produce positive results. By 1984, their market share erosion had been halted. In the same year their Mitcheldean manufacturing plant won a British quality award.

What was emerging from the effort to respond to the 'crisis' was the understanding that competitive benchmarking and employee involvement were two closely related phases of Xerox's rather unique approach to quality. The first phase – competitive benchmarking – enabled the identification of gaps between Xerox and the competition from which quality goals then might be established. The second phase – employee involvement – was acting to implement those goals through the experience of Xerox people at all levels. In marketing terms, they had defined their quality gap and followed this with 'gap-narrowing' activities.

One of the lessons Rank Xerox learned rapidly from competitive benchmarking was the importance of meeting customer requirements. They learned not to add features for the sake of it. Derek Hornby, former Rank Xerox Chairman, said, 'We used to like to go to our customers and say, "look what we've got for you now". The problem was, by the time the customer came back to say they didn't want it, a great deal of time and resources had been invested in making the new (unwanted) bells and whistles part of the product package.'[2]

Leadership through quality

At Xerox Corp. senior management and in particular David Kearns, their world-wide president, had become convinced of the need for a company-wide focus on the customer and for a planned developmental approach to total quality principles. He had observed the success of Fuji Xerox in Japan. In implementing total quality, their efforts had won them the prestigious Deming Prize back in 1980. Kearns recognized that if a world-wide strategy was to be successful and sustainable, it would involve a change in managerial behaviour and management practices at many sites in many countries. During 1983, Kearns and the top twenty-five executives of Xerox met and reached consensus on a comprehensive change strategy. They called it **Leadership Through Quality**. In that year, they established the Xerox quality policy, strategic objectives, supporting standards, guide-lines and processes. This global plan was communicated in a strategy document internally referred to as the 'Green Book'. Leadership Through Quality was intended as the integrating force which would encourage and focus the energies of all Xerox employees around the world. The key statement in the quality policy says:

> Xerox is a quality company. Quality is the basic business principle for Xerox. Quality means providing our external and internal customers with innovative products and services that fully satisfy their requirements. Quality improvement is the job of every Xerox employee.

The emphasis on conforming to customer requirements meant that customer satisfaction at Xerox started with knowing who your customers were and what they might reasonably expect. Following that, attention could be focused on consistently meeting those requirements. For many Xerox staff, their customer was and still is a person within the company. All employees therefore have customers. The Xerox quality policy implied that senior management did not have all the answers, hence quality improvement must be the job of every Xerox employee.

Making employees at all levels identify who their **internal customers** were forced people to recognize the need for change. In a very deliberate sense, Leadership Through Quality had one eye on the customer and the other on changing the organizational cultures of Xerox world-wide to suit that customer focus. Rank Xerox for example felt confident enough after the first two years to put 'customer satisfaction' as its first priority goal in its annual planning review, ahead of profits. Long-term profitability comes automatically, Derek Hornby had argued, if customer satisfaction is high.[3]

One expected flow-on effect of Leadership Through Quality was improved relationships with customers. Key customers were invited to visit Rank Xerox's headquarters each year to exchange information about their business outlook and strategic plans. The idea was and still is to achieve a better alignment of customer–supplier strategies.

The effects of Leadership Through Quality within the organizational fabric have been far reaching since 1984. Every person has received formal training in work processes, tools and techniques of identifying customers, specifying customer requirements and in using problem solving skills. There are systematic defect and error prevention processes in place and under continuous review, likewise, methods for measuring the cost of quality.

Training activity continues to expand through the company to all levels. This takes place in what are called 'family groups', comprising natural working teams together with their manager or supervisor who is responsible for ongoing training. The way skills are 'cascaded' down is interesting. Most executives, managers and supervisors receive two kinds of training. The first is an introduction to the particular principles and techniques involved. This at Rank Xerox is training at the **learning** level. The second level of training is at the **teaching** level, where the same people are exposed to the process of communicating and facilitating these same principles and techniques. This ensures that process facilitation skills are inspected at every level before 'cascading' to the next level. At Rank Xerox the quality training agenda covers eight key areas.

- Quality policy orientation and awareness
- Rationale for Leadership Through Quality
- Family group planning
- Problem solving processes
- Person to person skills
- The quality improvement process

- The role of the manager
- Application planning

In this methodical way, the first wave of Leadership Through Quality took five years to reach every employee world-wide.[4]

At Rank Xerox, each 'family group' measures its performance in terms of a number of key outputs, chosen to give an indication of customer satisfaction. Internal targets are set in cooperation with internal customers. To deal with special problems, groups form problem solving teams to work on difficult issues and raise quality to the target level or beyond. These teams are often cross-functional, that is, suppliers and customers may be co-opted to help solve particular problems. Each month, as project teams propose new ideas for raising quality, top teams are selected. Recognition and reward are executive responsibilities. For example, once a year there is a 'quality convention' at Mitcheldean, at which each of the year's top teams makes a presentation of the results of their work.[5]

The implementation of the quality strategy at Rank Xerox is incremental by its nature and is still evolving. Actual details of application in sites world-wide vary but they all conform to the Xerox quality policy and the essential quality principles. The goal is always to:

- Improve customer satisfaction
- Increase competitiveness
- Reduce the cost of quality

Two-way communication has been essential to the change process but to say 'communication is important' does not get to the heart of the matter. Derek Hornby believes that the most important factors to date in their success have been the involvement of everybody in identifying and making the changes needed, and the visible commitment of top management.[6] This last point is especially important. Top management have not abdicated their responsibility for the change process and have made a determined effort to act as role models. By their actions they mean to 'walk as they talk'. Senior management's 'behavioural' responsibilities are to:

- Promote the programme in every way
- Personally use competitive benchmarking techniques and employee involvement in problem solving
- Personally use the quality improvement process
- Seek feed-back on their own management style with reference to openness, patience, trust and team work
- Expand communications meetings and information sharing
- Hire and promote managers who actively practise Leadership Through Quality
- Recognize and reward Xerox people who exemplify Leadership Through Quality[7]

The organizational outcomes

It is difficult to establish direct cause and effect linkages between the change programmes and financial results, however, since the start of Leadership Through Quality, Rank Xerox indicators show:

- Improved customer satisfaction – up 35 per cent
- Cost of production – down 40 per cent plus
- Inventory levels – down from six months to less than one month
- Market share increasing[8]

It would be quite wrong to suggest that there are no tensions, contradictions or internal debates about the change process. For example, take the analytical technique called 'cost of quality'. Staff at Fuji Xerox disparagingly define cost of quality as 'something the Americans do'.[9] There are, however, more important issues. As Xerox stretches the cultural 'elastic', turbulence is encountered. At some sites, 'flexibility' has become a euphemism for staff reductions. They will need to solve the riddle of whether staff commitment and down-sizing of operations are compatible goals. Any perceived fear of being made redundant must affect feelings of commitment.[10] How these issues are handled seems likely to test the upper limits of Xerox's quality strategy.

One early Rank Xerox initiative was their **networking experiment**. This is a form of work flexibility for information workers whereby selected and trained volunteers leave their parent company to found their own businesses. By way of an informal partnership, the parent company becomes one of the clients of the new company.[11]

Through their concept of networks, they are in a good position to learn and extend relationships out further. Extending out to **supplier market relationships** is a recent step. More than 80 per cent of Xerox production cost is represented by purchased materials and their ability to stabilize quality and reduce cost directly depends on receiving defect-free purchased parts, on time every day. During 1986, Xerox materials management concluded that their suppliers might need to make a commitment to Xerox in terms of quality. Simply mandating suppliers to take on a total quality philosophy would not work. However, the Leadership Through Quality commitment provided a set of common language tools which were to form the basis of new supplier partnership relationships. They established a full-time consulting team to take the total quality philosophy to one hundred key suppliers world-wide, over a span of three years. That programme has been extended.[12]

No one at Rank Xerox argues that there is no room for improvement. Most of their problems are due to success, and that is a welcome change. There is potential to become more systematic and process orientated in quality improvement techniques. Although their training covers basic quality tools, the general thrust of the change strategies has been 'people driven', indeed marketing and HRD-based. This has given them a market orientation and a pioneering stance on culture changing strategies. Through their world-wide networks, they are in a good position to learn.

They have pushed human resource development to the point where the cultural 'elastic' has to respond. In the process, not all people have been happy with the new 'quality values' and relationship building approaches. Many have left. Some are asked to go. Staff commitment is the sensitive side of quality and no one can know how far the process of changing staff behaviour will go. Will 'acting the part' become just an act?

Many departments are shrinking as non-value waste is eliminated. There is recognition that they are becoming more productive and professional. The reverse side of this is that they constantly reorganize and people ask, 'when are we ever going to stop?' There is the issue of organizational **stress** developing as a corollary of organizational **flexibility**.[13] Better processes and systems are one answer, using Fuji Xerox as the window to Japanese quality management techniques. The world-wide Xerox family is an obvious resource. Rank Xerox for example are deploying their natural advantages in IT to develop information systems as an integral part of critical work processes. This frontier area is called IT-driven process redesign.[14]

With all that has been learned and applied at Rank Xerox there is still no sense of 'having arrived', notwithstanding their success. Their distant star still beckons. The ultimate challenge may be in exploring the nature of learning itself. Businesses of the future will need people who have learned how to learn. Xerox may well find their place in such a learning environment, secure within the network of relationships that they have set out so boldly to build.

References

1 Cullen J. and Hollingum J. (1989). *Implementing Total Quality*. IFS Publications, p. 3.
2 (1989). The quality of marketing. *Marketing Business*. April pp. 4–5.
3 *Ibid.*
4 Mercer D. S. and Judkins P.' E. (1990). Rank Xerox: a total quality process. In *Managing Quality* (Dale B. G. and Plunkett J. J., eds) Philip Allan/Simon and Schuster, pp. 303–4.
5 Cullen J. and Hollingum J., *op. cit.*, pp. 6–7.
6 *Marketing Business, op. cit.*
7 Mercer D. S. and Judkins P. E., *op. cit.*, p. 305.
8 Giles E. M. (1989). Is Xerox's human resource management worth copying? *3rd Annual Conference, British Academy of Management.* September, p. 25.
9 *Ibid.*, p. 26.
10 *Ibid.*, pp. 8–13.
11 *Ibid.*, p. 14.
12 Sugden R. A. and Parker J. R. (1989). Xerox supplier total quality strategy. *2nd International Conference on Total Quality Management.* IFS Publications.
13 Giles E. M., *op. cit.*, p. 14.
14 Davenport T. H. and Short J. (1990). The new industrial engineering:

information technology and business process redesign. *Sloan Management Review*. Summer, pp. 21–2.

INDEX